Tackling College Admissions

Tackling College Admissions

Sanity + Strategy = Success

Cheryl Paradis, Psy.D.
and Faren R. Siminoff, J.D., Ph.D.

ROWMAN & LITTLEFIELD PUBLISHERS, INC.

Lanham • Boulder • New York • Toronto • Plymouth, UK

ROWMAN & LITTLEFIELD PUBLISHERS, INC.

Published in the United States of America
by Rowman & Littlefield Publishers, Inc.
A wholly owned subsidary of The Rowman & Littlefield Publishing Group, Inc.
4501 Forbes Boulevard, Suite 200, Lanham, Maryland 20706
www.rowmanlittlefield.com

Estover Road
Plymouth PL6 7PY
United Kingdom

Distributed by National Book Network

British Library Cataloguing in Publication Information Available

Library of Congress Cataloging-in-Publication Data
Paradis, Cheryl, 1957–
    Tackling College Admissions: Sanity + Strategy = Success / Cheryl Paradis
and Faren R. Siminoff.
        p. cm.
    ISBN-13: 978-0-7425-4783-4 (pbk. : alk. paper)
    ISBN-10: 0-7425-4783-3 (pbk. : alk. paper)
    1. College student orientation—United States—Handbooks, manuals, etc.
    2. Education—Parent participation—United States—Handbooks, manuals, etc.
    I. Siminoff, Faren Rhea. II. Title.
    LB2343.32.P373 2008
    378.1'610973—dc22   2007037763

Printed in the United States of America

⊗™ The paper used in this publication meets the minimum requirements of
American National Standard for Information Sciences—Permanence of Paper
for Printed Library Materials, ANSI/NISO Z39.48-1992.

Contents

How to Use This Book

THIS BOOK is *not* a "how to get my teen into an Ivy League College" guide. Nor is it written for your teen. Instead, this book is written with you, the parent, in mind. It administers just what the college admissions doctor ordered: a little sanity and a lot of common sense. And, trust us, this is just what you and your college-bound teen need.

Why has the college admissions process become so daunting? The answer is found partly in the sheer number of applicants combined with the high cost of a college education. In past generations, only a relatively small percentage of the population attended college. Today, however, millions of parents and their teens enter the college admissions race each year. This race is akin to running the steeplechase: the path to the finish line is littered with obstacles and hurdles of all kinds—some anticipated, and some entirely unexpected—even for parents of the most focused teen. However, it is a race that, with training (and knowledge and humor), is entirely winnable, and virtually everyone can cross the finish line. The prize at the end? Admission to a college that provides the right fit for your teen.

We offer a simple, comprehensive approach to college admissions that can help your teen cross that finish line successfully. We've divided this book into two parts. In part 1: Training for the Race, we show you how to become an informed and effective coach for your teen. Here are your three crucial preparatory steps: first, discard destructive college admissions myths; second, understand your parenting style; and, third, assess your teen's strengths, challenges, and needs. Once you have taken these preparatory steps, you are ready to begin the race.

In part 2: Running the Race, we explain how to "run the race." We take you through the ins and outs of the college admissions process. We alert you to the pitfalls and hurdles you may encounter on the course and teach you strategies to overcome them.

Here is a sample of the strategies you will learn that can help your teen cross the finish line:

- Define and dispel destructive myths about the college admissions process
- Help you identify and work with your parenting style
- Help you identify your teen's strengths and weaknesses and the challenges he or she may face during the application process
- Teach you how to get the college dialogue started and how to keep it productive
- Advise you how to help your teen put together the best college list
- Teach you how to use the application and interview process to effectively "market" your teen
- Provide you with specific easy-to-implement strategies and tips for motivating, assisting, and working with your teen to overcome any hurdles
- Help you and your teen come to terms with your respective hopes and fears about college admissions
- Teach you how to gain and maintain perspective, a sense of humor, and inner calm during this stressful time

"I'm worried my teen won't get into a good college. Can this book help me?"

Absolutely. Most teens are in fact what we call "not-always-focused" (NAF) teens. NAF teens frequently have some real hurdles, such as less-than-stellar grades or SAT scores. Usually, they are not the editor of the school newspaper or the class president. They are, in other words, your typical teen. If this is your teen, don't feel crestfallen! The good news is that the vast majority of teens fall into this NAF category. And more good news: there is an abundance of excellent colleges to choose from, both private and public. This book will help you find the college that provides the right fit for your teen. And, contrary to what you may believe, most are accepted by one of their top college choices. Making that match is all in the approach, and this book will provide you with the perspective and skills to guide your teen into that good fit.

"My teen is an extremely focused student who has excelled throughout his high school career. Isn't that enough? Do I need to know more?"

Yes. Even if you have the seemingly always focused, or, as we like to call them, the "always-focused" (AF) teen, don't be lulled into a false sense of security by those great grades, long list of extracurriculars, and near-perfect SAT scores; they too can hit a roadblock. In addition, these teens also need to find the right college fit, and depending on your teen, this may or may not be the most competitive or elite institution. A final consideration: in today's admissions environment, even the AF teen will not necessarily breeze into one of the Ivies or other highly selective institutions scattered across the nation. In fact, only 3 percent of college-bound teens will attend one, and there are about ten or fifteen students applying for each slot. As of 2006, only 9 percent of applicants to Harvard made the cut, while the numbers at other institutions were as follows: Yale, 10 percent; Williams, 19 percent; Wesleyan, 28 percent; and Haverford College, a small selective school in Pennsylvania, 26 percent.

Does it seem unfair? Yes, of course. These AF teens appear to have done everything they were supposed to do and more. And in years past, most would probably have been shoe-ins. However, with the huge increase of echo boomer (children of baby boomers) applications, there are simply too few slots, even for the AF teen.

These numbers mean, as Wanda Blackman a school counselor from Jamesville-Dewitt High School, a suburban high school located near Syracuse, New York, forthrightly put it, "Ivy Leagues are reach schools for everyone." But if you are the parent of an AF teen, don't despair. There are literally hundreds of other colleges and universities eagerly awaiting your teen, where he or she will receive just as good an education and, yes, sometimes better. This book will not only help you put the whole Ivy craze into perspective but also convince you to forget about brand names so that you can focus on finding the best fit for *your* college-bound teen.

So, whether you are the parent of a NAF or an AF teen, this book has something for you. However, most important, for all of us—the parents who find ourselves running in the college application marathon—this book's message is that the "finish line" is admission to the college that best fits *your* teen.

PART I

Training
for the Race

N O QUESTION, the college application process is a huge undertaking in terms of time, money, and sheer emotion. So before you start, before those nerves begin to fray and tempers give way, before you even look over that initial college brochure, consider "warming up." No, we don't mean putting together the college list or even talking with your teen—all these things come later—first you need to "get in shape." There are three "warm-up exercises" we want you to do.

First, pick up and throw out the three big (and oh so destructive!) college myths out there.

Second, lose some weight! Recognizing and putting aside your own particular dreams and expectations for your teen's college career accomplish this. Once you do this, you'll feel lighter (and better).

Third, add some muscle by knowing your teen as a college applicant. Assess your teen's strengths and weaknesses and identify his or her unique challenges. This will help you identify and predict the obstacles your teen is likely to face. So, read over the chapters in part I and get ready to do some exercise to get into shape for the challenges ahead.

CHAPTER 1

Dispelling the Three Big College Myths

FIRST SEPARATE the myths from the realities. "Myths?" you might ask. "What myths? Isn't this a pretty straightforward process? Take the tests, fill out the required paperwork, see some colleges, and send the kid off to the best college that takes him." Well, sort of. In fact, the process is more competitive and stressful than ever, and buying into the three big myths only make things worse by causing you to lose sight of the real goal—the right college fit for your teen. Here are the three big myths:

- Only an Ivy Will Do
- Only *My* Teen Can't Get into an Ivy
- Let Them Jump without a Parachute

Myth #1: Only an Ivy Will Do

You know a myth has become pervasive when it has seeped into the popular culture. Nothing brought this point home more than an episode of the HBO blockbuster *The Sopranos* in which Tony and Carmela scheme to ensure their daughter's acceptance at Georgetown University. The message: "Only an Ivy will do" (even for mobsters). So we weren't surprised when our friend's daughter, on receiving an acceptance letter from an excellent state university, turned up her nose and declared, "It's not like I'm going to get all excited about it, Mom. It's only from a state school. It's not like it's from an Ivy!"

After hearing this story, we asked ourselves, "What is causing a seventeen-year-old to believe the key to her future success lies in attending an Ivy?" Unfortunately, she is not alone. Just like Tony and Carmela—and probably just like you—she has bought into this myth. Why the fixation? Well, we have the diagnosis: Ivyitis [Ivy-i-tis].

Ivyitis. We use this term to describe the condition that results from buying into Myth #1—the belief that future success hinges on admission to an Ivy. Ivyitis has infected parents, students, and even educators, who are now repeating the tenets of Ivyitis as if it were a mantra: "Only an Ivy will do, Only an Ivy will do, Only an Ivy will do. . . ." Even when not spoken openly, this is the message that is getting through. It's heard at college fairs, repeated in many high school guidance offices, discussed and lamented by students, and reiterated by millions of anxious parents getting ready to pack their teens off for their first year away from home. It's a troubling trend in college admissions and serves no other purpose than to add anxiety to an already stressful process. After all, if only 3 percent of the college-bound population attends one of these elite institutions, does this mean that most college-bound teens are wasting their time and their parents' money? Absolutely not! Here again is Jamesville-Dewitt High School counselor Wanda Blackman on Ivyitis: "I tell my kids that Ivy Leagues are reach schools for everyone. . . . I say, 'I know you have a 98 average; I know you took five AP courses, but Harvard is just a reach for you because that's just the way the numbers work out.'"

There is, however, an antidote to Ivyitis. It comes in the form of a little knowledge. So let's check out the realities of a college education and take the cure.

Remedy: Don't Buy into the Hype

There is an unbelievable amount of hype surrounding the necessity of attending one of the traditional or little Ivies. The first step to a cure is to understand the cause of Ivyitis. Hype for the Ivies comes from many quarters: the media, educators, peers, and parents. The media extol the value of an Ivy education almost to the exclusion of all others. If you don't believe us, just check out newspaper and magazine articles on the topic or simply stroll down the college guidebook aisle in your local bookstore. As you glance at the titles, you'll notice that one theme seems to dominate: how to get into an Ivy. Some big sellers' titles have that theme clearly emblazoned, while others simply imply it. Yes, of course, there are a few popular books with a realistic bent, such as *Looking beyond the Ivy* and *Forty Schools That Make a Difference*, both by the former education editor of the *New York Times*, Loren Pope. Most of the brisk sellers, however, tout the need to attend an Ivy. These sales indicate what we are buying and, more to the point, what we are "buying into." The message handed down is "Only an Ivy will do."

Adding to the hype are the many high schools, public and private, that are under increasing pressure to demonstrate "success," measured not only by the percentage of high school seniors going on to college but also by the colleges their graduates choose to attend. The futures of school counselors and administrators ride on these stats. However, the stats they don't list are the ones that tell you that one in every four freshmen will drop out after their first year and that up to half will not get a terminal degree from the school they originally entered. These stats point to the fact that for you and your teen's long-term goals, it is the college fit, not the brand name, that is critical for success.

Peer and parent pressure have also fueled the fires that have fed this myth. Surprised? Don't be. In 2005, 68.6 percent of high school graduates enrolled in an institution of higher learning (U.S. Bureau of Labor Statistics 2005). Unlike past generations, college has become the most common rite of passage for teens. This has imbued college admissions with a significance it did not have in the past. Everyone wants to tell family and friends that he or she is headed for "the best." Receipt of the college decision envelope is now seen as the finish line as opposed to a new starting line for teens. It is no wonder that teens are under pressure from their peers and parents alike to be perceived as "winners" in the college marathon.

Remedy: Get the Biggest Bang for Your Buck

A college education has become an enormous financial investment for most families. The cost of an Ivy can run upward of $50,000 per year, and tuition is rising faster than the rate of inflation. Even state-sponsored universities will take about a $20,000-per-year bite out of your pocketbook. For most of us, this is not an insignificant amount of change. The economics of college education has put additional pressure on parents and teens to believe that all this money is indeed buying "the best."

Are Ivies overpriced? Why spend $50,000 as opposed to half that at a state school or at another college that might be willing to give your teen a very attractive financial package? Obviously, it's because parents are convinced that they are buying the best. Here's what our school counselor Wanda Blackman told us: "I had a student who was accepted at two schools. A highly selective private university and an excellent state school where she was accepted into their honors program and awarded $4,000 a year. She turned down the state school because it wasn't a 'brand name.' I actually thought she would do better at the state school. It was a smaller setting, and she would have received a lot of attention, but I just couldn't convince her. Over the years I've discovered that students are willing to pay for that brand name."

Are Ivies really the best? Do you get what you pay for? Let's examine that proposition. Recent articles with titles such as "Who Needs Harvard?" (Easterbrook 2004), "The Worthless Ivy League?" (Samuelson 1999), and "A Prestigious Alma Mater Is Overrated on the Job" (Waldman 2004) show that Myth #1 is indeed just that, a myth. These articles examine the worth of an Ivy education and review the 1999 groundbreaking study by Stacy Berg Dale of the Andrew W. Mellon Foundation and Alan B. Krueger, a Princeton University economist. Looking at the data on 14,239 adults who entered thirty different colleges in 1976, they concluded that "students who attended more selective colleges do not earn more than other students who were accepted and rejected by comparable schools but attended less selective colleges" (Social Science Research Network, August 1999). In other words, the determinative factors for long-term success are student characteristics, such as ambition, drive, maturity, and discipline. They wrote, "Students who attend more elite colleges may have greater earning capacity regardless of where they attend school."

Success and the Ivies don't necessarily go hand in hand. Case in point: film director Steven Spielberg has been incredibly successful despite being rejected by the two most prestigious film schools on the West Coast: UCLA and USC. Dale and Kruger coined this type of success without the Ivy degree "the Spielberg effect."

Need more proof? Take a look at the entering class at the top medical or law schools across the country. In 2002, a full 61 percent of Harvard Law School's first-year class did not graduate from the Ivies. And if that doesn't convince you, did you know that Earlham College, a relatively unknown school of only 1,200 students, has a higher percentage of its graduates going on to receive doctorates than are graduates of Duke, Dartmouth, and Brown? Nor is an Ivy League education the ticket to elective office. Let's look at the U.S. Senate and Congress. Half of U.S. senators graduated from public universities. The same holds true in business. The majority of chief executive officers of the top Fortune 500 corporations and 2004 Rhodes scholars did not graduate from an Ivy (Easterbrook 2004).

So what's the cause of Ivyitis? Well, for starters, the baby boomers' children (often referred to as "echo boomers") are applying to college in record numbers, leading to a huge surge in applications since the mid-1990s. The number of applications is expected to continue to rise through 2010. Not only are today's teens attending college in record numbers, but they are also applying to more colleges, on average between six and ten. Yet even with this surge of applicants, the Ivies and other colleges have not created a significant number of new seats to match. It's not all in your imagination that selective colleges are more difficult to get into—they are.

As any parent who has been through the process before knows, the competition for these coveted slots has increased dramatically, leading to what we call the "trickle-down effect." Countless talented, smart, and successful students have "trickled down" to the other schools. So remember, your teen (smart and talented, of course) will have plenty of talented company even if he or she does not attend an Ivy.

Do the Ivies have the best professors and the best education? Not necessarily. What you see is not necessarily what you get. Many of the Ivies tout the advantage students gain studying with the "best minds" in America. Yet many undergraduate-level courses, particularly those all-important introductory ones, are taught not by these luminaries but by graduate students and adjunct professors. As a rule, senior faculty at the Ivies are far more focused on their research and graduate students.

Another important factor is class size. Many of the Ivies' introductory classes are, in a word, *huge*. Before being wedded to an Ivy, ask yourself if your daughter (or son) will be dismayed when, come September, she walks into her first-ever college class and finds herself seated in an auditorium alongside a hundred or more other freshman while the esteemed professor she was expecting is a graduate student. We hope she will have a sense of humor and think, "I don't remember seeing *this* classroom on the tour."

The fact is that excellent professors teach everywhere these days. Why? It's the law of supply and demand. In 1960, 10,545 new Ph.D.s were granted. By 2000, that number had skyrocketed to 45,000 (Mathews 2003). Combine this with diminishing numbers of tenure-track positions at the Ivies (or anywhere in fact), and you get the same trickle-down effect that we discussed earlier. Highly skilled faculty abound at all colleges these days. The winners, of course, are your teens, whether Ivy bound or not.

Here's a final thought about the financial cost of buying into Myth #1: don't forget graduate school. Increasingly, the bachelor's degree is not the end of the educational road, and young people are increasingly returning to universities for advanced degrees. You may want to save some money to help your teen through graduate school.

While the Ivies may look like gold to you, remember the old adage: All that glitters is not gold. Instead, approach the college admissions process with the idea that you are going to help your teen find the right fit. If it turns out to be an Ivy, great, but if not, don't sweat it. Your teen will and can succeed as long as both of you find the right fit, Ivy or not.

Remedy: Ask Yourself, "Will My Teen Thrive at an Ivy?"

As tempting as it is to encourage your teen to go for Ivy admission, first ask yourself, "Who is my child?" "What does my child need to succeed in college?" Remember, some students thrive in a highly competitive atmosphere, while others do not. Although it sounds like a cliché, the college–student fit is the most important factor to consider when applying for and accepting a college. Remember, approximately 70 to 80 percent of high school graduates begin college, but only approximately 50 percent graduate. Acceptance into one's college of choice is both the finish line as well as the start of a new race. Take a good hard look at a college's learning and living environment and ask yourself, "Should my child go there? Is this the environment where he [or she] will succeed?" The answer to these and other questions will be discussed in more depth in chapter 3, "Know the Common Challenges," where we help you assess your teen's challenges and provide strategies for recognizing the best fit for your teen.

Myth #2: Only My Teen Can't Get into an Ivy

Parents of not-always-focused (NAF) teens rarely feel comfortable enough to speak honestly with other parents about the college admissions maze and the challenges their teens face. In this hypercompetitive environment, no one should be surprised that many parents feel embarrassed and even reluctant to voice their fears that their teen's path to college acceptance may be a little (or even very) bumpy. No one brags about their teen's Bs and Cs, much less Fs. Yet statistically, most NAF parents actually form part of that "silent majority." Their NAF teens *are* the typical teens. So don't fall prey to Myth #2, "Only *my* teen can't get into an Ivy," and let these fears silence your voice.

Myth #2 leads to what we call "the Big Silence," which undermines the effectiveness of both parents and teens. As a result, the NAF teen may avoid college discussions with friends at all costs or feel defeated before the process even begins. The Big Silence is destructive for all concerned. It locks you behind a wall of isolation, keeping you and your teen from getting information you need. And, as you have probably already guessed, it is based on misinformation and mistaken assumptions. To get beyond the Big Silence, let's try to understand why you, along with countless parents out there, struggle with Myth #2.

Many parents feel alone and isolated in the false belief that only their teen is not Ivy League material. They tend to keep their feelings and concerns to themselves, forced

REMEMBER:

Many paths lead to success.

to squirm and listen as the vocal parents drone on and on about their teens who they firmly "know" are headed straight for an Ivy. You know who these parents are. In fact, everyone knows who they are—the ones with the kids with straight As, near-perfect SAT scores, a transcript filled with advanced placement courses, and a list of community-oriented activities that would even put Mother Theresa to shame. At "relaxed" coffee klatches, they speak as if their kids will breeze into one of the Ivies, while so many of the other parents just sit there, mouths shut, firm in the belief that their wonderful (but perhaps NAF kid) is the exception to the rule and not (what he actually is) one of the silent majority. One of those who haven't yet "peaked."

Dispelling Myth #2 is vital so that you can network with other parents and make use of the many helpful existing resources. We all know the value of networking. As an actively involved parent, perhaps you've often made use of other parents' recommendations regarding the best camps, schools, and even classroom teachers. In your personal lives, many of you have also found that career advancement and opportunities are, as often as not, secured from that network of contacts you have cultivated. Why, then, should this phase of life be any different? It's not. Knowledge truly is power. There is a treasure trove of knowledge out there that can be mined by networking with other parents. Through listening to other parents, you will uncover numerous strategies they have successfully employed to navigate the college application maze. That's why buying into the Big Silence is so counterproductive. If you think otherwise, consider what Ann, the mother of a high school junior, confided to us:

☀ A MOM'S TALE

"I was sitting with a group of mothers that had all known each other since our kids were in elementary school. Over the years, we had all confided our hopes and dreams for our children, and believe me they were all pretty lofty. We all imagined our kids getting into an Ivy college; we all believed (yes, sincerely believed) each one of our children would receive all kinds of awards, honors and scholarships! And now, here we all were, our kids are juniors in high school, and it was time to really start working on those college applications.

"For my part, as I sat there and listened to some of the mothers weaving their plans for their child's acceptance at Harvard or Brown, I wasn't so sure of my son's chances. He was only an average student at best. His first SAT score, 1,150, while decent, was not nearly good enough to qualify him for one of the Ivies. I had suggested an SAT prep course, or even a tutor, but he told me, 'I'll study on my own,' though I knew he wouldn't. To make matters worse, I couldn't get him to focus on the process at all. I had no idea what colleges he was interested in, and the college guidebooks I had left for him in his room had not moved! I couldn't possibly confide my concerns to these mothers whose children seemed perfect. I was convinced they wouldn't understand or would look at me as a bad parent. I felt alone and embarrassed with no one to turn to." ☀

After listening to Ann's story, we asked her if she remembered how many parents were actually speaking. Ann thought for a moment and recalled that there were probably about six mothers present, yet only two seemed to be doing most of the talking. As soon as she finished that sentence, she had an "aha" moment as she realized that many of the other mothers were just sitting there nodding, saying little about their own children's prospects probably because they felt embarrassed and were silenced.

Why should Ann (or you for that matter) feel this way? For one thing, in this hypercompetitive culture, parents often feel that their children's achievements are a reflection and validation of their own parenting skills. We all have asked ourselves this: "Am I good parent?" For better or worse, many of us measure ourselves by our child's accomplishments. The college acceptance letter has become, in many people's minds, the equivalent of the BMW or Porsche in the driveway. It is seen as the newest status symbol; a marker of parental success. No wonder you may feel anxious or discouraged if your teen hits a few bumps along the college admission course.

Another reason many parents falsely believe they are in the minority is that few guidebooks address the needs of the NAF teen. This reinforces the myth that you are indeed alone. Read over college-bound Amanda's mother story. If you are the parent of a NAF teen, we bet it hits home.

"I was in the bookstore with my friend whose daughter was also looking at colleges. As we browsed through the guidebooks my friend kept exclaiming, 'I'm sure Chrissie will get into Brown! She's done everything the books say she should do. And she's so organized! She's already working on her essay! All I have to do is write the checks for the application fees!' At this point in the story, Amanda's mother stopped, rolled her eyes, and then continued, "At that moment I just wanted to sink through the floor. Not only didn't my daughter have a clue where she wanted to go, she was only a 'B' student and hadn't yet filled out a single application. When I tried to discuss it with her she told me, 'don't worry, I'll get to it.' As I looked at the guides available in the bookstore, none of them addressed my child or her issues. Why aren't there any guidebooks out there for my type of kid?"

The answer, of course, is that many parents and teens have caught Ivyitis. Most college guides are simply a reflection of this. Unfortunately, these reinforced Amanda's mother false belief that her daughter is the exception and not the rule. So, unless you are totally convinced that your teen is one of the 3 percent who is headed for an Ivy, we want you to forget about all the guides, the hype, and those boastful parents. Instead, we want you to keep in the forefront of your thoughts that the teen years can be extraordinarily volatile at worst and simply transitional at best. Some teens are early bloomers and some late bloomers. Some teens struggle with emotional problems, but most rebound and do just fine. If you don't believe us, think back to your own teen years. Are you the same person you were? Chances are that most of you are already groaning remembering some of your own follies and problems from that

REMEMBER: You are not alone. Just keep your eyes on the prize: A good college fit.

era. But that's good because you can use those memories to give yourself some perspective. You have changed—and most likely for the better. And trust us, even if you have a NAF teen, give him or her some time and space, as he or she is not yet a fully formed adult, and positive change and growth is just around the corner. So, as you hit those bumps and face the hurdles on the race course, we urge you to network with other parents so that you can arm yourself with as much information as you can.

Myth #3: Let Them Jump without a Parachute

Would you let your child jump out of a plane without a parachute? Of course not. Don't let your child handle the college application process alone either. This is not the time to let a teen (even an always-focused [AF] teen) go it alone despite what some guidebooks and experts tell you. Indeed, doing this is counterintuitive to almost everything most parents know about their children. The teen years, as we all know, are one of the most turbulent times in any person's life. It is a time of rapid physical and emotional change, a time of being neither child nor adult, neither totally dependent nor independent. Applying to college is certainly no easy task, and most teens are simply not emotionally or intellectually equipped or savvy enough to handle such a complicated maze all alone. The college application process may be your teen's most important and challenging task to date. So, you need to cast out Myth #3 and remind yourself that selecting and applying to college involves tasks for both of you. This is not, however, a license to be either overly involved or protective. Do not become a "helicopter parent"—a parent who hovers over or micromanages their kid. Just keep your perspective and use your common sense, and you will find the perfect balance needed for navigating the process successfully.

Where does Myth #3 come from? If you look carefully, you'll see it and hear it all around you. It's found between the pages of that guidebook you just bought, and it's hidden in the "helpful" comment your friend just made suggesting that you let your teen "learn from his own mistakes" and passed along to you when the college assigns you to a "parent's-only" tour. The message? Back off and let the kid decide!

Your experiences applying to college, now decades in the past, may also push you to buy into Myth #3. Chances are you are a baby boomer, which means that you are part of a generation that rejected the age-old tradition of parental authority and control. You are part of the generation that fed on such slogans as "Don't trust anyone over 30" and "Question authority."

Maybe you chafed at the thought of being dictated to, particularly when it came to planning your life. The result of this cultural shift has had a tremendous influence on your child-rearing practices. As with most things, changes can be both positive and negative. On the positive side, today's parents seem more in tune with their teens' specific needs, strengths, and weaknesses. On the flip side, many baby boomers balk when faced with taking the reins. During the college admissions process, there is a time and place for taking the lead and for hanging back.

You need to feel confident that you, too, have a wealth of advice to offer your teen, just as, in retrospect, you now realize that much of your parents' advice was not so bad after all. And while it is true that no one can force-feed wisdom to anyone, the knowledge about life that you have gained over time is invaluable and worth passing on.

Today's parents are often not aware of just how complicated the application process has become. If you went to college "back in the day," it was a relatively simple process, and most of us handled it without significant parental assistance. More likely than not, you simply filled out an application, took the required boards, and waited for the envelopes. End of story. But times have changed, and it can be hard to really absorb the new reality and act on it. Therefore, it becomes so much easier to simply follow the advice of "let them go it alone."

While some teens can take full control over the process, needing little assistance from their parents, most teens are not helped by this "one-size-fits-all" approach. The questions you need to ask and answer are the following: How involved should I be? How much responsibility can my child take on? When should I step in and when should I back off?

These are important questions we will address in part II. For now, let's explore why Myth #3 is so destructive. Here is an example of what can happen when the "hands-off" approach is carried to extremes. Ellen and Ed, two extremely devoted patents, learned this lesson the hard way:

✸ A PARENTS' TALE

Ellen and Ed's son Tim had some academic difficulties early in his high school career. Tim attended a large public high school, and no matter how many times they went into the school to try to get Tim extra help, he was falling further and further behind. At the end of Tim's freshman year, his parents withdrew him and, at great financial sacrifice, placed him in a private school. Over the next three years, Tim flourished in a smaller environment. When it came time to apply for college, Tim had a solid, if not stellar, academic record. A well-constructed application would have given him a shot to be matched with any number of good-fit colleges. Tim's parents, however, after reading numerous popular guidebooks, decided to follow the prevailing wisdom of some of the "experts" and take a backseat (way in the back of the college bus) and let Tim take the lead. Not surprisingly, Tim chose inappropriate schools, missed deadlines, failed to schedule any tours or interviews, and generally prepared an application that did not reflect his genuine strengths and accomplishments. When rejected from all but one school that he had never even visited, he was crushed. Of course, it was too late to rectify the situation, and all Tim's parents could do was reassure Tim that he "could always transfer." Tim's mom later confided to us that she regretted their decision to let Tim undertake the process alone. She lamented, "Why didn't I follow my intuition? After all we sacrificed to enable Tim to succeed at high school, what a mistake to take a backseat during his senior year." ☀

The lesson of this story: Don't take your eyes off the finish line. The goal is not necessarily the Princeton decal on your car's rear window but a happy kid admitted to a school that's a good fit.

Remember, while your teen will be assigned a school counselor, many are simply overwhelmed with the number of students they are assigned, and their time is stretched thin. Most will appreciate any help you can provide, especially since they need to write recommendation letters for all their students. One mother, for example, "helped" the college adviser prepare her daughter's letter by sending a thank-you note—which included a well-written description of her teen's school accomplishments. Not only was the counselor appreciative, but it was likely that some part of the parent's letter was actually incorporated into the adviser's recommendation letter. Even at the most elite private schools, with the most involved and knowledgeable college advisers, you need to keep your eye on the ball. No one will be watching your child's progress as carefully as you.

The Homestretch

We hope we've convinced you to discard the three big myths: "Only an Ivy will do," "Only *my* teen can't get into an Ivy," and "Let your teen jump without a parachute." We hope you truly believe that "it's not where you go but what you do when you get there." The message to take to heart is that the college application process does not need to be overly stressful or frustrating. As you read the chapters that follow, you will learn how to identify your teen's individual challenges and learn effective strategies to successfully maneuver around predictable roadblocks. You will realize that one size does not fit all and that there are plenty of good choices for your child. In the end, it's the student, not the institution, who is most responsible for his or her future and long-term success. The message here is that we all need to stop obsessing over the Ivy diploma, thinking that one size fits all and ignoring our common sense during the application process.

CHAPTER 2

The Parent Trap

WHAT DO YOU want for your child? You know the only correct answer—to be happy—but is that all you want? Of course not. You, like almost every other parent walking the earth, want to feel proud of your child. You want affirmation that you are a successful parent. During your child's life, there have been numerous milestones that you have used to mark your child's progress and, by extension, your success as a parent: baby's first step, a great report card, winning that spelling bee—the list can go on and on. Your child's college admission is simply another one of these markers. We all want our teen to be a "winner" in the college marathon. However, we are suggesting that you change the definition of "winner." Your child *is* a "winner" when he or she enters that good-fit college. Your child *is* a "winner" when he or she is happy. Your child *is* a "winner" when he or she succeeds at college. So there is only one caveat we have for you—and it's a big one: don't fall into the "parent trap."

What do we mean by this? Parents fall into the parent trap when they allow their personal styles or traits dominate the process. So now it's time to identify those aspects of *your* style or traits that reduce your effectiveness. After all, if you cannot climb out of your own parenting traps, how can you assist your teen out of his or hers? So, let's begin. All parents—indeed all human beings—have their own unique personalities, styles, and traits. As you might suspect, some styles are more helpful and some less during this stressful time. Parents, we find, tend to fall into five styles:

- The Type A Parent
- The My-Dreams-Are-Your-Dreams Parent
- The Worried Parent
- The Procrastinating Parent
- The Laid-Back Parent
- The Ambivalent Parent

Of course, you may be a combination of more than one style. To help you identify your style, we've included a series of targeted "Parent Self-Assessment Questionnaires" below. After each questionnaire, we include "Roadblock Alerts" and strategies for making your style work.

To be clear, we know you can't change your style—as if that could be easily accomplished, possible, or even desirable. Instead, we advocate something much more reasonable and within your grasp: first, gain a healthy dose of self-awareness and acceptance and, second, use the helpful strategies we've included that are suited to your particular parenting style. You can help your teen best when your involvement in the process is crafted to suit your teen's particular personality and needs.

As a rule, only one parent tends to do most of the college application work, and, since you are reading this, we're guessing it's you. But remember, even if you are the more actively engaged parent, don't think your spouse or partner should skip this chapter since both parents can help or place additional burdens on your teen. This means that both of you should, ideally, complete these questionnaires. If your spouse or partner won't do the questionnaire, it's nothing to fight about. Most of us know our partners well enough to fill out something like this for him or her. The results may not be quite as accurate, but it will be useful nevertheless.

Tips and Strategies:
What's Your Style? The Type A Parent

Parent Assessment Questionnaire

1. Did you attend an Ivy or highly selective institution or program or major in a competitive field such as law or medicine?   YES/NO

2. Are you highly competitive, either at work or in the parenting arena—PTA, school committees, soccer coach, etc.?   YES/NO

3. Do you drive yourself very hard to become an expert at whatever projects you start?   YES/NO

4. Are you very demanding regarding your child's academic success/progress?   YES/NO

5. Do you have little patience with "failure" or imperfection even when you realize that a best effort was made?   YES/NO

6. Have people labeled you as a Type A personality?   YES/NO
7. Do you define academic success primarily by grade-   YES/NO
   point average?

If you answered "yes" to three or more of these questions, you probably are a Type A parent. This parenting type has high aspirations and standards, which can lead to perfectionism and a competitive or driven attitude. These types of parents tend to take on the college application process with the same zeal: like the invasion of Normandy! Still not sure if you fall into this category? Here are some more clues to help you decide if you are a Type A: Do you become very annoyed when your child is passed over for some coveted school or team position? Have you read more than four books on the college application process, and it's only your teen's sophomore year? Have you memorized the "Top List of Selective Colleges"—in order? Or it is fall of the junior year and you have already corralled your teen into twenty college tours.

Type A parents are fantastic at getting tasks done and are willing to fight for what they want. While this trait often serves them well in their professional lives, during certain times in their children's lives these very traits lead to family conflict. Type As struggle with the urge to push too hard. Yes, while it's true that some teens do thrive under the watchful gaze and vigorous prodding of the Type A parent, for others this may be a burden. Teens can become resistant and even rebellious under too much micromanagement. Remember what we talked about before? It's all about balance. The timing and manner of intervention is everything.

Why do so many Type A parents become so overinvolved and driven? While some might be hypercompetitive people, many do have realistic concerns about their child's future. After all, in today's rapidly changing economic climate, the future can seem uncertain. As a result, all types of parents are asking, "What is a safe career?" They worry that their children will be the first generation whose real earnings will be less than that of their parents. All this feeds the competitive fire of Type As, further reinforcing their belief that today's teens will need to fight to get ahead. Today's battle for them is getting into the best college.

How can you make your Type A style work for you and your teen? First, accept it. There is no need to change your style. This style, if managed correctly, can be incredibly effective during the college search. You are the parent who never misses a deadline and who ferrets out all the salient information and has a million ideas to get things done in the best possible way. This energy can be harnessed for the college marathon.

Roadblock Alert:
Don't Overwhelm Your Teen

When you imagine the typical Type A parent, does a woman's face come to mind? Most likely. But don't think dads are immune; they're not. Lindsay's dad, Brian, was the parent most involved in the college application process. After a hectic summer of studying for SATs, taking a general psychology course at a nearby college, and volunteering in a hospital, it was finally time for Lindsay to rest and go on vacation. Mom had asked dad to leave the college stuff behind, and he solemnly promised he would. As the family packed to leave, Lindsay wondered why her father's carry-on bag was so heavy. Her question was answered shortly after the plane took off. Dad opened that very heavy bag, revealing the newest books and magazines on college admissions along with SAT flash cards. Smiling, he turned to poor Lindsay and announced that she could "practice" during "any downtime" on their vacation. He also informed his now trapped and horrified family that "applications to college are up and acceptances are plummeting!" Fortunately, Lindsay, used to her dad's Type A ways, simply laughed and took a nap!

Solutions

Below are three basic strategies to make your Type A qualities work for you and your teen:

Harness and Strategically Use Your Energy and Drive

Most Type A parents have high levels of energy and drive and can make very effective use of these during this time. If you are one of these dynamos, you will efficiently and in record time complete the necessary background research needed to get your teen started. With your energetic "get it all done sooner rather than later" type of personality, you will read all the leading books and articles on the subject and make multiple calls to schools requesting to view books and applications along with scouring the Internet for colleges you think might suit your teen.

If both you and your teen are Type As, the results can go in two very different directions. When your collective energy works well together, both of you can become a very effective, well-oiled college application machine.

When it goes wrong, however, you might very well drive each other into a frenzy over college-related choices and activities. Keep in mind that frenzy does not make for clearheaded planning or decision making. The key to keeping it positive is to keep it under control. Take things step by step. Keep perspective and don't get ahead of yourself or obsess over things you simply cannot control.

What about the Type A parent with the laid-back or carefree teen? If this is your situation, again your teen might respond well to your energy and drive, relying on you to motivate and energize him or her. This is more likely to happen when you adopt a more behind-the-scenes approach and don't jump in at every turn. Remember, timing is everything. If you are not timely and measured in your interventions and management, you and your teen will butt heads, and he or she might shut down or rebel and become oppositional. One common mistake that Type A parents make—too much information, too early. Unless your teen is a willing partner to all these "go-get-'em" tactics, it is probably best not to bombard him or her with too much information too early. Use chapter 4 in this book, "The Dreaded Countdown," as your timing guide. This will help you decide when your teen needs to begin to absorb different types of information, fill out the applications, and make tour and interview appointments. Remember, your more laid-back teen probably does not view this process with the same do-or-die approach as you, and you simply need to accept this. So go for it but be smart and measured, and you will find that your Type A persistence and drive will work for your teen.

Build in an Escape Valve

You can't do college stuff 24/7. Be realistic; don't become obsessed. Look for the danger signs that you are going overboard: Are colleges and the application process the first thing on your mind when you wake up? Do you find yourself perusing the Internet to check out just one more college? Is the first (and the last) conversation you have with your teen about college? Has your teen had to tell you at least once a day to stop "bugging" him or her about this?

Make sure that you schedule time off from the college campaign; don't turn every family holiday or free weekend into a college search. Remember, while the college search and admissions process is extremely important for your teen, it isn't the be-all and end-all of life. There will be other challenges in the future—we promise. So schedule time off, and you, your teen, and the entire family will get through this stronger and better for it.

Find a "Reality Checker"

At their best, Type A parents are efficient and persistent. This is why they get the big projects done so well. Check out the PTA president, Little League coach, and parent in charge of the school benefit—all likely Type As. The danger for the Type A parent is losing perspective and going over the top, so you need a reality checker—someone to give you the heads-up sign when you need to rein yourself in. Ideally, the best reality checker is a person who has been through the process before because that individual is often best able to judge how much is enough and how much is too much. However, even more than prior experience, the most important quality to look for in your reality checker is someone whom you respect and will listen to. This needs to be someone you trust enough to rein you in.

Tips and Strategies:
What's Your Style? The My-Dreams-Are-Your-Dreams Parent

Parent Assessment Questionnaire

1. Do you feel you have not achieved enough either professionally or personally?	YES/NO
2. Do you berate yourself over "lost" opportunities?	YES/NO
3. Do you find your satisfaction is derived more from your child's than your own achievements?	YES/NO
4. Do you worry that your child is going to repeat your mistakes?	YES/NO
5. Do you find yourself pushing your teen too hard or demanding more than your child is capable of doing?	YES/NO
6. Are you pushing your child to pursue a career path that you wished you had pursued?	YES/NO

If you answered "yes" to three or more questions, you probably have the my-dreams-are-your-dreams style.

Many parents burden their already stressed children with fulfilling *their* dreams and don't even realize they are doing it. It is so easy to get overinvolved and live your life through your child. All parents have some tendencies to become deeply involved in their child's life. This bond can cause us to lose perspective and feel our child's struggles and aspirations as our own. While many parents may on occasion fall into this trap, the my-dreams-are-your-dreams parent falls prey to or frequently struggles with such feelings. Not surprisingly, the college application process often brings these tendencies into prominence and at the worst times. Here are some more signs that this might be you.

Do you talk at length about your teen's achievements but rarely your own? Have you become so involved with your teen's extracurricular activities (dance or soccer, for example) that you pressure him or her to "stick with it" even when it is obvious he or she wants to stop? Do you become so invested in your teen's life that you become equally or more upset or depressed whenever he or she suffers any kind of academic or personal setback?

If you are one of these parents, you really have it rough these days. Many guidebooks and college admissions experts now admonish parents to "remember who is going to college"—the teen, not the parent. Yet so many parents look to their children to compensate for their own perceived failings. The accomplishments they believe they missed, the dreams deferred. If you fit this pattern, this is not the first time you have struggled with that painful feeling that you missed the boat. Were you one of those stage parents? Or one of the parents the baseball coach had to "talk" to? Or how about when you signed your child up for the music or art lessons she never asked for and hated? Whose dreams were being realized? Hers or yours? It is so easy to lose perspective and become overinvolved, particularly now.

Certainly we have all either seen, heard, or read of incidents where a parent loses perspective. We've probably all witnessed an out-of-control parent coming to blows with their kid's Little League coach or the parent hysterically screaming from the sidelines to the utter embarrassment of their child. Do you remember the Texan mother Wanda Holloway who hired a hit man to kill the mother of her daughter's cheerleading rival? This cautionary tale of the parent who lives out her dreams through her child is told in many forms on television, in movies, and in books and magazines. Here is a true story of how unchecked "my-dreams-are-your-dreams" feelings can potentially derail a teen's college search:

☀ EMMA'S STORY

Emma was a B student with average but not spectacular SATs. Her mother, a Brown University alum, had her heart set on her daughter following in her footsteps. Mom was forever warning Emma that if she didn't "shape up," she would never make the grade. Junior year came and went, and Emma steadfastly refused to take the Brown tour, and the Brown catalog remained unopened on Emma's desk. Exasperated, Mom asked the school guidance counselor's help. A week later, the counselor called to tell her that after much prompting, Emma had "confessed" that she wanted to be an art major—apparently Mom had overlooked Emma's interest and talent in that direction—and attend a school specializing in visual arts. She also informed Mom that Emma had absolutely no interest in Brown. To Emma's mom's credit, she was able to take a step back and finally recognize that she had unwittingly placed her daughter in an untenable, no-win position. Mom began the reconnection process slowly by simply mentioning that she really admired Emma's artistic abilities and wondered if Emma had ever seriously considered doing something with her talent. This led to their first open and honest discussion about colleges with programs that would fit Emma's talents and ambitions. Together they drew up a list of prospective colleges where she had a good chance of being accepted (of course, Mom did her homework to research these colleges). Emma was energized and assembled a winning portfolio. By the beginning of Emma's senior year, Emma and her mom were taking college tours and looking forward to the choices Emma would inevitably have for college. Later, after Emma was settled in at college, Emma's mom told us that any residual feelings of disappointment disappeared as she watched her daughter flourish. ☀

Roadblock Alert:
Let Your Kid Dream

Laura had two my-dreams-are-your-dreams parents to contend with:

☀ LAURA'S STORY

"Applying to college was a very stressful time for me. They kept telling me it was important for me to get into the best college I could. That I needed to draw up the list and begin thinking about the whole thing right away. Neither of them finished college, and I grew up hearing what a mistake that was. My dad had actually started at an Ivy League but dropped out and was always whining about how different things would have been if he had finished. When I showed my parents my college list, it wasn't good enough. They added schools that I knew I'd never get into, and this depressed me. Why apply to a whole bunch of places you know are going to reject you? I felt they wanted me to do this just to make the point I was a big disappointment. My dad kept telling me that if I didn't go to a top school, 'I was going nowhere in life etc. etc.' It hurt me a lot." ☀

Another teen recalled, "College applications are very stressful. Not only because they're long and impossible but because you have to do them to satisfy your parents. It's hard to live up to your parents' expectations."

Solutions

Below are four basic strategies to help you put aside your dreams and focus on your teen's dream.

Look at Yourself

Today's teens are under a lot of pressure from their peers, a demanding and ultracompetitive society, and their own dreams and expectations. Many parents—some unwittingly, some because they simply can't contain themselves—place the weight of their own disappointments on their teen's as-yet-untested shoulders. The antidote for this is a strong self-administered dose of introspection.

First, take an objective look at your own achievements in life—professionally and personally. Do you feel successful? Are you content with your life? Do you find yourself thinking about or even mourning missed opportunities? Do you struggle with low self-esteem? Everyone feels this way sometimes, but it's when your aspirations for your child have crossed the line from "I want him to succeed and be happy" to "I really want to live out my unfulfilled dreams through her" that you need to take stock and stop yourself.

Second, confide your feelings to someone you trust and respect. Vent, if need be, your disappointments to that person. Enlist this person—your "reality checker"—and give him or her permission to rein you in if you begin to impose our dreams on your teen. You may need your reality checker—to tell you when you start pushing or controlling too much. Of course, it helps if this person can tell you this with kindness and humor. If you already struggle with self-esteem, the last thing you need is to be told that you are a less-than-wonderful parent.

Third, don't act on your feelings. We are not actually asking you to stop feeling these emotions. What's important is that you *not* act on these. So, even if you can't vanquish your strong desire to see your teen succeed in ways you did not, just don't place this burden on him or her. The first step is simple— simply recognize and admit that these feelings exist.

Listen to Your Teen—What He or She Says and Doesn't Say

A challenge for you may occur during the task of making up the college list. Your "dream school" may not be the best fit for your teen. If your teen is assertive and knows what she wants, she may tell you to back off. However, if your child is overwhelmed by the process or unsure of herself, she may feel pressured to choose a college simply to please you. It's up to you to really listen to your teen's spoken and, equally important, unspoken wishes. If you do this, we promise that little by little your teen will take more initiative for drawing up the college list.

Stop. There's an Elephant in the Room. Time for Honest Talk

Okay, you say, "let's say I realize I have the my-dreams-are-your-dreams style, what do I do about it?" The odds are that your spouse or your partner and your friends and acquaintances as well as your child all know you struggle with these feelings. So, since everyone knows, why not talk about it honestly? Talking about it gives your teen permission to tell you to "Back off!" when you are pushing his wishes aside. The fact is that giving voice to what has remained unsaid or unacknowledged can help both you and your teen develop some perspective and a sense of humor. Once you all can actually laugh about your my-dreams-are-your-dreams style, all the college tasks become much easier to complete.

Remember, There Are Many Ways to Win

So, you never made it in show biz, and, can you believe it, your child actually has talent. But wait. Before you get too excited, take a step back and ask yourself, "Have I pushed him into a field because I actually wanted to do this?" Your teen may have talents or strengths in a variety of areas and have dreams that differ from yours. So ask yourself, "Is this my dream or hers?"

Look for signs of ambivalence. Sometimes your teen will literally scream it out—"Mom, I don't want to go on any more auditions!"—or sometimes it can be subtler—"Well, okay Dad, I'll play ball again if you really think I should." These are signs that it is time for you to back off and take stock of what your child—not you—really wants.

A different twist occurs when your teen rebels and chooses a college or major simply to thwart your dreams. Mary Fleischer, chair of the Department of Performing Arts at Marymount Manhattan College in New York City, recounted how she frequently finds applicants auditioning for theater against their parents' wishes. She told us about parents who actually tell their teens, "You're going into the theater over my dead body." Dr. Fleischer believes that some teens actually choose a theater major out of "rebellion."

You need to constantly remind yourself that it is their life and that they will not be happy or successful pursuing *your dreams*. This point was brought home by a story that Clete Gualtieri, a school counselor at Jamesville-Dewitt High School, shared with us:

> Parents want their children to be happy, and they want their children to be successful, but sometimes we need to remind them that the child is going to be happy and successful at the place that is the best fit. I recently had a student that was accepted at his grandfather's alma

mater—Cornell—and also at Tufts. There was a lot of family pressure for him to go to Cornell because it was the grandfather's dream for at least one of his grandchildren to go to Cornell. The student was accepted at both schools but opted for Tufts. Right after the student decided on Tufts, I saw the grandfather, who said, "So you're the one that helped my grandson decide to go to Tufts." I was expecting this to be a difficult conversation, but the grandfather said, "Better he be happy at Tufts than go to Cornell and be miserable."

This is an important point because I regularly tell parents that in late September or early October of that college freshman year, your kid will be asking himself, "Why did I pick this place?" Remember that no place is as good as the fantasy. So, if the answer to that question is because Mom picked it or Dad wanted it, then the kid is not going to make it. But if your child can say, "I chose this, I carefully looked at all the options," then chances are your child will persist and be successful.

Tips and Strategies:
What's Your Style? The Worried Parent

Parent Assessment Questionnaire

1. Do you define yourself as a worrier? YES/NO
2. Do you see doom and gloom enveloping your teen even before anything bad has happened? YES/NO
3. Do you have unrealistic and unobtainable expectations of your teen? YES/NO
4. Do people describe you as overly emotional? YES/NO
5. Do you already feel overwhelmed just thinking about the college application process? YES/NO
6. Do you think nothing good ever happens to you or your teen? YES/NO
7. Do you have trouble enjoying the moment? YES/NO

If you answered "yes" to three or more questions, you probably are a worried parent. We all feel worried and anxious from time to time. This is perfectly normal. Some people, however, are just worriers. They are the "what if . . ." kind of people. Worriers are concerned about lots of things: bills, due dates, medical problems, what people think of them—the list is endless. Family members may tell stories like, "Remember when you were so worried we would miss the plane we actually had to wake up two hours early even though there was no traffic and arrived at the airport three hours too early?" Other clues that you are a worrier are a tendency to lose your cool easily or at the worst time.

Many of our students complain that their worrying parents asked embarrassing questions during the college tours, questions that were clearly reflections of their own anxieties and were not really pertinent to their teen's needs. Some of the embarrassing questions included these: "How often are students mugged?" "Will my teen be viewed as a minority?" "What are the services for learning-disabled students?" "What's the suicide rate here?"

Excessive worry can drive teens to distraction. Teens with a worried parent complain of incessant nagging that burdens them, especially when parents voice their fears of college rejections. For your own peace of mind and for the sake of your teen, it's important to keep those anxieties under control.

So, if you are a worried parent, does that mean there is nothing you can do about it? Absolutely not. While you may not be able to change an inborn tendency, you can manage your stress level and learn to productively channel your worrying into being effective during this challenging time.

Not surprisingly, the stress of the college application process leads to increased anxiety for almost everyone involved but can be particularly difficult for you. Chances are the more you hear about the college acceptance hype, the more worried you will feel. And if you have fallen into the trap of Myth #1—"Only an Ivy will do"—then your fears will be more exaggerated than ever. You may even ruminate that if you don't do everything right, your child's prospects of getting into the "best" college are over. As you already know from reading chapter 1, nothing could be further from the truth. But if reading chapter 1 did not dispel the anxiety, just keep reading because more relief is coming your way.

Roadblock Alert:
Don't Fall Prey to Your Fears

☼ ARIELLA'S STORY

"My parents interfered in everything. When I was writing the essay, they kept bothering me to reword it and wouldn't leave me alone. My dad actually went into my computer one day and rewrote the whole thing and made me send it in! I was very angry. Then when I went to an interview in Florida, my parents kept telling anyone around who would listen stories of things I had done in high school that I was not proud of. I asked them how they could say such things, and they told me they were worried the college would find out so it was better just to get it over with. Can you believe it? They made me crazy the whole time." ☀

Solutions

Below, for the worried parent, are three easy to implement strategies to quell those nagging concerns:

Knowledge Is Power

You can easily adapt some of the tried-and-true techniques of cognitive behavioral therapy to help you through this time. One of the key techniques is known as "bibliotherapy" or, more plainly put, "becoming knowledgeable." The more you learn about the real facts about college admissions, the more your unrealistic anxieties will dissipate. So, one way to lessen your stress about the college marathon is to read a number of good, informative, reassuring books about navigating the college application process—including this one. In addition to this book, buy one or two books that review the different colleges and universities.

REMEMBER:
Only read what you need.

A bit of caution, however, about the above advice. Sometimes worriers buy too many guidebooks in the fear they won't be getting *everything*. This can actually become a problem in and of itself when the amount of material becomes overwhelming. So, become informed in an effective way.

Don't Let Your Worries Set the Pace

Here's a behavioral technique we highly recommend for you, the worrier. Get a set of index cards—we'll call them our "worry cards." On one side of each card, write down one of your worst college-related fears. It might be, for example, "My child won't be accepted anywhere." Write that on one side, then flip the card over and answer your worry as objectively as you can using the real facts you know about your child as a college applicant and about college acceptance rates. A good reply to our hypothetical might be, "Of course she'll get in. Her college adviser told me her grades and test scores are well within the range of acceptance at any number of good schools." We recommend that you write out a set of five (at most ten) of your biggest concerns on your worry cards. Label one side of the card "Worry" and its flip side "Reality." So, for example, on the "Worry" side, write, "My teen won't get into the college he wants." Then on the "Reality" side, write, "Most teens are accepted by their first or second choice college, and I'll make sure her college list is realistic." When you try this exercise, you may find that you are great at writing down all the worries but draw a complete blank at writing the reassuring reply. Don't fret; that is a typical pattern for worriers. If this happens to you, its time to do the following:

- Search out facts that will help you reformulate your perspective. This type of information is easily available from your teen's school counselor, in this book, in other useful college guides, or on the Internet.
- Easier still, simply turn to someone who is not a worrier, someone who knows the facts, perhaps someone who has already wrestled with these types of fears.
- Most important, you don't need to share all your worries with your teen. Some things are best kept to yourself. After all, most teens are already freaked out enough during this time, and your job is to bolster their spirits.

One last piece of advice: don't try to keep your worrying style a secret from your child. First, trust us on this, your teen already knows. Hopefully, he or she thinks you are funny. Admit you are a worrier and explain that you realize there is nothing real to worry about, then try to laugh about it together. Humor is a great antidote for frayed nerves.

It's Time to Slow the Pace

Here's another major challenge that even the parent who is not a worrier must overcome—today's parents and teens are over-scheduled and overbooked. Most of us simply have too much on our plate, and, at times, it really does seem as if it all won't get done. Now is the time to reassess your commitments. Take out a piece of paper and write down all your obligations, dividing the list into "Have to's" and "Should do's." Ask yourself which ones can be postponed or dumped altogether. Make a concerted effort to get off committees, don't take on nonessential projects, and prioritize those activities and obligations that remain. In fact, this is a great exercise for all parents. The college process is nothing if unpredictable; it may turn out to be a breeze, or it may be time consuming. Since "everything" isn't under your control—remember there is a teenager intimately involved in the process—you need to conserve your resources. So don't squander your time and energy. Your watchword during this time should be "conserve, conserve, and conserve."

One last word about conserving energy. Worrier parents usually don't leave enough time for relaxation. As they run through their hectic day, they tend to leave out time for lunch with friends or time to relax. Pare down your obligations and don't forget to rest and have some fun.

Tips and Strategies:
What's Your Style? The Procrastinating Parent

Parent Assessment Questionnaire

1. Do you tend to put things off to the last moment?   YES/NO
2. Has your procrastination caused problems in the past?   YES/NO
3. Do you procrastinate so close to the deadlines that   YES/NO
   others pick up the job to complete it?
4. Do you feel anxious at the thought of doing or   YES/NO
   completing important tasks?
5. Have you missed important dates or deadlines   YES/NO
   for your child's school or outside activities?
6. Do you already feel overwhelmed about the prospect   YES/NO
   of filling out forms for the college application?
7. Has your teen been bugging you to start college tours   YES/NO
   but you haven't found the time?

If you answered "yes" to three of these questions, you should keep reading (don't put it off). Lots of good, loving parents are procrastinators. In the past, this has led to problems—big or small. Procrastinators put off for tomorrow what they could or should do today. Procrastination can lead to missed deadlines and opportunities. College applications are nothing else if not time sensitive.

Why do people procrastinate? Many avoid tasks when they feel overwhelmed by the job at hand. They worry that it is either too big or too difficult. Tasks often become so large in a procrastinator's mind that they avoid even starting. We often hear from parents that getting started is actually the most difficult stage of the entire application process.

For some procrastinators, the root of this problem lies in the desire for perfection. Many have unrealistically high standards and expectations. If you are a procrastinator, you may need to learn what we call the "good-enough" rule. When you complete one task, ask yourself, "Is it good enough?" If it is, tell yourself it is, then check it off your to-do list and go on to the next. In other words, learn when to stop and move on.

Another common pattern seen in the procrastinator is what we call "playing chicken." This is when he drags his feet so long that the deadline looms and someone else has to pick up the ball to save the day. We find that procrastinators are often married to Type A spouses who take over before a deadline is missed. While this marital pattern may have worked fine up until now, continuing to play chicken adds hurdles and obstacles to the college application race.

Roadblock Alert:
Is Time Passing You By?

Solutions

Here are five strategies to help you climb out of the procrastinating trap:

Divide Tasks Up

This is a simple but effective approach. Divide the tasks into smaller and doable parts and tackle these one by one. For example, when you buy that giant book describing every college out there, don't try to tackle it all at once. Look only at a few entries or a single section at a sitting.

Don't Beat Yourself Up!

Don't be so hard on yourself! Self-imposed unrealistic expectations can create and feed a cycle of false starts and stops.

Procrastination can actually cause more avoidance. A helpful strategy is to talk about this tendency with people you trust to gain a new outlook. Check with other parents of teens in your child's grade to see how you compare. Are you behind in terms of starting college application tasks? If you are, these honest talks will get you going. The goal always is to successfully finish the race. Don't make your procrastination worse being overly harsh with yourself.

Keep Lists

Not more lists! Sorry, but yes. Lists can help. If you are a true procrastinator, then completing all the application tasks seems overwhelming. Successfully navigating through the college application maze is a task not so different from others—it looks overwhelming at the beginning but, when broken down into doable tasks, isn't so difficult. Pay particular attention to chapter 4, which will explain everything you need to know about deadlines. After reviewing chapter 4, it's time to start a to-do list, and *don't* keep it a secret. Let your teen and/or spouse review the list and have some input. That way, if you start falling behind, someone will be there to get you back on course.

Organization Is the Key

Frequently we find that procrastinators are disorganized. They often make lots of lists, then misplace them. If this is you, pick up a wall calendar to keep track of all the important college-related dates, including dates of tours, interviews, and application due dates. We recommend a calendar dedicated to college stuff only and displayed prominently for all to see. A calendar stuck in the drawer won't be helpful for the procrastinating parent. You need frequent reminders of college task due dates. While your friends and job might be flexible and understanding about missed deadlines, colleges are not. They mean business with their deadlines.

Take a Breather

Are you the only adult who can help your teen through the application process? Of course not. It only feels that way.

Look around. Is there anyone to help you? Now is the time to honestly admit to your spouse or partner that you would like to divide the application tasks. If you're feeling overwhelmed, ask for help. If your school has an effective school counselor, meet with him or her and admit you are a procrastinator. The school counselor can be a great resource. If you don't have anyone jumping in to help and you can afford it, there are parents who have found that private college advisers can be effective in alleviating some of the college burden. However, before you engage a private college adviser, carefully discuss with that person the specific services provided. Make sure you are on the same wavelength or have the same philosophy. Fees can range from a few hundred to tens of thousands of dollars. So understand the financial commitment before obligating yourself. There are some who will, indeed, work with you and your teen throughout the college application process, keeping you both on track and organized. The best way to find a private college adviser is through word of mouth, at high school functions, and on the Internet. Just make sure to check their credentials and references.

Pass the Baton

If you have been blessed with an unusually organized always-focused teen, let him or her take the initiative and run the first leg of the race. A Type A or an efficient teen can take on more of the load. Yet don't be fooled and let him or her fly solo. Teens still need someone watching over them because even the most efficient, mature teen can be erratic or forget an important date. So, even if your teen can collaborate with you, keep your eye on the ball, and that means following the calendar and ticking off each task as it's completed. Be ready to take the baton when you see your teen's energy flagging or his or her energy focused solely on school and social activities.

What if you can't rely on your teen? What if your teen avoids and procrastinates as well? This is a fairly common situation, so, if this applies, then both of you need to sit down and have an honest discussion. It's also definitely time to read chapter 3. This will provide strategies for helping the procrastinating teen. If both of you share this style, you definitely need to bring a third person into this process—either a spouse, a friend, or a college adviser. You will need someone watching over the two of you to make sure the tasks get done.

Tips and Strategies:
What's Your Style? The Laid-Back Parent

Parent Assessment Questionnaire

1. Has your teen been pretty much in charge of his   YES/NO
   or her high school career without much direction
   from you?
2. Do you keep a wait-and-see attitude when your teen   YES/NO
   has problems, like a drop in grades or withdrawing
   from extracurricular activities?
3. Do you have implicit faith in your teen's ability to   YES/NO
   choose the college best suited to his or her needs?
4. Are you unruffled even when you discover that you   YES/NO
   don't know the ins and outs of the college admissions
   process and deadlines?
5. Do you find yourself surprised at high school events   YES/NO
   when you hear about activities that occurred, that
   you missed, and that you knew nothing about?
6. Have you forgotten to add your e-mail address for   YES/NO
   your teen's high school to send you important
   information?
7. Have you forgotten to check your teen's school's   YES/NO
   website for important college-related information?

If you answered "yes" to three or more of these questions, you probably are a laid-back type of parent. It may be hard for many parents to believe, but there are truly relaxed and easygoing parents out there who have successfully raised their children without reading many how-to books or lost endless hours of sleep worrying about whether their child will make the soccer team, and their children have survived just fine. Their children often thrive with their parents' love and support and without much overt control or supervision.

We frequently find that laid-back parents have relaxed children. It may be that having children with easygoing temperaments facilitates this type of parenting, but some people approach parenting this way no matter what type of child they have. These parents approach life in a relaxed manner, have sunny dispositions, and handle stress without getting too flustered.

If you are this type of parent, you probably recognize yourself without even doing the self-assessment questionnaire. Usually, other parents made comments like "I can't believe you're not worrying about this!" or "I can't believe you're so relaxed about college applications." Most likely you haven't even bought more than one book dedicated to the college application process.

However, with increased competition for college and with all the hype and myths we discussed in chapter 1, the laid-back parent tends to be in the minority. While being this relaxed may have its advantages, you run the risk of not being up to date and on top of all that you do need to know. A clue to this could be when parents use terms like "early decision," early action," or "rolling admission" and you don't know what the terms mean. While your tendency to "let things take care of themselves" may have worked well up to now, this is the time to take a slightly more hands-on approach. The application process is very complex and not fully understood without putting in some time and energy. If you wait for everything to fall into place, your teen may wind up scrambling to catch up.

Roadblock Alert:
Don't Go Off Course

☀ ALEX'S STORY

"When I started looking at colleges, I realized there was a lot of competition. I mean there were hundreds of other students with the same grades as me applying to the same schools. I wanted to know, 'What would make them choose me?' I also had a problem finding schools that offered the program I really wanted. I would call up a school and tell them what I wanted, and they'd say, 'yes.' Then, when I went to visit, it turned out the major was only for graduate students. I talked to my mom about this, and she said I probably misunderstood or asked the wrong questions. But no matter what problems I had—deadlines or some advice about essays or whatever—my parents didn't really help me. Maybe because they are pretty laid back and just thought I could pretty much do it all myself. I mean they paid for the applications and took me on tours, but they were kind of, well you know, just, 'Don't worry you'll get in.' I mean some of my friends complained because their parents were always on their backs, but I think I would have preferred that to the way my parents acted." ☀

Solutions

Check to See If Your Approach Is Working

Sometimes, your laid-back approach is exactly what your teen needs. The question is, How do you know? If your teen is organized and mature, he or she can gather the necessary information about potential colleges, application tasks, and deadlines. They can take the lead, and all you need to do is provide support, supervision, and guidance—and sign some checks. If this is your teen, great, you're lucky. Yet don't be totally in the dark; keep your eye on the ball because even the most organized teen can forget some details or become overwhelmed.

Know When It's Time for a Course Correction

Be ready to jump into the race. If your teen procrastinates or becomes overwhelmed or disorganized, you need to take on the leadership role. In any case, you need to read this and other guides, attend college information sessions, and talk with other parents who have been through it before. Basically, change your modus operandi. Don't worry; it's not forever. You can go back to being laid back if your teen gets back on track or after the acceptance letters arrive.

Know Who's on Your Team

Wouldn't it be great if you were married to someone with the same relaxed style? Maybe yes, maybe no. If both of you are laid back, you run the danger of not effectively helping your teen. If you and your partner differ in style, however, and this is often the case, there can be a conflict over how much to prod and push and when to back off and let the teen take the lead. It is essential that both of you talk honestly about your differing styles and come to some resolution of how you will work together. The last thing teens need during this stressful time is to get mixed messages from their parents.

Tips and Strategies:
What's Your Style? The Ambivalent Parent

Parent Assessment Questionnaire

1. Do you fit into two or more of the parenting   YES/NO
   styles described above?
2. Do you send inconsistent messages to your teen   YES/NO
   about what is his or her job and what is yours?
3. Do you get very frustrated when your child won't   YES/NO
   complete the tasks that you believe he or she is
   mature enough to handle on his or her own?
4. Does your spouse or partner complain you oscillate   YES/NO
   from spoiling to having unrealistic expectations?
5. Do you push your teen to act independently, only to   YES/NO
   intervene later?
6. Do you tell your teen, "I'll be happy if you do your   YES/NO
   best at school," only to show your displeasure when
   his or her performance is less than stellar?
7. Have you told your teen "choose whichever colleges   YES/NO
   you want" and then insisted that he or she tour
   schools you want?

If you answered "yes" to three or more of these questions, then you are probably an inconsistent/ambivalent parent. Some of you may recognize yourself in two or more of the parenting styles. You might realize that you are a flip-flopper, sometimes being laid back, other times worrying or controlling. How do you know if you have an inconsistent style? Do you try to let your child take the lead, then jump in to save him or her from disaster? Do you believe and expect that your teen should be taking on more responsibility and can't believe it when he or she acts so childish or immature? Does your spouse accuse you of doing too much for your teen, babying him or her? Do you react by pushing him or her out of the nest, perhaps too soon, and simultaneously worrying that he or she isn't ready? If these or anything similar describes you, then you have an ambivalent/inconsistent style.

Why do parents give mixed signals? It may be that the message we receive from society—that teenagers are independent and capable—just doesn't match reality. We all know that children mature at different rates. There are some sixth graders who can do their homework alone in their bedrooms, while others need to sit at the kitchen table with a parent there to provide encouragement and guidance. There are some ten-year-olds who are ready to go to sleep-away camp and some who are not. Deep in your heart, if you have a late bloomer, you know that he or she may need more than some other children. The bottom line is that the "one-size-fits-all" approach does not work.

Sometimes parents give mixed signals because they are tired or feel overburdened. Like most of your friends, your day-to-day life may be over-scheduled and overly pressured. The additional work of college applications can feel like one burden too many. You may feel ready for more freedom and time away from the parenting role and unconsciously be rushing your teen to leave the nest. In some cases, your teen may be ready to go, yet you're not ready to let go. So what happens? You try to pull him or her back, micro-manage, and overprotect. A clear sign of this is if you are still doing his or her laundry or cleaning his or her room.

Teens can also feel ambivalent about leaving childhood behind and send mixed signals. As a parent, you need to be aware of this and do your best to encourage him or her to assume as much independence as he or she is ready for. Jump in only when necessary.

One last cause of mixed signals occurs when there is a mismatch in styles. One parent or partner may push their teen toward independence while the other pulls him or her back. This style can be problematic partic-ularly when it confuses your teen about what college he or she should or should not consider.

Roadblock Alert:
Your Wires Are Crossed

☀ JON'S STORY

"My parents told me that I could go to *any* school I wanted. Any-where! So I decided it would be cool to go to college in Hawaii. I had family there, had visited a few times with my parents, and thought this would be fantastic. But when I told my parents I wanted to go to school in Hawaii, they acted shocked and told me that 'it was out of the question.' I just couldn't believe it! I wound up staying on the East Coast. I was very disappointed. I guess I was never really happy at my college because of this." ☀

Solutions

Know What Your Teen Can Actually Do

Learn to take your clues from your teen. Think about his or her past accomplishments, missteps, or falls. Know his or her general pattern of behavior. Now ask yourself, Is my teen mature for his (or her) age or not? Has he or she already started thinking about college choices, maybe even bought and read through some college guides, or is it not yet on his or her radar? Is he or she capable and independent, doing well in school and emotionally resilient, or does he or she require a great deal of "hand holding" to get things done? You need to understand where your teen is and work to adopt a consistent pattern of parenting to meet your child's needs.

Don't Be Unrealistic

Formulate realistic expectations. Compare notes with other parents going through the process. You will probably find it refreshing to honestly ask a friend, "Is your teen filling out the applications by herself?" or "Does your child go on college tours alone?" By talking honestly about your concerns, you will see that most parents are taking an active role in guiding and helping their teen complete all application paperwork. Once you know what to really expect, you can formulate a consistent strategy.

Accept It: You'll Be Doing More for Your Teen Than Your Parents Did for You

Some ambivalent/inconsistent parents expect their teens to be more independent during this process because they themselves did not need much help from their parents when they applied to college. Keep in mind that times have changed. Not only do teens face much higher demands today, but most do need some assistance from their parents.

Let's take a quick peek at college admissions past and college admissions present. When we were in high school, we took the SAT, but most of us didn't take SAT prep courses—now most teens do. Most of us took only the SAT. Today, in addition to this high-stakes exam, many students also take the SAT II along with advanced placement exams. We may have applied to six colleges; today many apply to ten or more. Add to this all the tasks involved in applying to college, and you can see how times have changed. Understanding the intense pressure your teen is under will allow you to be there for him or her, both emotionally as well as practically, to help with all the paperwork and logistics involved in the application process.

The Homestretch

Everyone's style is comprised of the "good," the "bad," and even the "ugly." The important thing to take away from this chapter is to identify your style, accept it, and work with it. After reading this chapter, you'll be able to see early warning signs that your *own* issues may prove a hindrance to reaching the finish line. You'll know when to call for reinforcements and when to step back. Self-knowledge really is power, and armed with a little insight and some sound advice from us, you'll find the path smoother and easier to travel.

CHAPTER 3

Know the Common Challenges
Assess Your Teen

What Is a Teen Assessment?

This teen assessment chapter helps you take an objective look at your teen and your family. It asks the important questions that will identify the six challenges your teen may face in the admissions process. Is your teen, for example, a self-starter or a procrastinator? Are there family or financial considerations that affect college admissions? Does he or she have communication problems? Is he or she mature for his or her age or not? Does he or she excel on standardized exams, in school generally, or does he or she struggle? The questionnaires included in this chapter begin with these and many other questions, jump-starting the "teen assessment" lap in the application race.

Assess your teen early to maximize success.

Why Is It So Difficult to Begin the Teen Assessment Process?

Assessing your teen seems like a commonsense idea, an easy thing to do that should take neither much energy nor much time. Yet, surprisingly, it is not so easy. Countless parents we have spoken with have difficulty fully and honestly evaluating their teens or simply don't know where to start. Why is this? One reason is that parents and teens struggle with the three myths we discussed in chapter 1: "Only an Ivy will do," "Only *my* teen can't get into an Ivy," and "Let them jump without a parachute." These myths combine to paralyze many parents and pose an obstacle to teen assessment.

Why Complete the Teen Assessment before Anything Else?

The college race should not be run before doing a teen assessment. As you probably already know, many teens are noncommunicative or unaware of their innermost thoughts and feelings—not only with you but also with themselves. They often can't identify their challenges. Their major racing challenges include communication, avoidance/procrastination, academics/extracurriculars, personality considerations, family issues, and personal considerations. If left unrecognized, these can turn into roadblocks that block your teen's path to the finishing line. Don't worry about the college application tasks now. We get to these in later chapters. First, let's focus on assessing your teen's challenges.

Understand the Teen College Challenges

Now that you are aware of the importance of teen assessment, let's more fully discuss the six common challenges that can stop teens in their tracks.

By completing the "Discover Your Teen" questionnaires, you will be able to predict which of these challenges are likely to be a concern for your teen. Just keep in mind that teens always surprise!

While this chapter reviews the teen challenges, the following list will give you a little "heads-up" on the college application tasks that await. Part 2 discusses each task and provides the strategies for overcoming any roadblocks your teen may face.

Challenges:
- communication issues
- avoidance/procrastination
- academics/extracurricular
- personality considerations
- family issues
- personal considerations

Challenge #1: Communication

The most common teen challenge is communication. This is typical. We hear over and over from parents comments such as "My teen won't talk to me," "I asked her how she

Challenges + Tasks = Roadblocks

feels and she rolls her eyes," or "When I ask him if he is ready to schedule the tours he answers, 'Whatever.'" It is understandable that many teens are reluctant to talk with parents about their college hopes and fears. Some are infected with Ivyitis and feel that "life is over" if they don't get into an Ivy. Others are concerned about disappointing their parents. No wonder they don't want to talk. This is simply too much pressure for many teens to handle.

This kind of pressure actually shuts down the lines of communication between you and your teen. While some teens continue to talk, it is often in an anxious, overwhelmed manner: "What happens if I don't get in *anywhere?*" and "There is too much to do!" Psychologists call this type of thinking "catastrophysing." It actually increases anxiety and creates more obstacles. Catastrophysing is, simply put, making a mountain out of a molehill and assuming the worst-case scenario. Other teens just shut down and lapse into utter silence or monosyllabic answers—"Yes, No, I don't know, I don't care." Either scenario creates an environment that breeds misunderstanding, bruised feelings, and missed opportunities for you to effectively partner with your child in the application process. Consider this family scenario in which open communication was blocked:

MUST-DO TASKS:

- Draw up the college list
- Submit high school transcript
- Submit standardized test scores
- Submit personal essay
- Submit college applications

SHOULD-DO EXTRAS:

- Carefully review college brochures and websites
- Visit colleges
- Do college interviews

☀ JENNY'S STORY

Jenny's parents immigrated from Korea twenty-five years ago. As Jenny told us, her parents endlessly reminded her that they left their homeland to provide her with a better life. They've worked fifteen hours a day in their retail store and saved every extra penny for Jenny's college education. They expected her to attend an Ivy and then go on to medical school. Unfortunately, these were not Jenny's dreams. She had never been able to tell them that she didn't want to attend an Ivy or become a doctor. In fact, Jenny wanted to study fashion design. However, because she couldn't honestly discuss her dreams with her parents, she felt frustrated and trapped. By her junior year, her grades began to slip, and she refused to discuss either her grades or the college search with her parents. This caused everyone to feel hurt and resentful. Just as importantly, without open communication, she compromised her chances to attend the type of college she really wanted. She never even prepared the required portfolio. In the end, neither Jenny nor her parents were happy. She did not get into an Ivy, nor did she go to a college with a fashion design major. Instead, she went to a large university where she majored in biology. Jenny dropped out after her sophomore year. 🌼

This worst-case scenario shows what can happen when family members don't talk openly.

A teen can feel anxious or worried about so many things: grades, SAT scores, peer pressure, and even the desire to please you, his or her parent. It's no wonder they don't want to communicate. Too many parents don't understand that mere words do not equal a discussion. A true dialogue involves give-and-take on both sides. To get this going, you need to take the initiative in a positive, constructive manner. Not only will you learn a lot about your teen's hopes, fears, and dreams, but you will be in good shape to leave the starting block and get into the race.

Complete this assessment questionnaire to determine whether and to what degree communication issues challenge your teen's college admissions.

Discover Your Teen Questionnaire: Communication Issues

My Teen:

1. Becomes upset or argues with me when I try to discuss college.   YES/NO
2. Avoids all or many discussions with me about important topics such as: grades, test scores, and preparing for SAT.   YES/NO

3. Keeps many of his or her thoughts and feelings to   YES/NO
   him- or herself.
4. Has been very moody lately but won't tell me what's   YES/NO
   bothering him or her.
5. Won't even talk to me (or to anyone) about making   YES/NO
   a college list or scheduling tours; he or she finds a way
   to avoid the discussion.
6. Has actually made a college list but I can't figure out   YES/NO
   the selection criteria! Some are urban, some rural,
   some small, others large, and so on.

Challenge #2: Avoidance/Procrastination

Avoidance and procrastination is the second most common challenge many teens face. How do you know if this is a problem for your teen? Chances are this has been your child's long-standing approach to other school tasks, chores, and obligations. Typically, the teenage avoider/procrastinator is "too busy" to attend to the college application process. He is busy with other things: friends, schoolwork, sports, and so on. When pushed to begin or complete college applications, he insists that he will get to it when he has more time. Or, better yet, he tells you he's "workin' on it" when you know he hasn't even given it any consideration at all. By the spring of his junior year or the fall of his senior year, he still has not "found the time." When forced to sit down, he may agree to work with you and even be enthusiastic about making "to-do" lists: things for you "to do" and things for him "to do." The problem is, you get your list completed while he still hasn't gotten to his—"Later, later . . ." he constantly assures you.

What is stopping him from moving forward? You know he really does want to go to college. But fears, worries, and concerns, some real and some imagined, are typically at the root of his pattern of avoidance and procrastination. Mariana correctly diagnosed what was at the root of her son's Sam's procrastination: "I think," she told us, "he was in denial about going to college. He was terrified he wouldn't get in anywhere good, and he was terrified of leaving high school. He never said this to me directly, but I knew he was scared of growing up and having to deal with a whole new environment. Going somewhere where he didn't know anyone. I knew that this was why he didn't send in the applications until the very last minute— February 1!"

This pattern of avoidance and procrastination can affect any type of teen at any time during the application process. Even the teen who has never been prone to procrastination is not immune. Even the always-focused teen who seems to have it all together can suddenly fall "into the void." Here's what happened to Rebecca, a seemingly independent A student who had Ivy League aspirations:

☀ REBECCA'S STORY

Rebecca and her mother had an appointment to meet with the school counselor to discuss her college applications. Rebecca knew this was an important meeting because she attended a large, public high school where these appointments were hard to come by. As she was leaving for school on the day of the appointment, her mother reminded Rebecca that they would meet in front of the counselor's office at 1:45. Yet, at the appointed time, Rebecca was a no-show. At 2:15 the counselor told Rebecca's mother she had to move on to her next appointment. Mom struggled with feelings of embarrassment. "I can't understand where Rebecca could be," Mom proclaimed, "she's usually so punctual." The school counselor smiled sympathetically and advised Mom to take this as a signal that Rebecca was not as secure, calm, or focused as they had all assumed. She probably needed, the counselor advised, more direct guidance and reassurance from her parents. ☀

Discover Your Teen Questionnaire: Avoidance and Procrastination

My Teen:

1. Has a pattern of avoidance and procrastination.	YES/NO
2. Has college information packets piling up on the dining room table and tells me daily, "I'll look at them later."	YES/NO
3. Took the PSAT, his or her score was "not so hot," and he or she still won't commit to taking an SAT prep course.	YES/NO

4. Has avoided visiting any colleges saying, "I'll do   YES/NO
   it later" or "I don't need to."
5. Has visited colleges but with resistance (refused to go   YES/NO
   on the tour, did not schedule specific interviews,
   did not get out of the car, and so on).
6. Won't schedule or misses appointments with the   YES/NO
   school counselor.
7. Avoids asking teachers or coaches for recommendations.   YES/NO

Challenge #3: Academic and Extracurricular

Common hurdles encountered on the college racetrack are less-than-stellar grades and college board scores and few extracurriculars. When we ask our college students about their worst application experience, the number one reply is "The SATs!" Even teens with stellar grades can run up against the SAT barrier. In terms of grade challenges, your teen may be a C student or have an inconsistent academic record. So many teens will get As or Bs in classes they like but Cs and Ds in those they don't. Or there are teens who got off to a "slow" start in their freshman and sophomore high school years and began to earn good grades only during their junior year.

Then there are the kids with few outside interests other than spending time with friends or "leisure" activities. These are the ones who have resisted their parents' suggestions to join clubs or do volunteer work. It's "no biggie" for them, but by the junior or senior year, you may be in a panic: What extracurriculars can be put on the college application? How will it look if your teen leaves it blank? Here is a creative approach one mom used.

☀ A MOM'S TALE

Janice's son, Keith, went through high school without participating in a single extracurricular activity. Other than his interest in music and playing the guitar, his summers were spent in an equally uninspiring fashion. No amount of suggestions, prodding, or even warnings that he would need something to put down on his college applications motivated him. At the beginning of Keith's junior year, Janice felt it was "now or never" to get Keith involved in something. Janice looked for opportunities for her son and discovered a music program at a nearby college that was looking for volunteers to help with a Saturday outreach program with eco-nomically disadvantaged children. Janice contacted the program director and explained that she wanted her son to participate but was worried that if the suggestion came from her, he would reject it. The director (a sympathetic woman with a teenager of her own) agreed to call Keith personally and invite him to volunteer. The call from the director worked. Keith was flattered by the invitation and agreed to try it. Keith stayed with the program until the end of his senior year and was popular with the children and full-time staff. When it came time for Keith to apply to colleges, not only was he able to put his experience into his applications, but the director wrote him a glowing recommendation. ☀

Keith's experience shows how a bit of creativity and initiative can work miracles. Janice understood, after several unsuccessful attempts to involve Keith in outside activities, that her suggestions would be rejected out of hand. She wisely enlisted the assistance of the director. The approach Janice took was effective because she realized something important.

Teens will often accept help and advice from any-one but you.

In this case, it was evident that, deep down, Keith wanted to come out of his shell but couldn't bring himself to do it or directly discuss the matter with his parents. Through the director, Janice was able to indirectly guide and assist Keith. The lesson is that you don't always have to go it alone. When appropriate, you can enlist others to assist your teen overcome challenges.

Discover Your Teen Questionnaire: Academic and Extracurricular Challenges

My Teen:

1. Doesn't perform well or up to potential on standardized tests because of either inadequate preparation, anxiety, or a learning disability.   YES/NO

2. Has an "uneven" academic high school record (some poor grades or low SAT scores).   YES/NO

3. Doesn't have an impressive record of after-school activities or achievements.   YES/NO

4. Doesn't have strong teacher recommendations.   YES/NO

5. Has some actions or entries on his or her high school   YES/NO
record that will be a problem (suspensions, expulsions,
transfers, and so on).

Challenge #4: Personality Considerations

Every person, including your child, is unique, and no two adolescents have the same personality. On the other hand, there are a number of common personality traits that you need to consider as you participate in the college marathon. Is your teen outgoing or shy? Do you have one of those teens who appears so mature that you almost think of him or her as a little adult? Or does yours still act a bit like a baby? Some teens, for example, love new environments and eagerly anticipate change, while others appear to be real homebodies. These are not necessarily "good" or "bad" traits. They simply are some of the many component parts that make up any personality. This guide does not advocate trying to change these. On the other hand, some of these traits facilitate completing the college admissions process, while others do not. Certainly these personality characteristics need to be factored in when making the college list.

The teen who is outgoing, mature, and open to new and larger environments generally has an easier time both completing the application process and finding a "good fit" than those who are immature, shy, or more fearful of new environments. If your teen's personality has any of the latter traits, this is a signal that you are going to be needed as their aide-de-camp. You should be aware that the more immature teen needs more hands-on guidance and emotional support; the shy teen may have a harder time with tours and interviews, and the teen who is more cautious about new environments will probably do better at a smaller rather than a larger college.

A cautionary note about personality traits. Simply because a given trait does not lend itself to all things for all purposes does not mean it is not a desirable trait. For example, caution and prudence can, under certain circumstances, be just what is needed. On the flip side, wild and adventurous can be a great trait but at times may prove to be an impediment. The college admissions process is no different. Jake's story is a good example of this:

☀ JAKE'S STORY

Jake appeared to be a fairly outgoing teen. He had a large number of friends and even appeared adventurous in his choice of activities: skiing, skateboarding, and windsurfing ranked among his favorites. When Jake insisted that he wanted to attend a large university, his parents acquiesced, and off Jack went. Much to his parents' chagrin, Jack came close to flunking out at the end of the first semester of his freshman year. Naturally, they asked themselves, "What had gone wrong?" ☀

When Jake's parents looked back on Jake's teen years, they realized that they had missed some of the markers that were clues to Jack's key personality traits. True, Jake appeared outwardly adventurous and open to new experiences, but in reality his real-life adjustment had been uneven and unpredictable. His first year in high school was rocky, though he did great his last three years. They recalled that Jake hardly ever went to parties or attended events where there would be large crowds. He preferred to stay home and have friends visit. They also remembered that Jake had resisted college tours and interviews and that he had put them off with the excuse that he was "too busy" with schoolwork and could not afford the time away from his studies. In retrospect, his parents realized that they had been fooled by some of Jake's activities, which they interpreted as a sign of an overall adventurous personality. A more careful assessment of Jake's personality style would have revealed that Jake was actually somewhat shy and a bit fearful of new and large environments.

Fortunately, all was not lost for Jake. Remember, it is *never* all lost. College students can always get another chance. His parents encouraged him to withdraw from his university and enroll in their local community college, where Jake did quite well. They then looked for smaller colleges and insisted that Jake tour them. By the spring semester of his sophomore year, Jake had transferred to a small college and went on to successfully complete college.

As you can see from Jake's story, it is critical to consider your teen's personality traits for drawing up the best-fit college list.

Discover Your Teen Questionnaire: Personality Considerations

My Teen:

1. Doesn't handle change well (e.g., has had difficulty   YES/NO
   going to sleep-away camp or never lived away from home).
2. Has a birthday late in the year or is somewhat immature.   YES/NO
3. Becomes anxious in public speaking situations or does   YES/NO
   not talk in large classes.

4. Becomes shy when meeting new people.   YES/NO
5. Doesn't like situations where there are crowds.   YES/NO
6. Has difficulty being assertive in a school situation   YES/NO
   (e.g., trying to get a class changed or approaching
   a teacher for assistance).
7. Has difficulty making new friends.   YES/NO

Challenge #5: Family Issues

These days, many teens come from families of single or divorced parents, while others live in unconventional or blended families. The college admissions and selection process can cause old issues or conflicts to resurface—or new ones to emerge. For example, questions such as "Who's going to pay how much, for what?," "Who will take the kid on college tours?," and "Whose job is it to fill out all the paperwork?" can crop up at the worst possible moments. Failure to identify these challenges ahead of time leads to serious roadblocks:

☼ ROBERT'S STORY

This critical delay happened to Robert, whose parents divorced when he was ten. His parents had difficulty talking openly and avoided discussing many issues about Robert. Their conversations often focused on old, unresolved hurts. While they never clearly discussed college costs, Dad had promised to pay his son's college tuition. Robert was not only counting on it but also setting his sights on an expensive private college. Following his college counselor's advice, Robert sailed through the application process and was accepted at an excellent private college. Even though he did not receive any scholarships, he and his mother were ecstatic. When the time came to put down the deposit, Robert's father announced he would not pay for a private school. "Yes," he agreed, he had said he would pay Robert's tuition, "but not for such an expensive private school." Unfortunately for Robert, he didn't know about this stipulation ahead of time, and now it was too late to apply to one of the many fine state universities. He and his mom had to scramble to find the money for this expensive college, and, not surprisingly, Robert's relationship with his father was badly damaged. ☀

Robert's example is typical and perhaps one of the most common family issue. In today's society, where families come in "all shapes and sizes," there are a myriad of challenges that can crop up. Blended families face unique issues. Let's say that a newly blended family has two teens applying to college the same year. With different biological parents, there may be disparities in economic resources. The teens may have very distinct strengths, weaknesses, and dreams. Factor in the sheer logistics of it all—two sets of applications, competing times and places for college visits, competing voices, along with the double expense—and you really have a complicated stew in your pot. Sorting out the who, what, when, where, and how is certainly a challenge, but it's vital that you try to resolve these issues early on, before you begin the college search.

Perhaps the least discussed issue is that concerning families with gay and/or mixed-race parents. This can be a touchy subject. Teens, no matter how much they love or are proud of their families, struggle with "I want to fit in" or "I don't want to stand out" feelings no matter what they may publicly voice or say to you, the parent. College visits may be triggers for these feeling. An extra burden for them may actually be admitting these feelings to you. They may fear that you will feel hurt by these perfectly understandable feelings.

☀ A PARENTS' TALE

Ruth and Larry, a mixed-race couple, confronted this issue when they began to plan their son Ben's college visits. The first visit was to a large urban university with a very diverse student body. On visit day, Ben announced, "I think I just want Dad with me. You [Mom] can stay home." Mom was stunned. She attempted to argue with Ben, but he just dug in his heels and finally told her that if she insisted on coming, he would not go at all. Mom was hurt but resigned. When Ben and Dad returned, Larry told Ruth that students actually asked whether he was the father or the stepfather. Larry is black, Ruth is white, and Ben takes after his mother. During the visit, Ben confided to his father that he thought that if the kids on campus saw them together without his mother, they would realize "who he *really* was." Ben had never voiced this kind of concern about his racial identity and mixed loyalty before. Not surprisingly, a whole range of issues surfaced during the application process. ❋

Another family challenge involves financial issues. High tuition and living costs are a burden for almost all families. Few can shoulder the entire burden alone. Most families need some type of financial aid in the form of either loans or scholarships. So discuss financial issues early and ask yourselves, "Can we afford a private college?," "Should we only look at public colleges and universities?," and "How will these obligations be shared or apportioned?" We suggest that you first discuss the financial constraints with all the adults involved so that all of you are on the same page before discussing it with your teen. Only then can you draw up the college list.

Discover Your Teen Questionnaire: Family Issues

My Teen:

1. Comes from a single-parent household.   YES/NO
2. Comes from a divorced-parent household.   YES/NO
3. Has parents with very disparate ideas on college   YES/NO
   choice and application.
4. Has divorced or separated parents who have not   YES/NO
   clearly established who will take the teen on tours,
   complete the application paperwork, assume
   financial responsibility, and so on.
5. Has major financial concerns (e.g., how college   YES/NO
   tuition will be paid).

Challenge #6: Other Personal Considerations

Many teens have personal considerations that are not addressed in most college brochures or books. Some personal considerations include ethnic, racial, religious, and sexual identity. Others include specialized interests such as engineering, culinary arts, music, and theater. The highest priority is to find a college where your child will be happy and succeed. For example, if your child is an African American, does she prefer a historically black college or a more integrated school? These same concerns can also arise among many other ethnic groups as well as for gay teens and those whose religious affiliation or political bent are defining factors in their identity. Remember, college may be a drastic geographic, demographic, and cultural change from high school. Your first job is to figure out which colleges will provide the best environment for your teen. Then you need to be aware that your teen can emphasize some of these personal characteristics in the application. When and how these issues can be effectively raised will be included in chapter 7.

A final personal consideration is your teen's peers and their influence. All of us think or hope that we, the parents, will be the most influential advisers in our child's choice of college; however, teens often place tremendous importance on the advice and opinions of friends. An issue that commonly affects a teen's choice of college is where friends are applying. Unfortunately, what may be a good match for a friend may not be as great a fit for your teen. Your teen may not have the same academic record and test scores as his or her friends, or there may be other considerations and factors that will affect his or her choice of college and chance of acceptance. There are times when you will have to maneuver around your teen's friends and romantic attachments. Here is a small example of the disastrous consequence of a teen simply following her heart in her college selection:

☀ A MOM'S TALE

Joan remembered that from the time her daughter, Nancy, was a child, her passion was music. She played piano from age five, and, unlike so many other kids, her mother never had to ask her to practice. Even during those mercurial teen years, Nancy steadfastly stuck to the piano and her love of music. When it came time to go to college, Joan had no doubt that her daughter would apply to a music conservatory. She did and got into several fine ones, including her first choice, which was the New England Conservatory of Music in Boston. Imagine Joan's surprise when her daughter announced that she wanted to attend University X—a fine state university but not strong in music performance. "Why in the world do you want to go there?" Mom wanted to know. The answer (and we're sure many of you have guessed it) is that there was a boyfriend. "Bob is going to University X, and we have to stay together," Nancy said. As you can imagine, Mom was not happy but decided to let Nancy make her own decision even though she was certain her daughter would regret it.

Nancy went off to University X with Bob that fall, and at the end of the first semester, they broke up. By the spring semester, she was thoroughly miserable. Her attempts to gain admission at the highly competitive music conservatories that had accepted her just a year earlier were unsuccessful. Unfortunately, not every story has a happy ending. Discouraged by her failure to transfer to a conservatory, Nancy abandoned her dreams of a professional music career and settled for a degree in music education. Joan told us that, to this day, Nancy regrets not going to a music conservatory. ✺

The moral of this cautionary tale is that, while there are times when you can (and should) allow your teen to make mistakes or even "fail," you have to use your judgment to assess when you should step in.

Discover Your Teen Questionnaire: Other Personal Considerations

My Teen:

1. Is an ethnic/racial minority student.   YES/NO
2. Is gay or bisexual and wants to be in a highly   YES/NO
   diverse and accepting college community.
3. Has strong religious values and cultural identifications   YES/NO
   and prefers colleges with a high percentage of students
   of similar cultural values.
4. Has friends who have scored either much higher or   YES/NO
   lower on the SATs and/or have higher grade-point
   averages.
5. Has friends all of whom are going to local colleges   YES/NO
   (or going away to college).
6. Has goals that would be enhanced by attending a   YES/NO
   different college than his or her friends.
7. Has specialized interest in the arts or athletics that is   YES/NO
   not shared by her friends.

The Homestretch

If you're like most parents, your answers to these questions demonstrate that your teen has one or even a number of challenges that need careful consideration during the application race. By identifying both your own parenting style(s) and your teen's challenges, you have taken the first crucial steps in successfully finishing the college admissions race. Equipped with this information, you have empowered yourself to effectively partner with your child and guide him or her around the roadblocks that stand in the way to the best-fit college.

We hope that after reviewing part I, you genuinely realize that you are not alone—the vast majority of teens face some challenges, whether they reflect personal preferences or family circumstance. Remember that none of us, no matter how hard we try, are the perfect parent or can provide our teen with the perfect environment. All we can do is try our best. So don't feel discouraged. You have actually taken that first crucial step in helping your teen "win" the race by identifying and addressing your and your teen's challenges and are now on the fast track to the finish line.

So read on. Part II includes crucial information about college tasks and descriptions of strategies you can easily apply to overcome the obstacles and roadblocks your teen may encounter. And don't worry! For every roadblock or challenge, we will provide you with numerous tips, strategies, and creative, easy-to-follow solutions. Remember, you and your teen can finish this race and win.

How to Train for the College Application Race:

1. **Make you teen #1 in the process.**

2. **Discover your teen's abilities, potential, and dreams.**

3. **Assess your teen's challenges and get ready to overcome the roadblocks.**

Running the Race

YOU'VE GOTTEN into shape, and you are ready to run the race. What is the most important thing to know before you begin? Familiarize yourself with the course. The course is made up of a variety of tasks. Part II takes you through these in an easy-to-digest, commonsense manner. We lay out the course for you so that you know what to expect and also alert you to any challenges or obstacles you might encounter on your way to the finish line. And, so that you don't become discouraged if you do have to jump over a hurdle, we provide the strategy for doing so.

Briefly, here is how to run the course. First, check out chapter 4, "The Dreaded Countdown," and familiarize yourself with all the basic tasks and when and who needs to do these. Second, gear up and prepare your teen for the high-stakes tests. Chapter 5, "Let the Tests Begin," will not only explain the what, when, and where of these but also provide you with *options* with regard to these. Your next decision is to decide the path you and your teen think you might want to take to the college finish line. In chapter 6, "Drawing Up the College List," you will assess the wide variety of options out there and select a manageable college list. Finally, you will go and check out the course. These are the college visits and tours. In this race, you get to look over the course before starting to run. Chapter 7, "Taking It on the Road," tells you what to look for when visiting colleges.

Chapter 8, "Packaging for Success," takes you through this process step-by-step, alerts you to any obstacles you might encounter, and shows you how to overcome these. Chapter 9, "Personal Considerations," is a continuation of particular concerns and issues that many families have that affect college selection and admissions. Chapter 10, "Crossing the Finish Line," discusses making the decision.

CHAPTER 4

The Dreaded Countdown
College Tasks from Freshman through Senior Year

MOST PARENTS (except the Type As) are not fully engaged in the college admissions process until their teen's junior or senior year. So, if you're reading this guide, most likely your teen is either a junior or a senior and you have begun to feel the college countdown clock ticking in earnest. There seems to be so much to do and so many application tasks to finish. You may be asking yourself questions like "When should my child take the SAT for the first time?" and "When do we need to begin visiting colleges?" You may also be a bit harsh on yourself, wondering, "Why don't I know these things?" The truth is that no one who hasn't gone through the process has more than a kind of general, passing knowledge of what to do and when to do it. Most first-time parents running in this race feel as if they are late leaving the starting block. But don't panic. This chapter succinctly and clearly lays out the high school to college timetable. We'll take you step-by-step through the countdown—from the freshman through the senior year. The section on the freshman and sophomore years are brief and dedicated to those ambitious college parents who begin to prepare for college applications during their teen's freshman year.

Many of you may be thinking, "Freshman and sophomore year? My kid is already a junior. I'm hopelessly behind. The race is already lost!" Don't panic. In fact, welcome to the club. Before our junior year, most of us were not paying too much attention to college either. However, even if your teen is a junior, you may want to read the freshman/sophomore section before you move on to those sections dedicated to the junior and senior years because there are many organizational suggestions and ideas that you can still use.

Freshman/Sophomore Years

Many college guides focus on getting your child's résumé up and going early in their high school years. Certainly, we agree that it is very helpful to start organizing your teen's materials early so that you won't have to frantically search for them during the fall of their senior year. It is also good to be aware of the best classes and extracurricular activities they might enjoy and guide them into these if they are willing. Here are a few racing tips to jump-start the college application process:

Tip #1: Prepare the College Drawer

Start putting together a separate file, drawer, or box for college application materials. Make one file in which to save and organize all the programs, playbills, honor certificates, awards, and other materials documenting those extracurricular activities and special academic recognition. Label it, for example, "Résumé Materials." Don't worry if your teen doesn't have a file full of honors during these early high school

When in doubt, file it.

years, as most won't. What you can do, however, is save or file away certificates of attendance/participation that are routinely distributed as well as a record of anything your teen participates in or has accomplished, even if no certificate comes with it. All of this will come in handy for putting together that all-important résumé.

Tip #2: Get Your Teen into Shape with Extracurriculars

Many not-always-focused (NAF) teens are not involved in extracurricular activities. If possible, try to encourage your teen to join school clubs, become involved in sports or the arts, and volunteer or work for pay. Colleges do value students who will contribute to their college's community. Don't interpret this recommendation as a green light to push them into activities for the sake of the college application. Extracurriculars are important to teens, to their social life, and to their self-esteem. The key is to help them find activities that match their interests and engage them. Teens are happier when they are busy doing things they enjoy. As a bonus, extracurriculars enable teens to learn more about themselves, and this will ultimately make the college search easier for all concerned.

Tip #3: Know the High School Classes That Are Right for Your Teen

Become aware of the range and challenge level of your child's classes. Many liberal arts colleges, as well as specialized college programs, have specific high school prerequisites. Glance at (don't memorize yet) a few college brochures to see what classes they expect applicants to have taken during high school. The general rule is a minimum of three years of sciences, three years of language, four years of English, and four years of social studies.

If your child is both motivated and capable, you can encourage him or her to take honors and advanced placement (AP) classes. Not every teen is ready for these highly rigorous classes. Make sure you consider whether your teen will respond positively to and is capable of succeeding in these types of classes. While successfully completing such advanced courses looks great to a college admissions officer, it is counterproductive to try to force or pressure a teen to take such courses. Compelling a reluctant teen to take on these challenging courses could result in your teen developing an antagonistic, negative attitude toward school or you or simply doing poorly in that AP or honors course. This is not a battle you need to fight. Doing well in "regular" courses is far preferable to doing poorly in advanced courses. So remember, when weighing your child's activities and academic options, use your common sense. Push when helpful and back off when not.

Tip #4: Consider the PSAT/PLAN

High schools give teens the option to take a practice PSAT or PLAN exam during the fall of the sophomore year. The scores provide you with a ballpark indication as to how your teen will do on the SAT or ACT. These practice tests are great because they are risk free; the scores will not be sent to any colleges. We recommend that you encourage your teen to take it, but don't go overboard. We have seen parents push their teens to study for this test during their sophomore year, and this is usually a mistake. Too much test prep too early will lead to test burnout. In fact, you actually want to see how your teen does on this type of standardized entrance exam uncoached. It will help give you a realistic idea of how much assistance your teen may or may not require to prepare for the SAT or ACT. We discuss these tests in depth in chapter 5.

Tip #5: Help Keep Their Grades Up

Last, as we all know, the bottom line is grades. If your teen is an always-focused (AF) teen who has studied hard and earned good grades during these first two years of high school, then your child is entering those critical final two years in great shape. If, however, your teen is more a NAF teen, don't despair. Keep in mind that he or she is one of the silent majority. Keep your sense of humor and perspective, especially since most teens don't. Hopefully, your teen has developed positive friendships, matured a bit, made some academic progress, and started to work through some of those adolescent woes. There are still another two years to go. And don't forget: "It ain't over 'til it's over."

Freshman and Sophomore Tasks:

1. Choose the "right" courses and keep up the grades
2. Organize the college file or cabinet
3. Take a practice PSAT
4. Get involved in extracurriculars

Junior Year

Now we come to the first of the two critical years in the search for the best college for *your* child. Now the race begins in earnest. You are probably facing an overload of information and tasks that need doing. Fortunately, the college admissions process is not rocket science. Armed with accurate infor-

"I'm already overwhelmed. What do I do first?" Just follow the racing tips.

mation, a lot of patience, and just a pinch of creativity, you can skillfully guide your teen into a good-fit college that both you and your teen will be happy with. So let's get ready to run.

Tip #1: Organize, Organize, and Organize

The calendar is your most important tool, and luckily it is both low cost and low tech. The calendar you purchase should be dedicated to the application process. Post it in a place where you will see it frequently. Don't tuck it away in a drawer. Dedicate it for college-related deadlines and activities *only*. Use it to list all the tests, tours, interviews, auditions, and application due dates. As you begin to fill in this calendar, you'll see that all this is really too much to keep track of in your head. Of course, in an ideal world it would be preferable for your teen to assume this responsibility, but, with few exceptions, most teens cannot keep track of all of these deadlines and dates.

Tip #2: Buy a File Cabinet or Clear Out a File Drawer

A college file cabinet or drawer is an indispensable tool in the college application race. This is especially important for the procrastinating or worried type of parent. However, if you follow these tips, by next year you will be in shape to fill out those applications. Your college file cabinet will be filled with all the materials you need to get the job done in as painless a way as possible. Let's organize the college file drawer.

The Résumé File

This file is for all the information you need to make your teen's résumé. Into this file will go all the playbills, programs, awards, certificate of participation, copies of report cards, and any materials they receive about both their outside activities and their academic record. This is especially helpful if your child is involved in sports and visual or performing arts. Some students or parents started the résumé construction process way back in the freshman or sophomore year. Don't worry if you haven't. Just start collecting these materials, and if you didn't keep anything from the freshman and sophomore years, see if you can get them from the high school, friends, or pertinent organizations. This may take a few phone calls or sorting through piles of old papers, but trust us: it's worth the effort. If all else fails, you will have to reconstruct it from memory. Remember, be honest about your child's activities and accomplishments and don't worry if you don't have that "magical" piece of paper to back you up—supporting documentation is not required for student résumés.

A few last thoughts about teen summers. Chances are your teen has gone to camp and done interesting things. Just because he or she didn't win some award or prize doesn't mean it won't be something that can be presented in a favorable light in the student résumé or on his or her college application. If your teen developed a unique relationship with outside-of-school supervisors or employers, you can encourage your teen to request a letter of recommendation. Just file these letters or certificates away in the résumé file for later use.

Supporting Application Materials

Even though you probably don't know which colleges your child will eventually choose to apply to, there are materials you can collect that will be sent to all the schools, including a graded paper and recommendations. Toward the end of the junior year, your teen can ask favorite teachers for recommendations. Some may have an essay they wrote for a class that could be used as the basis for the personal essay or as a supplement to the applications. You should, after making copies, file these away. When the time comes to fill out those applications, you'll be happy—and relieved—you did. (For information about what materials to send to college, see chapter 8.)

College Information File

You also need to make separate files for college materials. These will be your "College Information Files" for collecting and organizing the college brochures and view books. Don't worry if you are constantly adding and subtracting from this file. In fact, if you find yourself doing this, it means that you and your teen are getting a sense of which type of college he or she is or is not interested in. You will be amazed at how much information colleges send. Once you and your teen are really interested in a particular college, you can make separate files.

Financing File

Now is also the time to start thinking about financing your teen's college education, and you need to create a separate file in which to collect that information. You can certainly include information about scholarships and aid. It will make your life easier later.

Tip #3: It's Time to Open Up Those College Brochures

Most teens just throw the college brochures away or let them pile up, unopened on a dining room or kitchen table. Is it okay for you to open them? Yes—if your teen gives you permission. Most could care less as long as you don't pester them too much. If your teen won't open and organize the college brochures, then you should do it. Remember, your teen will be sent loads of materials, and you probably can't or shouldn't keep all of it.

Not surprisingly, the procrastinating teen is particularly resistant to beginning the college search process. Eventually, you do want your teen to at least glance at those college materials or college websites. When broaching the subject, we suggest you emphasize that your teen should "just look at it." Make it clear to your teen that "looking at" a college brochure is not tantamount to a commitment to attend that school or even filling out the application. Now is *not* the time to pressure your teen excessively; your goal is to have some sort of pared-down list by the spring of the junior year or fall of the senior year.

Tip #4: Get a General Sense of the College Costs

Here comes a subject we all dread: the cost of a college education. We're sure you don't need to be reminded how expensive it is—but it's so important, for many reasons, to get a general sense of the costs, your family's college budget, and the available financing options. As you start to look at the many college options, you will see there is a big difference in the price tag between community, state, and private colleges. Private colleges can cost anywhere from $25,000 to $50,000 per year inclusive of room and board, the average running about $35,000. On the other hand, community colleges and four-year state colleges can cost between $3,000 and $25,000, depending on your state of residence.

Clearly, unless you have saved significant amounts of money before the junior year or are extremely flush in the pocket, you may not be able to afford a private college without a little—or a lot of—assistance or financial aid. Now is the time to explore scholarship opportunities. You might be able to swing a private college if your child has demonstrated financial need or has some kind of "hook." These hooks include athletic or artistic talents, stellar grades or test scores, minority status, and even demonstrable abilities such as leadership. You also want to familiarize yourself with the federal loan program and other types of assistance that are available on a state-to-state basis. This guide does not discuss financial aid issues in depth. If you need more information, we strongly recommend that you read one of the specialized guides and websites. There are numerous guides available, from general guides such as College Board's *Guide to Getting Financial Aid* (2007) to more specialized guides such as Berry's *Minority Financial Aid Directory* (1995).

We strongly suggest that you honestly and assertively discuss these financial issues with all the adults you expect to contribute to "the college fund" *before* you broach this sensitive issue with your teen. Different family circumstances will prompt a range of considerations. If you are a single parent, are there grandparents or other family members who can help? If divorced, will your ex pay part, most, all, or nothing? If your resources are limited, can you afford a private college, or should you and your teen consider only a state or community college? Remember, try not to discuss finances with your child until you have a firm idea of how much you can afford and how the costs will be covered. We emphasize doing this in the junior year because you don't want to encourage your teen to apply to private colleges only to find out, after the applications have gone out or acceptance letters received, that you cannot swing it financially. It is essential, from the start of the process, that everyone have realistic expectations.

Even if finances are an issue, this *does not* mean that you should discourage your teen from applying to any private colleges. Remember, scholarships are given, especially for those with a demonstrated financial need or some hook, and loans are readily available. Just be clear about what the options are and the implications of taking out loans if that is the only way you can swing it; also make sure that your teen also applies to state institutions in case the needed financing for a private college does not materialize. This way, your teen does not enter the process with unrealistic expectations that can lead only to serious problems and disappointments later. Putting the financial option cards on the table from the beginning will go a long way to ensuring that when those college acceptance letters arrive in the spring of his or her senior year, both you and your teen will be pleased.

Tip #5: Get Your Teen Involved

We haven't forgotten that we promised earlier to tell you *when* you need to complete college-related tasks, and that time has arrived. By the junior year, your teen should be involved in some form of extracurricular activity. If your teen is already involved in extracurricular activities, great. If not, a few suggestions to "join a club" could be just what a shy or underinvolved teen needs. Remember, being involved in school activities is rewarding in and of itself. Reluctant teens will be more likely to join if they feel they are doing it for the pure enjoyment of the activity as opposed to doing it simply to satisfy some unknown college admissions officer. If, however, your child remains adamant and doesn't want to join clubs or do sports, then try volunteer work. If your teen is truly too busy during the academic year, think about interesting activities your teen can do over the summer. Don't worry if he or she doesn't become class president or the editor of the school newspaper; what's important is finding an activity that has meaning for him or her and something he or she can stick with.

Now a word about teens with learning, emotional, or physical disabilities: remember, for these teens, keeping up and/or excelling with their schoolwork may be as much as they can realistically do. If this is the case, then you need to set aside your fears that without extracurricular activities, your teen cannot compete with others in the application process. In other words, we are urging you not to overburden or pressure your teen. Don't let your fears infect your teen. Instead, try to space and achieve a balance between academic requirements and extracurriculars. After all, isn't that what summers are for?

And what about the teens who simply love to read, kids who want to spend their free time with their nose in a good book? If this description fits your teen, don't worry, it really is okay. The most important aspect of *all* teens' lives is that they have friends and are developing into happy young adults. Try to nudge them to turn their love of reading into an extracurricular activity—maybe volunteering to read to children in your local library or become a reading tutor.

If you just can't get them to do much outside of their schoolwork, it may be that this is a challenge you have to live with. Some NAF teens, no matter how you emphasize that a lack of extracurricular activities may hurt their college applications, simply won't budge. Other than giving them this choice, there may not be more you can do. If you are a worried or Type A parent, it may be especially difficult to accept this, but, more important, you need to keep your composure and let it go. Remember, sometimes you just can't control everything.

And, as always, even without many extracurriculars, all is not lost. In chapter 8, we will discuss the ways to address all these situations on the college application. Don't lose sight of the fact that there is something unique about every teen, something worthwhile that can be highlighted in the college application.

Tip #6: Get Acquainted with the Standardized Tests

Exam fever usually sets in during the fall of the junior year, when most teens take the PLAN or PSAT. Most high schools will give your teen the application and administer the test during the school day. What should your attitude be about these tests? Most NAF teens will not seriously study for the PSAT/ PLAN. How should you handle it if your teen will not study for it? Remember, this PSAT/PLAN score is used only for the National Merit Scholarship Awards and will not be sent to colleges as part of their applications. For most teens, this is their "wake-up call," their dose of reality; it is their first *real* score. If your teen gets a high score without preparation, great; if not, don't worry, as a disappointing PSAT/PLAN score will usually motivate a teen to study for the "real" (SAT/ACT) test. While the PSAT/PLAN may not be designed for this purpose, we find it to be the perfect kick in the pants for many procrastinators. Read chapter 5 to learn all about the various tests.

Teens usually take the SAT/ACT for the first time during the spring of the junior year. You and your teen need to decide about SAT/ACT test preparation. There are several options: private tutors, commercial prep courses such as Princeton or Kaplan, and self-studying. Of these three options, we recommend only the last for the most organized, mostly AF teens. Of course, these teens are usually the ones eager for a prep course.

So how to decide which test prep approach best suits your teen, and how do you motivate him or her to do it? It is up to you to assess which option is best for your teen. Ask yourself questions such as "Is she generally good at studying with a group?" and "Can she be counted on to do the SAT practices assigned?" If yes, then one of the commercial prep courses will probably do. However, if your teen needs more individualized attention to keep her on track, then you might want to consider a one-on-one tutor or a smaller-group situation.

Another consideration is, of course, your financial circumstances. If money is a concern, ask your school's guidance counselor if the school provides a test prep class. Some community organizations and churches also provide reduced price prep courses or resources to help defray the cost. Additionally, some of the commercial prep courses will provide a lower rate for those with a demonstrated financial need. Remember, never be afraid to ask. If you don't ask, you don't get. The worse thing anyone can say is "no."

You may be thinking, "Well, this sounds great, but my kid won't even agree to take a prep course." Don't panic. Most of the time these NAF teens—even the procrastinators and avoiders—will agree to a prep course once the first disappointing test result comes in. Most teens (NAF or AF) do take the SAT/ACT a second time and sometimes even a third time. Test prep can always be arranged during the summer or even as late as the fall of the senior year. The great thing is that these tests are given frequently, and the turnaround time for the score is usually no more than a few weeks. Consequently, even the most obstinate teen has the opportunity to procrastinate and get in his or her best score before colleges make their final decisions.

What if your NAF teen has test anxiety? Many teens are overly concerned about how they will score compared to their friends. If this is your teen, we strongly recommend that you steer him or her toward individual tutoring. Many teens avoid prep courses not because they are lazy or don't want the help but because they, understandably, don't want to be embarrassed in front of other teens. If you suspect this might be the case, talk about it openly and ask the right questions. There is no reason for the words "test prep" and "torture" to be synonymous.

Don't forget about the SAT IIs or subject tests. These are twenty additional tests of specific academic areas including the sciences, foreign languages, history, and other high school subjects. Most colleges do not require SAT IIs, while some of the Ivies request up to three. Since the SAT IIs assess specialized knowledge, it really is important that your teen take the SAT II exam immediately after finishing the related course. He or she has the best chance of a high score when the material is fresh in his or her mind.

A general rule of thumb, most high schools *do not* register teens for the SAT or the SAT IIs. It is up to you and your teen to decide *when* your teen takes the SAT and which SAT IIs to take. Of course, your teen should choose those SAT IIs that he or she has the best chance to score well on. Once this decision is made, you can go ahead and schedule one or two exams. Even though three can be taken on one day, we don't recommend it, unless your teen has lots of energy. And one last thought about these exams: some teens opt to take the ACT. The ACT is used mostly in the Midwest and is a standardized college entrance exam used to assess mastery of the high school curriculum. It includes questions in math, science, and reading and an optional essay. Your teen can always take the ACT in the spring of the junior year.

If your teen has a physical or learning disability, now is the time to learn about, consider, and apply for testing accommodations. Many parents have already completed the necessary evaluations and paperwork for accommodations. However, if you have not, you need to deal with this issue *now*, before the dreaded high-stakes exams must be taken. In chapter 5, we discuss the advantages and disadvantages of the SAT and the ACT as well as issues specifically for students with disabilities.

Tip #7: Start Touring by the Junior Year

The best time to begin the college tours is during the junior year. While some teens (particularly AF teens) have been eager to visit colleges and began touring during their sophomore year, most do not. Should you push? Now that your teen is in his or her junior year, yes, but gently and tactfully. By the end of the junior year, it is best to have seen enough schools to have a general notion of the colleges that will be a good fit. While some teens are able to do this through "virtual" tours by reviewing college brochures and surfing the Internet, nothing can really substitute for a real, boots-on-the-ground visit. Most need to actually see the campus (and, most important, the students there). In addition to taking tours with you, encourage your teen to go on organized tours with their high school, church, or other community organizations. Another popular option is to organize a group of teens to take some tours. This not only makes touring more enjoyable and less stressful for your teen but also is a great way to share the costs in time and money. Read chapter 7 to learn more about how to arrange tours and make the most of these visits.

Tip #8: Don't Forget the School Counselors and Other Mentors

The school counselor can be a wonderful fount of knowledge and a useful ally. Encourage your teen to meet with the counselor as often as possible, but don't insist. Many, especially the overworked ones, don't want to meet with juniors until the spring semester. School counselors can often make suggestions that your teen will "hear," even if he or she has ignored the same recommendation from you. They can also be helpful regarding locating prep courses and tutors and can give you tips about financial aid and suggestions of good-fit colleges.

If your teen doesn't have a good working relationship with the counselor or refuses to ask the counselor for assistance, consider encouraging your teen to speak with alternate mentors. This can be a close friend, a relative, a private college adviser, or anyone your child is willing to listen to.

Tip #9: Don't Forget to Use the Summer

If your teen is very busy with extracurriculars and/or schoolwork, you should consider using the summer between the junior and senior years to get some of the college visits and interviews completed. We find that teens learn more if they tour while college is in session, but if that definitely cannot be arranged, do what you can. Certainly, if your teen has already identified one or a few colleges he or she definitely plans to apply to, summer is a great time to get those interviews done.

Now is also a good time to schedule the fall interviews. Don't wait too late, or you'll find the best times taken.

Senior Year

At the start of the senior year, you and your teen need to choose your teen's application option. These are the following:

• Regular action
• Early decision
• Early action

Regular Action

Regular action is applying to college according to the traditional time line: most applications due sometime between the New Year until February 15 with a decision coming sometime between early and mid-April. Teens applying regular action typically include a good number and range of schools.

Early Decision

Early decision (ED) is an option where the student applies early—usually in November. Notification of acceptance (or not) is also early—usually in December. The student who applies and is accepted ED is spared the waiting-until-April anxiety. But you know that old saying, "There's no free lunch." This is true: you get something, but you give something in return. The ED option is binding. Your teen signs an agreement letter that he or she must attend if accepted and withdraw any regular action applications submitted.

One other thought about ED. This program has come under increasing fire in recent years. Many educators believe that it favors well-to-do students and puts the rest of the population at a distinct disadvantage. Harvard University apparently agrees. In September 200, Harvard announced it would drop its ED. A few days later, Princeton University announced that it too was eliminating its ED program. The changes in their admissions policies may affect students applying for the fall of 2008.

Early Action

Some colleges have instituted an early action (EA) option. Early action means that the college will let the applicant know early whether they have been accepted, but there is no binding agreement. Unlike ED, the applicant does not have to accept or reject the offer until the regular decision time in April. There is really no downside to applying EA. Just make sure to check when the EA applications are due since colleges have different application dates.

Tip #1: Don't Forget All Those Tests

The fall of the senior year is the time for many teens to *retake* the SAT/ACT. Many SAT IIs are directly course related and should be taken in the spring after the teen has completed the course. Other SAT IIs, such as literature, are not directly course related and can be taken at any time. If your teen did not take any SAT IIs last spring and is considering a college that requires them, schedule them now. Refer to chapter 5 to learn all about the different tests. It is not too late to schedule some tutoring or prep classes.

Tip #2: Working with Your School Counselor

Now is also the time to check on how your teen is working with his or her counselor and if he or she has requested and gotten those teacher recommendations. If you sense a problem, you may want to speak with the school counselor directly. As much as we don't like to say it, senior year is crunch time, so it's time to get moving. If the tasks are not being completed on time, you need to run faster and jump higher. Obstacles during the fall of the senior year can be serious and can have an adverse impact on getting into a good-fit college.

. Also keep in mind that many high schools have their own deadlines for putting together the college application materials. Find out about deadlines from the college office and mark these on your calendar. Inform yourself about any available college application assistance provided by your teen's high school and, more important, what they will not do. Some small or private high schools will do almost all the paperwork for you, while others (particularly large public high schools) do only the bare minimum.

Tip #3: Select the Colleges Your Teen Wants to Apply To

Now is the time for you and/or your child to pare down or, in some cases, create the college list. Read chapter 6 about how to help your teen do this. Hopefully, you started a college file during your child's junior year. It's time to take out all those brochures and view books you filed away and make a separate file for each college you will be sending an application to. Now is also the time to take out your calendar and enter each college application deadline on it. Also, don't throw out college brochures from schools you think your teen is not interested in—he or she may change their mind—and it's easier to retrieve it from your file cabinet than request it again. Just put them away, out of your teen's sight for now.

If your teen hasn't done so already, now is the last opportunity to schedule tours and interviews. Don't wait until too late because the open dates get taken. Better to schedule and cancel. Encourage your teen to visit colleges and read about college tour strategies in chapter 7.

What can you do if your teen flatly refuses to visit? Take a deep breath and look for your sense of humor. Remember, even your NAF teen *will* go to college. Together, you will select colleges by looking at the brochures, talking with knowledgeable parents and students, consulting with the high school college adviser, and reviewing the Teen Assessment Questionnaires you completed. Remember, many teens apply to and are accepted by colleges they have never seen or been interviewed by. The good news is that most colleges today offer the opportunity for your teen to visit once he or she has been accepted. In our experience, even the most tour-adverse teen will visit colleges that have accepted him or her.

Tip #4: College Interviews, Auditions, and Portfolios

Not all colleges require interviews. As a rule, the most competitive colleges usually recommend interviews, while many large public universities do not have them at all. If a college "recommends" it, this means your teen should make an all-out effort to interview. Many colleges send admissions counselors around the country—referred to as "away" interviews—to conduct interviews in the applicant's local area. Type A and worried parents may question whether their teen would lose some "edge" by taking advantage of this time- and energy-saving way to interview. We don't have any clear advice for you in making this decision. If you have the time to schedule the interview at the college, do it. If you or your teen doesn't have the time or money, use your common sense and take advantage of the "away" interview. Again, it is up to you to inquire as to the availability of an away interview in your area. And don't forget: put those interview dates down on that calendar.

If your teen is applying for a specialized program, such as in the arts (music, theater, dance, or art) or architecture, then your teen will probably need to submit a portfolio or audition. You need to ascertain the deadlines for these so that you can make the appropriate preparations and, as always, mark their deadlines on your college calendar. Again, if you live in or near a large metropolitan area, your teen may be able to audition locally. While some colleges accept a tape or video, in the arts, if at all possible, have your teen do a live audition.

Tip #5: College Costs

You need to learn about the costs of each college your teen is considering. Investigate the possibility of financial aid or merit scholarships. Most teens have difficulty ferreting out this kind of information and rely on your advice. You can discuss these issues with the financial aid offices of prospective colleges.

Tip #6: Application Deadlines

Different schools have different submission deadlines; however, most are somewhere between January 1 through February 15. Of course, if your child is applying for early admission, the application deadline will be earlier, usually in mid-November. Some colleges have what's known as "rolling admissions," meaning that your teen can apply at any time until the college closes its incoming class. And one last deadline wrinkle: audition and portfolio submission dates do not always coincide with the application date. You need to know and keep track of these deadlines. As a rule, both NAF and AF teens rely on you for this.

Let's take a look at who actually fills out the dreaded paperwork. If you can get past Myth #3 and have an honest discussion with parents of both NAF and AF teens, you will find out that it is the parent who does much of the routine paperwork. Why? It's simply because the paperwork is too voluminous and repetitive for most teens to deal with. A timesaver (and a nerve saver) is the *common application*. This is a single application form that is accepted by 298 colleges—even Harvard and Yale accept the common application. Using it will help conserve needed time and energy for other tasks.

Tip #7: Make Sure the Applications Arrive

You might consider sending the applications by FedEx or return receipt requested. After the applications are sent in, it is a good idea to check with each college to make sure that everything was received. If your child won't make these calls, you can do it. If you are a Type A or worried parent, you may be tempted to call frequently. Don't! Most schools will notify you if something is missing, and you don't want to annoy the admissions staff. For the procrastinating parent, don't make the mistake that no news is good news. Don't put total trust in the admissions officers. Check to make sure everything arrived.

I'm Already Overwhelmed!

If you're already feeling overwhelmed, join the club. As you can see, there is a lot to do. Let's review what you've accomplished to date. Use the checklist we've provided below for that review but don't let this list make you more anxious. We suggest you also use it as a basic organization tool. And remember: if you approach this task in the manner we suggest, you'll see that there's plenty of time to finish the race on time. So get organized, get going, and simply take it all step-by-step; you'll get through it all.

Calendar-Checklist

FRESHMAN YEAR

1. Check your teen's class schedule:
   - ☐ Is he or she taking courses at an appropriate difficulty level?
   - ☐ Are all the needed courses included?
2. Encourage involvement in school activities/clubs.
3. Encourage other extracurricular activities.
4. Start a "Résumé" file.
5. Consider formal psychological/psychoeducational evaluation if indicated.
6. Arrange interesting/productive summer plans.

SOPHOMORE YEAR

Fall
1. See items 1 to 6 in the freshman year checklist.
2. Take advantage if the high school offers practice PSAT or the PLAN exams.

Spring
1. Register for appropriate AP/SAT II exams.
2. Obtain a Social Security number for your teen if he or she does not have one.
3. Make sure that your teen's classes are those required by colleges.
4. Begin reviewing college materials to draw up the college list.
5. Attend college fairs and high school college events.
6. Encourage your teen to meet with visiting admissions officers.
7. Create individual college files for your college drawer.

JUNIOR YEAR

Fall

1. Make sure that your teen is registered for the PSAT/NMSQT or PLAN.
2. Arrange for either a prep course or tutoring.
3. Encourage extracurriculars activities but don't overprogram.
4. Begin touring colleges.
5. Just for you: review college application forms.
6. Investigate financial aid and scholarship opportunities.

Winter

1. Register for the spring SAT/ACT.
2. Register for spring SAT IIs and advanced placement exams.
3. Continue (or begin) college visits.
4. Schedule interviews at colleges your teen definitely plans to apply to.
5. Send thank-you letters/e-mails to the college interviewers.

Spring

1. Arrange prep course or tutoring for SATs/ACTs.
2. Take the SAT/ACT.
3. Continue college visits.
4. Request teacher recommendations.
5. Schedule TOEFL (Test of English as a Foreign Language) if needed.
6. Check your teen's class schedule for the fall:
   ☐ Are they taking classes required by colleges? Don't forget science, math, and language.
7. Take SAT IIs if indicated.

Summer

1. Continue college visits.
2. Schedule interviews.
3. Begin application paperwork—specifically the personal essay.
4. Collect applications for each prospective college. Consider the common application.
5. Register for the fall SAT/ACT if necessary.

SENIOR YEAR

Fall

1. Retake the SAT or ACT if necessary.
2. Consider additional test prep if it is necessary.

3. Take needed SAT II exams.
4. Make a final college list. Make sure to include two "safeties."
5. Continue college tours, interviews, and auditions.
6. Collect the applications for each prospective college.
7. Collect recommendation letters.
8. Make ten copies of all application materials to be sent to the colleges.
9. Keep track of the application deadlines.
10. Just for ED or EA applications:
    ☐ Complete applications and submit to all the colleges.
    ☐ Arrange for College Board scores to be sent to all the colleges.
    ☐ Complete Free Application for Federal Student Aid (FAFSA) and send in financial aid forms to all the colleges.

Winter
1. Complete and submit college applications by deadline dates.
2. Arrange for College Board scores to be sent to all the colleges.
3. Complete FAFSA and send in financial aid forms to all the colleges.
4. Keep copies of all the application materials.
5. Check to make sure that all applications have arrived.
6. Relax and celebrate. Nothing to do until April.
7. Just for ED applications:
    ☐ If accepted: relax and celebrate.
    ☐ If wait-listed or not accepted: complete and submit other applications.

Spring
1. Let your child open the college envelopes.
2. Attend accepted students' days or weekends.
3. If wait-listed at number 1 school, return the wait-list card and send additional materials.
4. If financial aid or merit scholarship insufficient, appeal and try to improve the package.
5. Help your teen decide which colleges offer to accept. Send reply card.
6. Don't miss the May 1 deadline to send in deposit.
7. Let other colleges know your teen will not accept their offers.
8. Complete and return all forms sent by the chosen school.

CHAPTER 5

Let the Tests Begin
Those Standardized Tests and Beyond

MOST PARENTS (and teens) cringe at the thought of the college entrance exams. Psychologically, these tests appear akin to a huge locked door between your teen and their college dreams. To this day, Sara, a college junior, still shudders when she thinks about her SAT experience: "The SAT was the worst experience ever. I took it three times and never scored higher than 1,050. I know that's why I didn't get into any of my first choices. My parents refused to pay for me to go to a prep course. Now that was stupid! I was really pissed off. I think they thought it wouldn't make a difference, and eventually I believed it too. I had the test prep papers. I left them on the kitchen counter all the time, but they ignored them. I think if they had let me take a course, I could have done better." Even three years later, despite the fact that this college junior was happy and successful at her college, she spoke about the SAT experience as if it were a fresh trauma.

In fact, she is not alone. It appears that the high-stakes exam experience stays with people—for better or for worse—for a long time. This doesn't have to be your teen's story. Sara's experience reflects a common misperception—that the test scores define who you are and who you will be. Why have these exams taken on such importance? Its part and parcel of Myth #1, "Only an Ivy will do." Everyone realizes that an applicant needs a top score on these high-stakes exams to even have a chance for admission at a highly competitive school. Unfortunately, many parents and teens mistakenly feel that these scores actually predict future success and measure one's worth as a person. As with Myth #1, "Only an Ivy will do," nothing could be further from the truth. And just as you have (we hope) shelved Myth #1, we hope you can do the same to its companion misconception, that the SAT defines who you are and who you will be.

What This Chapter Will and Will Not Do

"How can my teen raise his test scores?" We recognize that this question is on every parent's mind during the college application process. This chapter starts with an explanation of the college entrance exams—and not just the SAT. Yes, there is an alternative to the dreaded SAT—the ACT exam—and we will explain why your teen may choose this route. We then explain different types of test prep programs to help you select the most effective program for *your* teen. Finally, we describe effective strategies to get a recalcitrant or emotionally overwhelmed teen to accept help and study effectively.

Some teens are actually great standardized test takers. If this sounds like your teen, you're lucky. Certainly, if he or she has consistently and effortlessly scored well on such tests, then this chapter is less important for you. However, don't put this chapter aside too quickly since most teens *do* experience some test-related roadblocks and can use your help to improve their scores. At a minimum, you need to be aware of different types and scheduled test dates.

Although this chapter is not dedicated to teens with physical and learning disabilities, we do provide some necessary information. Parents of these teens need to know the ins and outs of obtaining accommodations if necessary. We also review the advantages of having a teen officially evaluated or diagnosed as learning disabled.

You will learn to assist your teen to maintain a balanced and realistic perspective about these tests. This perspective is essential so that the SAT need not become the defining event in your teen's quest for college admissions. So, while we wish that we could tell you not to worry about these tests at all, given the reality of the college admissions process we can't give such advice. Instead, we can provide you with racing tips to assist your teen to do his or her best, and in chapter 7, we include tips on how to prepare the application to minimize the impact of any disappointing scores.

Decisions, Decisions, Decisions: Choose Tests Wisely

Did you know that your teen has a choice about whether to take the SAT? It's true. While most parents in the eastern United States are familiar only with the SAT, there is an alternative: the ACT. The standardized tests, sometimes referred to as "high-stakes tests," include the PSAT, SAT I (usually referred to as SAT), SAT IIs, PLAN, ACT, and the advanced placement (AP) tests. Let's go through each test one by one.

The PSAT, or Preliminary SAT/National Merit Scholarship Qualifying Test, which your teen will probably take in October of his or her sophomore year, includes 131 questions to be completed in 130 minutes. The score is used to award National Merit Scholarships but is *not* forwarded to the colleges. In other words, except for being the basis of one scholarship award, it is more akin to being a practice test in preparation for the SAT. It provides you and your teen with an indication of how he or she is likely to score on the SAT.

There is one other important thing to note about the PSAT. Unlike the other college exam tests, the high school will register and administer it. Phew! One fewer task for you to add to your "to-do" list. This doesn't mean, however, that you are off the hook. You still need to stay informed and involved. A low score serves as your first warning sign that your teen is not a natural test taker and will probably need extra preparation. Remember, if the PSAT is your teen's first real taste of these high-stakes exams, it could be a wake-up call. The college admissions race has officially begun.

What can you do? At a minimum, make sure your teen is present at the exam and is at least somewhat prepared and well rested. And don't forget a good breakfast. Some schools provide some coaching, but most do not, so check with your child's counselor.

What You Have Been Waiting For: The SAT

Mention the term "SAT," and almost any parent of a teen will free-associate "college admissions." The two terms seem to go hand in hand and with good reason. In 2005, 1.5 million students took the SAT, a record number. This exam, along with its "little sister," the PSAT, are owned by the College Board and written by the Educational Testing Service. They are considered by many to be the "gold standard" of assessment tools.

The letters S-A-T used to refer to the Scholastic Aptitude Test. Today, only the acronym is used since most educators agree that it does not actually measure aptitude or innate mental abilities. Despite this, many college admissions officers believe that SAT scores are relatively accurate predictors of a teen's likely success at college. Couple this with the fact that the Ivies receive many more applications than they can interview or accept, and you see why the SAT score is used as a cutoff point for applicants. With this in mind, it is not surprising that a study done by the National Association for College Admissions Counseling found that colleges ranked SAT scores as the second most important admissions criteria. And, if all this weren't enough to raise your anxiety, many colleges also use the score on the SAT or ACT for awarding academic scholarships. No wonder these tests are the single greatest source of anxiety for both parents and teens during the college admissions race. So, if the mention of this test fills you with anxiety, don't forget that you are certainly not alone.

All that said—and despite the fact that most college-bound high school seniors will take the SAT—the exam itself remains controversial. Racial, socioeconomic, and gender biases have been reported and associated with this exam over the years. The College Board itself has reported that women score approximately forty points lower than men, while African Americans score almost 200 points lower than whites. The strongest indicator of success on the SAT is the income and education of the parents—the higher the level of education and income, the higher the student's score. This should not surprise anyone since the more economic resources at a family's disposal, the more likely that family can afford to pay for excellent schools and high-priced, intensive test prep tutors.

In response to all this criticism, the College Board made significant changes to the test. In 2004, it unveiled the "new" SAT, which, except for some changes, looks very much like the old SAT. The most noteworthy changes are its length and the addition of a writing section. The test has now become a grueling three hours, forty-five minutes long—up a full forty-five minutes from the "old" SAT exam. Quite a long haul, even for the most focused teen. On the old SAT, a perfect score was 1600, now it is 2400. However, the College Board still describes the SAT as a "reasoning" test comprised of verbal, math, and now writing sections. The dreaded analogy questions have also been deleted, and new verbal and math items were added. The math section covers basic algebra, algebra II, and geometry. The writing section includes a multiple-choice grammar section, a multiple-choice syntax section (student must choose the most well-constructed sentence or paragraph), and a twenty-five-minute essay on an assigned topic (scored on a scale of 1 to 6). Two readers score the essay, and if their scores differ by more than two points, a third reader is called in.

Will these changes allay any fears you may harbor about this exam? Probably not. Indeed, not everyone is happy with the new SAT. In fact, a recent report showed a drop in overall SAT scores since the new SAT was unveiled. Many academics point out that the essay is fairly formulaic and susceptible to coaching. The socioeconomic bias continues since the child who can afford tutoring on the verbal and math sections can certainly be taught how to write the essay in the format the SAT graders look for.

Recently, another problem with the SAT was reported. In the winter of 2006, the College Board admitted that scanning errors caused thousands of SATs to be incorrectly scored. Yet this was not the end of the matter. Many people felt that the real scandal was not the technical glitch but rather how the College Board handled the matter. Despite being aware of the problem in the fall of 2005, they did not notify the colleges until well into 2006. This meant that colleges had relied on these incorrect scores in their selection process. When news of the scanning errors—and its subsequent "cover-up" became public—it reignited an ongoing debate regarding the SAT's pivotal role in college admissions.

One other SAT test remains to be discussed: the SAT IIs or subject tests. These are hour-long achievement tests that assess material covered in a single high school subject, such as American history, biology, and Spanish. There are actually twenty-one separate SAT IIs, and you can find a complete list of these is available on the College Board website at www.Collegeboard.com.

Most teens take SAT IIs after completing the actual high school course, at the end of the junior year, or at the beginning of the senior year. Don't fall into the trap of encouraging or permitting your teen to take too many of these since all scores are reported to

Don't forget the ACT. It can have advantages over the SAT.

the colleges. Indeed, most colleges don't require any, and even the most selective institutions require only two, with only a handful that require three such exams. Be strategic about choosing which SAT IIs to take. Remember too that preparation here is also the key to success on these tests. On a more encouraging note, research has found that the SAT II is a better predictor of college grades than the SAT. Many educators also believe that it is a fairer test because it is less affected by socioeconomic background or less subject to short-term tutoring fixes.

A final and important consideration about both the SAT and the SAT II tests: your teen can't choose to drop a low score. Unlike the ACT, once your teen takes these exams, no matter how many times, all the scores, not just the highest, will be sent on to every college requested.

A Real Alternative: The Act

Many parents are not aware that there are alternatives to the PSAT and the SAT: the PLAN and the ACT. These standardized college entrance exams are widely administered in the Midwest; some states in this region even mandate them for their statewide assessment programs. They assess mastery of the high school curriculum and include questions in math, science, and reading. The ACT also contains an optional essay part. The scores range from 1 to 36. The PLAN is a pre-ACT test and can be a good predictor of the ACT score in much the same manner that the PSAT is a predictor for the SAT. It is also typically administered in the fall of the sophomore year.

In 2002, 1.1 million students took the ACT. We just told you that the test is mostly used in the Midwest and if you live outside that region, you may be tempted to jump to the next section, but don't! Almost all colleges in the United States accept the ACT, and there are advantages to this test over the SAT. First, the ACT can be taken many times, and, unlike the SAT, the student can choose which score to submit to a college. Colleges do not have access to a student's other scores. So, if your teen is willing, there is nothing to lose by trying both exams. If your teen scores higher on the ACT, then by all means send the ACT and not the SAT score. Of course, this strategy will not work if your teen is applying to one of the highly selective Ivies, which require SAT IIs. Bear in mind that once your teen takes the SAT, you cannot request the College Board to only send the SAT II scores and not the SAT I; it will send both. This means that if your teen is applying to a highly selective college that requires SAT IIs, you have to make a decision if you want your teen to take the SAT at all. But then, this is what practice tests (PSAT and PLAN) are for.

Let's talk racing strategy for a teen aiming for an Ivy but who is not a test-taking wiz. If he is cooperative or ambitious (probably an AF teen), you can arrange for him to take the PSAT and the PLAN during his junior year. If he does appreciably better on the PLAN, he can then opt out of the SAT and take the ACT. To fulfill the requirements of the Ivies, he will take only the required SAT IIs.

The vast majority of teens, the not-always focused (NAF) teens, won't agree to take both the PLAN and the PSAT. The first sign of an obstacle ahead may be a low score on the PSAT. If this happens, then encourage your teen to try the ACT early, before the SAT. If he or she scores well, great. Then don't bother with the SAT. If later you find that a college requires an SAT II, he or she can take it alone without ever taking the SAT.

As you can see, you and your teen are not locked into a do-or-die dance with the SAT; there are creative alternatives.

Passing through the College Exam Portal

Now that we've reviewed these tests, it is time to switch gears and identify common testing challenges and the strategies to overcome them.

While many educators are aware of the multitude of problems we've discussed with these tests and have made efforts to de-emphasize their importance in the admissions process, you know that many colleges still place a great deal of emphasis on these scores. As much as we don't want to overfocus on standardized test scores, it is important to review the four common challenges that can turn into a roadblock, that is, a disappointing score: 1) test anxiety, 2) moodiness 3) resistance to studying, and 4) learning disabilities. As always, we don't simply identify potential problems but provide you with practical strategies to overcome them.

Testing Challenges:
- **Test anxiety**
- **Moodiness**
- **Resistance to study**
- **Learning and physical disabilities**

To find out if these tests will pose a challenge for your teen, complete the following questionnaires that relate to the four most common testing challenges.

Teen Testing Assessment Questionnaires

Teen Testing Assessment Questionnaire

Challenge #1: On the High-Tension Wire: Test Anxiety

Take this questionnaire to discover whether your teen's performance on the high-stakes tests will be compromised by anxiety.

1. I know my teen is a worrier.	YES/NO
2. My teen has panic attacks.	YES/NO
3. My teen gets that petrified look in his eyes whenever the SATs are mentioned.	YES/NO

4. My teen has frequently told me that she feels   YES/NO
   "spaced out," "jittery," or "nauseated" or has
   anxiety attacks during standardized tests.
5. The closer my teen gets to taking any type of   YES/NO
   standardized test, the more frequently she cries.
6. My teen frequently suffers from what are referred   YES/NO
   to as "anxiety-related" physical maladies, such
   as headaches, gastrointestinal problems, hives,
   and so on.
7. My teen is having difficulty falling asleep and/or   YES/NO
   seems to worry excessively about all the things
   he needs to do or focuses on things that might
   go wrong.

If you answered "yes" to three or more of these questions, it is likely that your teen's test scores will be affected by anxiety. Now let's discuss what this means, the implications for your teen, and possible strategies around this challenge. Much of the excess emotion surrounding these tests is due to the tremendous hype and pressure surrounding these tests specifically and the college admissions process in general. Your teen certainly knows that these tests mean a lot. So it should come as no surprise that most teens experience heightened anxiety at this time.

You first need to determine whether your teen has a "garden-variety" case of nerves or actually suffers from a genuine anxiety disorder. While this book is not meant to provide psychological treatment, we can explain how any concerned parent can ask a few pointed questions to see if one's teen is seriously affected by anxiety. Below is a discussion of patterns of behavior that should alert you that your teen may need professional help.

Panic attacks are experienced as short periods of extreme anxiety during which the sufferer can have palpitations (heart beating rapidly), a sense of difficulty breathing, or fear of going crazy or dying. Panic attacks or feelings of high anxiety are quite common and are frequently experienced by adolescent girls and women.

If your teen experiences these types of attacks, you need to ask how frequent and distressing these are. Do the panic attacks interfere with routine activities or prevent him or her from doing or succeeding at activities or tasks, such as schoolwork, test performance, or enjoying his or her social life? Do the panic attacks affect your teen's mood? Does your teen either withdraw or even become angry when facing situations that trigger this level of anxiety?

If your teen has panic attacks, our first piece of advice to you is to stay calm. Panic attacks, as upsetting as they can be for the sufferer, are not cause for alarm. Most individuals actually get over them in time, while others may benefit from either reading self-help books or getting professional help. There are many such excellent books, which can be found in almost any bookstore or easily ordered online. *Don't Panic: Taking Control of Anxiety Attacks* by R. Reid Wilson is one we recommend.

Many teens who suffer from anxiety are actually not aware of what is happening to them. Most will be extraordinarily relieved to learn that they are *not* going to die or have a nervous breakdown and that anxiety symptoms respond very well to behavioral techniques.

If your teen is having frequent or severe panic attacks, we do recommend having a professional evaluation. Many teens benefit from counseling or psychotherapy—cognitive behavioral treatment can be very effective in either eliminating or reducing anxiety symptoms. This type of treatment is usually short term and typically covered by insurance. If your teen does not respond to any of these therapies, there are also highly effective medications available today. You can also ask your pediatrician or general practitioner for a referral to a private practitioner or clinic.

Anxiety tends to go hand in hand with avoidance. Not surprisingly, many students with test anxiety actually resist preparing for tests since, as we all know, we tend to avoid what makes us anxious. Unfortunately, the more the anxious teen avoids, the more nervous that teen will become when he or she has to take the test. If this sounds like your teen, he or she needs the reassurance that test anxiety is normal and can be overcome by becoming very familiar with the test structure and the types of questions.

If your teen experiences either test anxiety or panic attacks, he or she needs to start test prep earlier than most—even up to six months before the test date. Exposure and familiarity with the anxiety trigger (the test) is precisely the same method that behavioral psychologists use to treat individuals with elevator or subway phobias. The idea behind this treatment method is that the longer the anxious individual is exposed to the trigger, the better he or she will cope with any anxiety that arises when confronted with it.

Even after you have helped your teen become familiar with the test format, you need to prepare him or her for the unexpected "surprise" questions. The SAT includes an "experimental" section—either math or verbal—that include new types of questions that the College Board is "trying out." Your teen will not be informed during the actual test that this is an experimental section or that his or her performance on this section will not count toward their score. If your teen struggles with anxiety, he or she might feel uncomfortable guessing and be more easily thrown by the unexpected. You can help your teen by becoming familiar with the ins and outs of these exams so that you can give him or her a "heads-up."

Teen Testing Assessment Questionnaire

Challenge #2: Frustration and Moodiness

This questionnaire will help you assess whether your teen is experiencing normal emotional "aches and pains" or if the range of moods you see in your teen is indicative of something that requires more attention.

1. Does your teen frequently remind you of a two-year-old with lots of temper and moodiness? YES/NO
2. Recently, is your teen getting into more frequent arguments with her friends? YES/NO
3. Does your teen sleep excessively or wake up too early, feeling tired and unable to focus? YES/NO
4. Does your teen seem sad with little energy or interest in the world around him or her? YES/NO
5. Has your teen lost interest in his friends or normal activities? YES/NO
6. Does your teen blame everyone but him- or herself for his or her problems? YES/NO

If you answered "yes" to three or more of these questions, you need to decide whether this is a case of normal teen blues and moodiness or something more serious. Teens must be at the top of their game to successfully run the college application race. Strong emotions pose challenges when they interfere with effective test preparation and getting into the test taking "zone."

If your teen is crying frequently, particularly over friendship and relationship problems, or getting into frequent or serious verbal or physical altercations, this indicates that he or she is struggling emotionally. The first thing to do, of course, is have an honest conversation with him or her.

Don't let moodiness become a hurdle.

Ask the hard questions about his or her thoughts, feelings, and behaviors. Clear signs that a professional mental health counselor needs to be consulted include insomnia, excessive sleeping, bulimia, anorexia, self-mutilation (cutting), and excessive alcohol or drug use. Any such serious concerns indicate the need for a professional assessment with a psychiatrist, psychologist, social worker, or counselor. They are in the best position to determine whether your teen needs treatment.

Of course, most moodiness doesn't require professional intervention. Most teens have their ups and downs and find the college application process stressful. Reduce stress by scheduling enjoyable activities, letting them take a break from touring colleges, and asking yourself whether some of the stress is coming from you or your spouse. Are you putting too much pressure on your teen to score high, perhaps unrealistically high? Trust us, many teens feel frustrated or dejected about their tests scores, and your disappointment can only make it worse.

Teen Testing Assessment Questionnaire

Challenge #3: My Teen Resists Studying: He's on "Teen Time"

This questionnaire will help you judge whether you have a teen who simply needs more downtime, is more likely than not to come through during this crunch time, or if you need to devise some resourceful and effective strategies to get her going.

1. Is your teen a boy?   YES/NO
2. Is your teen a procrastinator?   YES/NO
3. Did your teen receive a low or disappointing score   YES/NO
   on the PSAT, but even that didn't "wake her up?"
4. Does your teen regularly "miss" his or her SAT   YES/NO
   prep classes?
5. Has your teen refused to sign up for a SAT prep   YES/NO
   course or promised to study "independently" but
   done neither?
6. Have you bought all the prep books but your teen   YES/NO
   just refuses to open them?
7. Is your teen so busy with extracurriculars that he   YES/NO
   or she simply doesn't have time for a prep class?

If you answered "yes" to three or more of these questions, it is likely that your teen is struggling with procrastination. "Teen time" or the perennial parental lament "He just won't study" is an extremely common challenge. We don't need to tell you how particularly frustrating this problem can be. If your teen tends to be on teen time, then chances are he or she will also have difficulty putting aside enough time to study for these exams. In fact, this can be a problem even for the always-focused (AF) teen who is overscheduled with extracurricular activities, television, "face books," and e-mail distractions. Teens are notorious for living for today. Many find it difficult to delay instant gratification—certainly not for SAT prep. You can argue all you want about the importance of test prep and how important the score is for college admissions, but your well-thought-out arguments may fall on deaf ears. This type of teen may be the procrastinating type we described in chapter 3. They are on teen time, while you are on "the rest of your life" time.

If you are still reading this section, then you are probably concerned about your teen's time management skills. Some of you may have been a little surprised or puzzled by the first question in the questionnaire: "Do you have a boy?" If you have a son, we hope that you are not offended by our first question. Or, perhaps you are relieved that we have acknowledged the elephant in the middle of the room—teenage boys tend to procrastinate more than girls. These days it is mostly the girls who are eager to study, who buy lots of test prep books, underline the questions, and practice, practice, practice. Why should this be? Research shows that boys tend to mature later in many respects, and many educators are concerned that the current education system is not designed to meet the needs of boys. We certainly recognize that there are plenty of girls who also procrastinate, and all our advice applies equally to them; however, this is an issue more prevalent in boys than girls.

If you realize that your teen is a procrastinator, then you realize that he can't put off all the college tests—eventually the high-stakes test will arrive, and eventually the applications will be due. He needs to take these tests and do his best. So it is up to you to try to help him prepare. If you can afford it, we strongly recommend signing him up for a test prep course. You can ask the school counselor at high school or friends for recommendations. If money is an issue and your local high school cannot assist, check with local religious groups or youth-oriented organizations. You can also ask the major test prep companies for a discount. Another option is to put together a small group of students and hire a private tutor to teach the group. The benefit is that it will save you money but still provide more individualized attention than a large commercial class.

We cannot emphasize enough the benefits of these prep classes or tutoring. These tests are very long and exhausting, and only practice will show your teen the importance of pacing. Additionally, a prep class or tutoring situation will provide your teen with the many "tricks" embedded in these exams. Learning the tricks of these exams is particularly important if your teen is taking the SAT. Your teen needs to be aware that the SAT is scored on the basis of more than just how many questions are answered correctly. For example, did you know that since all questions are worth the same amount, your teen should skip the most difficult questions, focusing instead on the easy to midrange ones? This means that the toughest questions should be tackled only after the easiest questions are answered and your teen has time to go back to the most difficult ones. Another strategy they need to learn is when to guess and when not to guess on the SAT. Your teen is penalized for guessing incorrectly, yet it is possible to learn how to eliminate the patently wrong answers and make it worthwhile to venture a guess. The ACT, on the other hand, is the opposite. It is better to guess than to leave and answer blank. After just this brief discussion of test-taking tips and tricks, you can tell that your teen will benefit from a test prep program (class or tutoring). Most respond positively to the right test prep group and approach.

Let's say you've won the first battle: your teen agrees to the prep course or tutor. Now how do you make him or her go, and, just as important, how do you get him or her to do the homework assigned? The first step is to think through the strategies that have worked best for your teen in the past. Applauding parents? Having friends for company? Material goods as rewards? Our advice: do anything that is ethical and works. There is no right or wrong approach here.

Help your teen free up some of his or her time for test prep, particularly during the winter and spring of the junior year. We recommend that you follow the schedule from chapter 4 and try to have your teen take the SAT/ACT during the spring of the junior year. Even if your teen waits until the summer after the junior year, he or she may still have time to take the SAT/ACT a second or third time. You probably realize that it isn't ideal for your teen to wait until the summer of the junior year to take a prep course. However, let him or her do so if he or she is particularly resistant. In the past, this was a problem because the test-result turnover time was long. Now, however, with board results available in about two weeks from testing, even that teen will have time to take the test again either in late fall or into early winter. Only a teen applying early admission cannot afford to wait so long. But since most early admissions applicants are usually AF teens, they typically take the high-stakes tests as early as feasible. Remember, every situation (every teen) is unique, and ultimately you need to exercise your best judgment and instincts. So, if that summer is the only time possible to schedule a prep course, go for it.

Some of you may be thinking, "Well, this is all very nice, but I can't get my kid to go to a course or tutor!" One of the most common reasons for this is due not to procrastination but to embarrassment. If your NAF teen has been a poor test taker, he or she may be embarrassed to practice for these tests in a group. This is perfectly understandable, and we don't blame them for wanting to avoid such a situation, and neither should you. If this is your teen, private tutoring is usually the way to go. This is also the way to go for the superbusy AF teen whose schedule won't fit into a test prep class.

We've mentioned the benefits of a private tutor so many times that by now you may be wondering, "So, how do I find one?" It's actually not hard. Look in your local "penny saver," ask your school counselor or the head of your high school's math or English department, or ask other parents (yes, you can, because you've vanquished Myth #2, "The Big Silence"). In addition, tutors are available through the commercial test prep services, such as Princeton Review and Kaplan. If not, ask around for a college or high school senior who tutors for these tests. You can even find advertisements online, but be sure to check their references.

One last word on tutors: the most important variable is the teen–tutor match. If your teen despises the tutor, it won't work. Don't waste your money and your teen's limited study time trying to make a bad relationship good. Either the chemistry is there or it's not. Don't hesitate to try a few tutors, and let your teen choose. Another benefit to this approach is that it will give your teen some sense of control—by permitting him or her to choose which tutor to work with. In this way, your teen will feel more invested in the process.

What can you do if your teen absolutely refuses to prepare for these exams? Give up? Certainly not, but you might need to bide your time. He or she will probably reconsider his or her stance after doing poorly on the PSAT or the SAT. While you might have hoped to avoid this, many procrastinating teens need the low score to break out of their denial. It is the roadblock that serves as a wake-up call. Only then will your teen agree that he or she needs some help. So, even if your teen refuses to take a course or accept a tutor, don't wait to find one. Do your research ahead of time and have "Plan B" waiting in the wings. Naturally, you don't have to tell him or her about this new racing strategy, but when your teen finally sees the light, you'll be prepared to immediately put tutoring or a prep course in place.

Teen Testing Assessment Questionnaire

Challenge #4: Learning and Physical Disabilities

If your teen has a physical disability, you probably have already started the paperwork required for accommodations. While this may also be true if your teen has a learning disability, these students are more likely to fall through the cracks. We find that many intelligent and hardworking students' learning disabilities go unrecognized, especially through elementary school. However, as the course load increases and timed standardized tests are introduced, their disabilities can become more apparent. Often, however, the learning disability issue emerges only at this time—when these high-stakes tests loom. Answering the questions below can be helpful in determining whether your teen would benefit from a professional evaluation and/or accommodations.

1. Do you know or suspect that your teen has a learning disability? — YES/NO
2. Does your teen have a history of scoring below his or her potential on standardized tests? — YES/NO
3. Have your teen's scores on standardized tests been erratic, and do you never know what to expect your teen to score on a test? — YES/NO
4. Does your teen frequently tell you that he or she knows the material but can't finish the tests on time? — YES/NO
5. Has your teen always been a slow reader? — YES/NO
6. Does your teen have a physical disability? — YES/NO

If you answered "yes" to any of these questions, then you may want your teen assessed or officially classified as disabled. Surprisingly, many learning-disabled students, especially from families with limited resources, have never been evaluated or accurately diagnosed. Certainly, one of the most common red flags is a history of low or uneven standardized test scores despite the fact that your teen studies or genuinely knows the material. Ask yourself, "Has he always had problems with timed tests?" "Are the low-test scores mostly with exams, which are primarily language based, math, or both?" "Could he have an unrecognized or undiagnosed learning disability that causes test anxiety—from mild to severe?"

Many bright, industrious students earn good grades but are brought up short by these pressured tests, which often rely on speed, concentration, and excellent reading and math skills. Some very smart, successful people will tell you honestly that they are "slow readers." This can be an indication of a "learning disability" or a teen who simply learns in a nonconventional manner. Such teens score lower than expected on standardized exams. These are the teens we frequently hear comments about, such as "Why did he score so low; he has very high grades?" or "We never expected the SAT to be a problem; his teachers always say how bright he is." Unlike the work submitted in a school setting or typical school exams, which cover classroom course work, these timed tests do not accurately measure the abilities of many students with learning disabilities. With the time pressure, many are unable to use the strategies they have found effective in the classroom setting.

Parents are often afraid of the label "learning disabled" because they believe that it will stigmatize their child. The good news is that times have changed. A generation ago, children were indeed stigmatized by the learning-disabled label. Over the past decade, however, the number of college students with learning and physical disabilities has increased dramatically. The U.S. Department of Education reports that for the period 1989–1990, 7.7 percent students reported at least one disability. In 2003–2004, the number jumped to 11.3 percent. Since the Americans with Disabilities Act was enacted in 1990, barriers that blocked their admission to and success in college have been reduced but, many would say, not eliminated. Title II of the act states, "No qualified individual with a disability shall be excluded from participation in or be denied the benefits of the services, programs or activities of a public entity."

Never forget that if your teen has a learning or physical disability, he or she is legally entitled to appropriate accommodations. These include large print for the vision impaired, audio versions of tests for the hearing impaired, and extended time for being learning disabled. Approximately 2 percent of all teens taking the SAT receive some accommodations, mostly extra time. Parents and teens are reassured to discover that, as of October 2003, the College Board no longer flags the exam as "Nonstandard Administration" when the scores are sent to the colleges. Therefore, a disabled teen has nothing to lose by taking advantage of needed accommodations.

What do you do if your teen has a documented disability? You need an up-to-date psychological evaluation (or medical evaluation). You can then contact your school counselor to prepare the necessary paperwork.

What if you suspect that your teen has a learning disability but has never been formally assessed? There is nothing to lose by having an evaluation. If you can afford it, we recommend using a private psychologist rather than the school-based psychologist. While this route is expensive—any-where from $500 and up—it is also confidential. If your teen wants to keep the results private, the high school and college need never find out. If you cannot afford this private evaluation, however, you can request that it be completed at your child's school.

Confidentiality can be especially important since many if not most learning-disabled teens struggle with embarrassment or low self-esteem. Their strong feelings frequently lead them to hide their disabilities or refuse evaluations and accommodations. We recall one mother who was very frustrated by her daughter Sara's attitude:

☼ A MOM'S TALE

"Although my daughter Sara had reluctantly agreed to be evaluated in the eighth grade, she had great difficulty accepting the results. It appeared she almost preferred the label 'lazy' to 'learning disabled.' She refused to allow me to alert school officials or request the extra time accommodation she needed and was legally entitled to. It was only the low score on the PSAT and the approaching SAT that pushed her to accept accommodations. Luckily, I had documentation of a diagnosed learning disability and was able to petition the Educational Testing Service for accommodations. The extra time—and lots of individual tutoring—made a big difference, and her SAT score was much higher than predicted by her PSAT score. Once Sara got over the hurdle of asking for the accommodations she needed, she was better able to accept her learning disability and continued to ask for the extra time she needed at college." ☼

It is essential that you begin the evaluation and documentation process early, by ninth or tenth grade at the latest. The Educational Testing Service is suspicious of teens who are diagnosed with a learning disability within a year of taking the SAT or who never received testing accommodations in high school.

Many teens resist being assessed for a learning disability. After all, many think, "Why has this learning disability never been a problem before?" Others are simply embarrassed or feel tarnished by a growing tendency among hypercompetitive parents to have their teens get unneeded extra time to give their teen an "edge." They don't want their peers to think they are "cheating."

What should you do if your teen resists the idea of evaluation or accommodations? You need to tread lightly—this is a powerful issue, one that definitely affects self-esteem. Your strategy can include two steps: 1) get the evaluation done; and 2) if your teen has a learning disability, arrange for accommodations. If your teen doesn't want the evaluation, you can explain that "none of your friends need to know" or "it is only information; we won't do anything without your permission." If the evaluator concludes that your teen has a learning disability and would benefit from accommodations, you (or the psychologist) can explain the advantages to your teen. Again, your teen (and you) need not tell anyone. He or she can even take the SAT/ACT exam with accommodations at a different site from one's friends if he or she desires total confidentiality.

Confront learning disabilities sooner, not later.

Should you encourage your teen to talk about their learning disability with teachers or friends? We believe that keeping it a secret makes it seem worse than it really is. But again, timing is everything. You can't push your teen to disclose this very personal information before he or she is ready.

We have found that most learning-disabled teens also struggle with test anxiety. As we discussed earlier in the chapter, test anxiety is not that unusual, especially during these high-stakes tests. Reread the applicable sections in chapter 3 on the tried-and-true techniques for reducing anxiety. Any teen with learning disabilities will definitely benefit from them.

You'll find a discussion on how to find the good-fit college for a teen with disabilities in chapter 6. For now, you need to be aware that disabilities certainly affect a teen's ability to score well on the high-stakes exams.

The SAT/ACT Score Does Not Define Your Teen

A final word about the value and meaning of the college entrance exams. While most colleges consider these exams highly important, the SAT/ACT scores are *not* the best predictor of either college grades or future success in life. We find that when a teen does not score well or as high as hoped for, his or her confidence crumbles, often for years. Therefore, it is essential for you, the parent, to help your teen keep these test scores in perspective. It is vital that your teen both understands and genuinely believes that while a disappointing score may present an additional roadblock in the college admissions process, it is not a measure of who he or she is as a person. It *cannot* and *does not* predict future happiness or success in life.

If you still have trouble believing this yourself and continue to obsess over a less-than-perfect score, look at the growing number of colleges and universities that no longer require either the SAT or the ACT. Some use the scores for class placement only, and many do not request these scores at all.

A leader in this trend to minimize the impact of high-stakes tests was Bates College, a small, highly selective college in Maine that has not required them since 1984. In fact, many of the top liberal arts colleges no longer require the SAT. Numbered among these are Bard College, Bennington College, Bowdoin College, Connecticut College, Dickenson College, Franklin and Marshall College, Hamilton College, Mount Holyoke, Pitzer College, and Sarah Lawrence College, and their numbers are growing yearly.

The Homestretch

Here's the minimum to take away from this chapter. First, don't make these tests into something they are not. Your teen's life does not rise and fall on a standardized test score, and if you can internalize this message, so will your teen. Second, if your teen scored lower than both of you hoped, remember that he or she is much more than the sum of test scores and that there are many good-fit schools that will recognize this. Third, since these tests are a fact of life, there are test-taking strategies that will help your teen maximize his or her score. We have provided you with a number of these strategies targeted to your particular teen and his or her needs and goals. Finally, if you keep perspective, so will your teen, and both of you can get back in the race and move ahead in a more positive, constructive manner.

CHAPTER 6

Drawing Up the College List
So Many Schools, So Little Time

Exercise: What Is Your Teen's Ideal School?

Before we even begin discussing how to draw up the college list, take a moment to complete this exercise. We want you to get a genuine picture of your teen's ideal learning and living environment. Find a quiet room where you can be alone. Close the door. Take a few deep breaths. Just relax. Next, put everything you've heard about the Ivies and the importance of the brand name out of your mind. Now conjure up in your mind's eye the ideal college environment for *your* teen. Where do you see your teen thriving? What type of learning and environment do you think or know your teen truly needs? Does he or she need a nurturing environment or a more competitive one? Does he or she need lots of activities and stimulation or a calmer, slower-paced setting? Does he or she thrive in small class settings or prefer the anonymity of larger lecture classes? Is he or she ready to go far from home, or is he or she not quite ready to cut the cord? Let your mind wander to consider all of what you believe would help your teen mature and succeed. Take a few minutes to jot down your thoughts, and we'll come back to them later.

_____

_____

_____

_____

_____

Now that you've completed this exercise, it's time to learn strategies to find that ideal college: the one you just conjured up in your mind. First, the good news: With hundreds of excellent colleges and universities to choose from, your teen has options. Now, the bad news: there are hundreds of excellent colleges and universities to choose from. Options mean choice, and while we all think we like choices, it actually causes stress because it adds the burden of responsibility. This perhaps explains why so many parents and teens are susceptible to relying on "the buzz"—the hype about this or that college. You need to discard "the buzz" and begin to build an individualized college list. To do this, here are some basic considerations—some tangible and some intangible—to think about.

Type of Institution

The very first thing you need to consider before going any further is the type of institution: public or private? Four-year or two-year school? University or liberal arts college? Specialized school or institute?

Liberal Arts College, University, or Specialized Institute?

We hear these terms bandied about all the time. But really, how many of us have ever thought about what these imply? Therefore, before you even start to draw up that list, let's clarify what these really are. A liberal arts college focuses on the education of undergraduates, while a university has both undergraduate and graduate students. Liberal arts colleges tend to be relatively small and are not subdivided into smaller school units, while universities are larger institutions that contain within them a wide array of "schools" or "colleges" (such as a business, law, medical, engineering, and architecture). Some students want the variety and stimulation that comes with a university, while others prefer the intimacy of the liberal arts college setting.

There are also highly specialized institutes or schools that focus on specific careers. Perhaps the best known is the Massachusetts Institute of Technology, but there is also a wide range of institutes for the student focused on the culinary arts, music, and even fashion. The student who selects this type of highly specialized educational setting must be very certain of his or her career path.

If your teen has demonstrated specific interest or talent, you can certainly support his or her decision to include specialized schools or programs on his or her college list. If, however, your teen has a particular interest but you have reason to suspect that he or she might not stick with it, make sure to include other types of institutions on the list. For example, you can steer him or her to a larger university setting that contains a school that meets your teen's interest but that also offers the opportunity to transfer into another school within that university in the event your teen changes his or her mind. At Oberlin College in Ohio, for example, a student can earn a double degree—a bachelor in music degree and a bachelor in arts degree. Students get the best of both worlds. They live in the dorms and take liberal arts classes with non–music conservatory students. The advantage of this type of specialty program is that it gives your teen the opportunity to pursue his or her dreams without foreclosing the possibility of a change if interests wane.

Public or Private?

Almost all states have a range of public colleges and universities, many of them excellent and some highly selective. For many teens, a public college is the only option because of the prohibitive costs of private institutions. Other teens choose public institutions because of the caliber of the education, an excellent reputation, or the fact that they are the biggest "bang for the buck." The tuition range is from approximately $2,000 up to $15,000. Add approximately $8,000 for room and board if needed. Almost all states offer a wide range of options, and you need to look at these just as carefully as you would if you were selecting a private school. And don't think that all public colleges are huge institutions where your teen will be just a number. Your research will find some smaller gems, such as Geneseo, a New York State honors college of 5,600 students, which more closely resembles a small, private New England college than the stereotypical image of the large impersonal state university.

Four-Year or Two-Year College?

Your teen can attend either a four-year college or a two-year community college. Four-year colleges typically issue the undergraduates degrees known as bachelor of arts (BA) or bachelor of science (BS). The two-year college grants a degree known as an associate of arts (AA) or an associate of science (AS).

Why choose a two-year community college over the standard four-year program? One major consideration may be financial. A public (community) college is very inexpensive. Many people simply can't afford a four-year college (not even a public one), and the community college tuition is within most people's grasp. Community colleges permit students to complete the first two years relatively inexpensively and then go on to complete the last two years at a four-year institution.

Many students benefit from attending two-year colleges (public or private). Some teens are simply not emotionally ready to leave home at the end of high school, and two-year colleges permit that teen to adjust to the higher academic and social demands while maintaining the support of home. You may also be unaware of the excellent education available at many community colleges. The professors are frequently high caliber and provide substantial support for the teen/student. The classes tend to be relatively small. "Late bloomers" or students who have simply struggled through high school usually benefit from the support offered in this environment. While it's true that community colleges may not have the prestige the four-year colleges have, this route can be an excellent stepping-stone to long-term academic success. Another well-kept secret: highly selective colleges are quite open to and likely to accept as a transfer a good student from a two-year college.

Location: Near or Far?

Location is an extremely important consideration in drawing up the college list. No matter how wonderful a college appears, it isn't a good fit if the distance is wrong (either too near or too far). Some teens want to attend a college far from home and are able to do so, but others do not and cannot. First, let's discuss what is "far" from home? Far is a subjective concept and personally defined. Most teens and parents define it in terms of actual travel time between the college and home. Others, however, feel that any distance requiring air travel is too far. In reality, many colleges situated near or in major cities can be a faster commute by plane than other colleges "in the middle of nowhere." However, many teens feel more secure if they or, more likely, their parents can reach their college by car, even if the drive is eight or ten hours.

A good rule of thumb is that "near" is within a four-hour drive from home. You probably already know if your teen can handle being far from home. By now, your teen likely has given you all the cues you need to figure this out. For example, your teen may not be ready to venture too far from home if she has never adjusted well to summer camp or has resisted or did not enjoy sleepovers, traveling, or new situations. Your teen may have dropped other hints embedded in such questions as "Do you think I'll be able to come home for weekends?" or "How many hours will it take to get there?" These are signs of a teen who is probably not ready to attend a college across the country. And don't be fooled by false bravado. Many teens are simply too embarrassed to admit it or are genuinely clueless that they are not ready to attend a college too distant from home. However, you may be lucky. Your teen may honestly and assertively insist that he or she doesn't want to go to a college more than three or four hours from home. This makes drawing up the college list so much easier.

What should you do if you have reservations, yet your teen insists on going the distance? You may have to simply put your anxieties and fears aside (or at least tuck them away somewhere) and let him or her try. You and your teen are now embarking on a new phase. He or she stands on the threshold of adulthood and needs to try new things and take *reasonable* chances. Remember, if it doesn't work out, it is not the end of the world. Your teen can always transfer.

☀ MARIE'S STORY

Marie, an 18-year-old teen, told all her friends she was eager and ready to "finally get away from home." She was a shy and somewhat anxious teenager who had never been away from her parents for more than a few days prior to moving to New Orleans to attend Tulane University. While aware that she was prone to homesickness, her mother supported her determination to go yet was not totally surprised by her frequent calls, tears, and panic. Her mother sheepishly explained to me that Marie had been calling her every day, then impulsively dropped out of college after the first week. There was a happy ending, however. Marie (and her mother) got to work to quickly enroll her in one of the excellent city universities in New York City, which had accepted her the previous year. With the support of her family, she was able to catch up to the other students and did well in her first semester. As she regained her confidence, she rethought her college list and transferred to a college closer to home where she could have it both ways—separation from her family with weekend visits whenever homesickness arose. ☀

Let's discuss the teen who appears ready to go the distance. If your teen has been adventurous, independent, and self-reliant and adjusts well to new situations and environments, then he is an excellent candidate to attend a school far from home. Even with this type of teen, there are still a few special considerations because there is no way to predict with 100 percent certainty how he or she will adjust. The distance can initially throw "off their game," even the most independent teen. During the first few months of the freshman year, you may need to stay closely involved to make sure your teen is adjusting.

Last thought: we always recommend including on the list a few colleges that are relatively close to home. At the last minute, your adventurous, independent teen may get cold feet and choose one from the list that is within easy driving distance from home.

Size: Big or Small?

Most likely, you know whether your teen feels most comfortable and performs better in a smaller or a larger setting. Some students can handle being one of up to 200 students sitting anonymously in a large lecture hall. Many actually prefer not being in the limelight. Others, however, require a smaller, more intimate environment and a low teacher-to-student ratio. There are many reasons for this. Some teens are easily distracted in a large environment or feel lost or isolated. Other teens simply enjoy the opportunity to easily engage with their professors and fellow students that a smaller environment readily provides. Additionally, smaller colleges tend to be liberal arts colleges. This means that professors are focused on the undergraduate population and not diverted from these types of teaching/mentoring duties, as often occurs in the larger university setting where the professors' attentions are divided between undergraduate and graduate students.

On the other hand, some teens do enjoy the hustle and bustle of a large university setting. These schools can provide a great variety of exposure to many academic fields as well as a broader range of on-campus activities. Greek societies, a wide range of division and nondivision athletic activities, as well as numerous political, social, religious, ethnic, and community service clubs are typical to the large campus experience. The teen who can maintain balance in this type of environment and who can learn to navigate independently in the larger more impersonal institutional setting can do well and enjoy this type of environment.

College Community: The Learning and Living Environment

A number of factors go into the making of a college community:

- Location and surroundings
- Religious, social, and political atmosphere
- Coed or single sex
- Party scene

As you look these over, you'll notice that these concerns are not that different from those you would consider when choosing where to live. You would not rent an apartment or buy a home in a neighborhood where you felt uncomfortable, unsafe, or don't think your family would thrive, would you? Of course not. Translate this type of reasoning into making the college list. You are going to help your teen choose a college social environment using these same considerations.

Location and Surroundings

There are essentially three types of college settings: urban, suburban, and rural (small town). When considering the right setting, you have to balance your teen's desires and what you believe is best for him or her. Some teens have some very strong preferences. Some, for example, want to try a different environment from the one in which they grew up, while others want to stay in a more familiar setting. You may also have some strong opinions about what is best for your teen. Some parents, for instance, are absolutely opposed to their teen living in an urban environment, while others think this is a great opportunity. So let's look at each of these environments.

An *urban environment*, by definition, has a faster pace and a wider variety of off-campus activities than those found in suburban or rural communities. Many parents are concerned that the boundaries between the urban campus and the surrounding city are often "blurry," the edges of a city campus and the city itself tending to merge. On the other hand, some parents see a city setting as offering college students a wealth of enriching experiences and opportunities that act as a supplement to the academic environment. Some urban colleges even describe their institution as having a "city as campus." To decide if the urban environment is right for your teen, you need to take into account expenses (city living tends to be more expensive, but, on the plus side, no car is required), the ability of your teen to function in a more hectic environment, and, most important, whether this is the location your teen desires.

The *suburban and rural environments* also have advantages and disadvantages. There is less going on outside the campus, which makes the campus itself the focus of college life. This can be a strength or a weakness, depending on the college. Students spend most of their time on campus, and this encourages the formation of strong bonds with other students. If the student body is small, however (less than 1,000), some teens find that after a brief time everyone knows everyone and that some excitement is missing. On the other hand, many teens thrive in a small, close-knit student body. Marlboro College, for example, is a small liberal arts college nestled in Vermont with a student body of approximately 315. It can be a unique and fulfilling experience for the right kind of student.

How can you tell whether there is enough going on in a small or rural campus? Look carefully at the campus activity offerings. A college that has a "thin" selection of activities or that does not have a strong administrative division that oversees this may not be ideal for many incoming college freshman.

Another important aspect when considering a rural or suburban college is *the car*. Whether to bring a car to campus is an important question. More and more college students in these rural/suburban settings have cars. Some institutions will not allow freshman to keep a car on campus, while many permit this by the sophomore year. Even if you sent your teen off vowing not to get him or her a car, you may quickly find this decision under siege. The pros of having a car can be more mobility, either for work or for internships, as well as more choice in off-campus housing. The cons are the distracting nature of a car and, of course, the expense. If your teen is the type always doing favors for others, we recommend that you discourage him or her from bringing a car, especially during the freshman year. We find that many of these "really nice" teens end up becoming their friends' chauffeur, and their academics suffer.

So when considering the college setting, keep in mind this axiom: "one size does not fit all." The school environment that you may prefer or that is appropriate for your neighbor's teen may not be right for your teen. Look at your teen; explore with him or her the pros and cons of the urban, suburban, and urban environments; and then let this, along with all the other factors, be one of the considerations that help you and your teen make the college list.

Single Sex or Coed?

While most teens prefer coed schools, some are open to considering or even prefer single-sex schools. There are many women's liberal arts colleges but only four men's liberal arts colleges. Most of these are small institutions. What are the advantages? Students rave about the small classes, the sense of community, and the close relationships with teachers. Students also highlight greater leadership opportunities. In fact, these colleges have a documented history of mentoring students, with a high percentage going on to graduate school and into high-profile positions later in life. While many teens might be concerned about the social life at single-sex schools, most have some cross-registration opportunities with nearby all-male or all-female and/or coed colleges. Many single-sex schools are situated adjacent to and affiliated with each other. Examples of this are Barnard College and Columbia University in New York City and Spelman and Morehouse colleges in Atlanta.

If you think this environment might be right for your teen, don't let an unenthusiastic teen summarily dismiss the idea. Take your teen for a tour of a single-sex college that looks like the best potential fit. If your teen is particularly resistant, combine that tour with another nearby school or even do it in an informal "just-passing-through" manner. Many teens, on touring a single-sex school, become enthusiastic about this type of setting.

Needless to say, if your teen is dead set against it, drop it. It isn't a battle you need to fight. For many teens, particularly if they are attending a single-sex high school, only a coed college will do. Even if you and your teen have decided on a coed college setting, you need to be aware that many do not have equal male-to-female ratios. Why? This is because fewer males are applying to college, and the female-to-male ratio at many colleges is 60 to 40 or even 70 to 30. While this might be a "dream come true" for many young men, this may not be so acceptable to many young women. Today, only the most highly selective colleges with the largest applicant pools are able to maintain a balanced male-to-female ratio. Consequently, even if you and your teen want a coed environment, it is best to be aware of this growing gender imbalance and look closely at the gender ratios of all coed schools.

A recent brouhaha in the *New York Times* exposed the practice we have dubbed "affirmative action for boys"—accepting young men with lower grades or SAT scores than those of similarly situated young women. This practice has been silently going on for many years, yet it only recently hit the press. A *New York Times* editorial by the dean of admissions and financial aid at Kenyon College, Jennifer Delahunty Britz, titled "To All the Girls I've Rejected" illustrates the controversy surrounding this practice. Dean Britz writes, "The reality is that because young men are rarer, they're more valued applicants." This means that girl applicants are not judged on the same basis as boys. Girls have to meet a higher admissions standard at the highly selective colleges. So, if you have a girl, this information may help both of you keep the proper perspective and reduce some of the pain of a rejection letter.

College RSPs (Religious, Social, and Political Atmosphere)

Every school has what we like to refer to as an "RSP": its religious, social, and political atmosphere. A college's RSP are those intangible factors that go into whether a college will be a good (or not so good) fit for your teen. The RSP varies from school to school and is rarely discussed openly during the college tour. Yet a school's RSPs are, in large part, what gives a school its own character and "flavor." Again, the one-size-does-not-fit-all rule applies. There is a good RSP match for your teen, but you need to look at these factors carefully to determine how your teen may fit into every college you consider.

Some colleges have a well-deserved reputation for being politically or socially liberal or conservative. Some schools are more "neutral" or diverse. Some teens care deeply about these issues, while others do not. Sometimes a college's RSP atmosphere is so obvious that you know it by reputation or can sense it even on the college website. Some schools have a formal religious affiliation. Others may have an unofficial but definite religious bent. Some campuses are more and some less diverse racially, ethnically, and religiously. There are many liberal campus communities that are welcoming of gay, lesbian, bisexual, and transgendered students. Sexual orientation will not be an issue there, while at other campuses these students may feel uncomfortable.

How can you gauge a school's RSP? It is typically not printed in the college brochures and fliers but can be found in the many official or unofficial guidebooks. And as you have probably already guessed, one of the best ways to get the lay of the RSP landscape is to take a tour (we'll give you some pointers about the tour in the next chapter).

Parents of teens with strong religious beliefs also have concerns about the RSP atmosphere and should consider the large number of colleges with a particular religious affiliation. Even if both of you are positive that a religious environment is optimal, you may want to tour the campus. Sometimes the teen who is totally positive that she wants to attend, for example, a Baptist-affiliated college may change her mind after the tour. While you may think that your teen would thrive in a religious college setting, you may find her resistant to the idea. This could mean that she is looking for a more diverse setting. This is an important issue that both of you need to resolve. A good compromise might be to encourage your child to consider nondenominational institutions, which offer many religious activities and organizations, such as Hillel and Christian Fellowship. Of course, some teens without strong religious affiliation could feel uncomfortable or out of place in a college where a particular religious identity is emphasized or most of the student body is made up from one religious background.

Religious and ethnic minorities may also have some special concerns. According to the 2000 U.S. Census, 69 percent of the country's population is non-Hispanic white, and 88 percent identify themselves as Christian. This means that most American campuses will reflect this profile. For those teens of color or those who are not Christian, the issue of student "diversity" tends to be an important consideration in drawing up the college list.

If you have a teen of color or a teen who is not Christian, you need to determine what type of setting, in terms of ethnic/religious diversity, will be the best fit. Read college materials to determine the ethnic breakdown of the student population. Ask yourself and your teen how important this issue is. For some teens of color or non-Christian teens, this is a crucial consideration, while for others it is not. Their comfort level and wishes may stem from their high school experiences. Have they attended a diverse high school or one that was primarily comprised of minority students? Did they have a positive experience? Do they want to replicate this in college or try something different? For instance, many African American students will choose to attend one of the many excellent historically black colleges, while others will choose a more diverse environment.

Lesbian, gay, bisexual, and transgendered (LGBT) teens face many challenges rarely addressed at college fairs or during their high school's ubiquitous "let's-get-ready-for-college" sessions. In the past, most LGBT teens did not "come out" until either during or after college. In a new book geared for LGBT teens, *The Advocate Guide for LGBT Students* (2006), Shane L. Windmeyer says that today up to half of LGBT teens come out before, not during or after, college. These teens also need to consider how a college's RSPs will impact their college experience.

The political environment of a campus can also be a make-or-break issue for some teens. Some teens are set on an environment that they believe mirrors their own political ideals and values, while others don't care. Some students enjoy the "challenge" of being a "liberal" on a "conservative" campus (or the reverse), while others do not. On some campuses (certainly not the majority), politics forms a core of the campus' identity and "feel," while on others it is a nonissue. Again, know your teen and what he or she is looking for and plan accordingly.

Before you take the college tour, look online at the college website and see what activities are listed under student life. When you do take the college tour, don't forget to look into the college commons and cafeteria during peak hours of use. Stop and speak to students if you are comfortable doing so. Are students from seemingly diverse groups eating or studying together, or do they appear to have self-segregated into homogeneous groups? Is there an active African American club or society, Gay and Lesbian Alliance, Asian American society, Muslim student association, or Hillel? Are there political clubs, newspapers, or other organizations geared to allow your teen to explore his or her political ideals? What types of campus structures (student run and administrative) exist on the campus that will support your teen? Does a school have course offerings geared for your teen? Is there a nondiscrimination policy along with programs and support services in place that can assist your teen? What are the housing opportunities for your teen? Factor all these in when considering how your teen will fit in. Remember, there is more to any school than its racial, ethnic, religious, political, or sexual orientation makeup. Your teen needs to like the whole atmosphere, and, as with any new environment, your teen needs to actually see it and experience it. This same approach holds true for teens of all ethnicities or religious denominations or political persuasions.

The bottom line for all teens is look carefully at the RSPs. If a college's RSP mix is not a good fit for your teen, why waste your time driving to a tour, going through an interview, or filling out an application? You don't want your teen to feel isolated or estranged from his or her peers. Making the RSP fit may be an important determinant of a good freshman-year adjustment.

Is It Party Time?

Now comes one of the most feared (at least by parents) characteristics of college life—how much alcohol and drug use is there? We've never heard anyone on the tour ask, "Is this a party school?" Yet it is a question on the mind of every parent. True, alcohol and drugs can be found on all college campuses. And yes, some schools by reputation are known as "party" schools. However, don't think that because a school doesn't have that reputation there will be no parties. There will be parties even on the most academically rigorous or religiously oriented campuses. For teens who either abstain from alcohol and drugs or use these only in moderation, they may feel uncomfortable and isolated attending a party school.

Most teens are exposed to drugs and alcohol by high school, and most parents know if drug and/or alcohol use is a problem for their teen. Consequently, while some parents feel confident in their teen's ability to control (or even abstain from) drinking and drug use, other parents have real concerns. If you realize that your teen is not that mature, has a proclivity for reckless behavior, or tends to follow the crowd, you need to examine the college party scene carefully.

How do you find out? Again, while you won't see this fact advertised in the glossy college brochures, many college guides do identify the party schools. You can also explore the possibility of a substance-free dorm. Many colleges have responded to parent and student concerns by opening such dorms.

Educational Environment

There are many aspects to consider when examining the educational environment of a college, including level of academic challenge, relationships with professors, class size, who teaches, advisement, academic flexibility, issues relating to disabilities, and specialized programs and athletics.

Level of Academic Challenge

Colleges differ greatly in the degree of academic challenge. The question to ask yourself is not "What is the *best* college my child can get into?" but "Where will my child *succeed and be happy*?" You want to avoid what Walter E. Williams from George Mason University described as an "academic challenge mismatch." This occurs when a student feels overwhelmed competing with students substantially better prepared academically. Another consideration is whether your teen is driven to study 24/7. If thrown into a setting where other students are significantly more academically driven or talented, your teen can flounder. There is nothing more demoralizing for a student accustomed to earning As and Bs in high school receiving mostly Cs or even failing a course in the first semester of college. Adjusting to college is hard enough without adding this additional academic and psychological burden.

How do you know if your teen will succeed at a particular institution? You may even think that an academic challenge—a wake-up call—is exactly what your teen needs. Again, review what you learned in chapter 3. When choosing the academic challenge that is right for your teen, remember who your child is. We believe that most teens work harder and take on more academic challenges if they are not overwhelmed, are underprepared, or are anxious. Just like Goldilocks sampling the bears' porridge, find the one that's "just right."

Relationships with Professors

There are many ways in which students can connect with their professors. In smaller class settings, students get a chance to actively interact with professors to exchange ideas and more fully explore intellectual interests. The mentoring relationship is something most parents hope their teen will find at college. Many still dream of their teen finding the "Mr. Chips" style of professor who will guide them through their college years. Colleges tap into this by marketing the existence of these mentoring relationships. The comment that "students often have dinner at their professors' houses" is so ubiquitous on college tours that we struggle to keep a straight face when we hear it.

Class Size

Many colleges also point to their small class size to demonstrate the amount and quality of contact between students and their professors. To support these claims, they cite their college's average class size, yet these statistics can be misleading since these include upper-level classes, which typically are smaller even at large universities. The critical adjustment and retention period occurs during the first two years of college, when the sizes of the introductory classes are significantly larger. Most college brochures don't specifically address this, so you may need to ask during the tour or call the school.

Who Teaches?

Another factor to consider is the percentage of classes actually taught by full-time faculty, as opposed to teaching assistants, typically graduate students or adjunct professors who work part time on campus.

How important is it to have a famous professor or one with name recognition? As with so many of these issues, it depends. Certainly, it can be inspiring for your teen to be exposed to some of the most well-known academics. However, it is equally if not more important to be actively engaged with professors. You want your teen's professors to be focused primarily on your child's education, not on his or her next appearance on *The News Hour* or Comedy Central. Again, depending on the school, faculty is often pulled in different directions. Have you heard the phrase "publish or perish"? In many institutions, faculty are under enormous pressure to conduct research and publish, leaving less time for teaching or student needs. Many have notable professors, famous in their respective fields, who have little contact with undergraduates. While this may be great for the reputation of the college or university, it may not meet the needs of your teen.

So how can you find out this information? The percentage of full-time professors is listed in brochures and guidebooks. You may need to ask some pointed questions since many college freshman and sophomore classes are not taught by full-time faculty. One way would be to inquire directly about professors' teaching loads or the percentage of teaching assistants. You can also inquire about what opportunities are available for faculty–student collaboration on research.

Do you need to cross off your college list all institutions that rely heavily on teaching assistants or adjunct faculty? Absolutely not. Often these teachers bring exciting, specialized knowledge. What you definitely need to be aware of, however, is whether the part-timers are happy, satisfied, and well treated. You don't want your teen to be taught by unhappy or overburdened teachers. Some colleges have a history of very poor relationships with teaching assistants or adjunct faculty. There have even been strikes and court cases demanding the right of adjunct faculty to unionize—notably at such prestigious institutions as Yale University and New York University. The bottom line: investigate and assess the right teaching mix for *your* teen.

Advisement

An important college characteristic rarely considered by parents or teens is advisement. Most teens do not know what courses are required and need faculty advisement. Almost every college provides yearly advisement by faculty; however, some colleges go a step further and have a built-in mentoring program. This is a faculty member who meets regularly with the student, not just prior to registration. Sarah Lawrence College, for example, has a don system in which students meet with an adviser weekly during their freshman year and biweekly thereafter. If you believe that your teen needs or would benefit from such a relationship, you should look carefully at the advisement system of each college you consider.

Academic Flexibility

Another key aspect of the educational environment to consider is the degree of academic flexibility. There is a wide range of options that fall into three general categories:

- *No requirements*—Some colleges are totally flexible, permitting students to create their own majors or course of study.
- *Distribution of general education requirements*—Some colleges require that students choose from a range of courses to fulfill the requirements in the sciences and liberal arts.
- *Required core curriculum*—Some colleges require that all students take specific, required courses in the sciences and liberal arts.

These terms may be confusing, and colleges often describe their curriculum requirements in unclear or misleading ways. We suggest that before you go on that all-important college visit, you review the college's curriculum requirements, programs, and majors. Does the college have the programs that fit your teen's needs and interests? Do you have questions about the school's general requirements? You can research these questions using printed or online materials or ask appropriate questions during the college visit.

How do you know which academic program fits your teen's needs and interests? Is one style better than another? Only if you believe that one size fits all (which by now you know we don't). Many high school seniors already have a set focus or direction and are resistant to being required to take too many courses too far afield from their interest. Significant numbers of students in the arts and sciences fit this mold. If they have a talent (e.g., theater, instrumental music, vocals, art, or athletics) or a clear career path mapped out (e.g., business, engineering, or computers), this may be their number one consideration when making the college list. If your teen is interested in studying only computer science, you may try to convince him or her it's important to study Shakespeare, but it just might not work. Remember, at this point in your teen's life, you can encourage, but you can't dictate. And never try to trick him or her into enrolling at a college with a core curriculum if he or she is dead set against it. This is a recipe for disaster. The college experience works best when your teen is both a willing and an eager participant.

Issues Relating to Disabilities

If your teen has a learning or physical disability, the availability and type of support services offered are of paramount importance. Since every college is different, you need to look at the supports provided at each college you consider. While the Disabilities Rights Act requires that each college provide accommodations, the extent and quality of those accommodations differ greatly. Almost all provide basic accommodations, including extended time for tests and books on tape. Others provide learning specialists, counseling on study skills, and the most up-to-date computer software. Landmark College in Vermont, for example, is a private two-year college that specializes in the education of students with learning disabilities. The bottom line here: there is a wide variety of options and support available, but you have to do a little digging to find the ones that might best match your teen's needs.

Don't neglect the specialized guidebooks that review different programs and colleges. Use these as a starting point for drawing up your college list. Once you're familiar with what's out there, it's time to expand your horizons by tapping into other resources, including your teen's teachers, advisers, or tutors. You can also contact the college coordinator of services for students with disabilities. We will provide tips on what to look for during the campus visit in chapter 7.

Specialized Programs and Athletics

Many teens have specialized talents in such fields as music, the arts, or athletics. If your teen has expressed a desire to pursue this type of interest or hopes to receive a scholarship based on a specialized talent or skill, there are multiple considerations for you and your teen. First, ask yourself, How talented is my teen? One indication of above-average level of talent is if your teen has already been recognized in his or her field. For example, if your teen has already signed with a talent agency and is working in the "business," is a starter on a varsity team, or has won any types of awards or honors for her specialization, she has talent.

But talent alone is never enough. Your teen must always meet some minimum academic standard to enter college. So don't assume that your teen can just "coast." Make sure your teen is academically sound and don't neglect the standardized exams. Even the best athlete, for example, can be shut out of his dream school if he doesn't "make the grade."

Second, don't take your teen's assurances at face value. Sure, if a college coach is actively recruiting your teen, you know he or she has talent. However, don't forget that in his excitement your teen may hear more than the coach meant to convey. This is not unusual. Teens often hear what they want to, leading to the false impression they are definitely "in." Remember that no matter how interested a coach may be in your teen, he cannot guarantee admission. As we mentioned, your teen must be accepted by the admissions department of the college. Bottom line: don't let your teen to be lulled into academic slumber as happened to Jared:

☀ JARED'S STORY

"I really wanted to go to college and even though my grades weren't so good. I always assumed I could get in because I am an athlete. I was a little disappointed because I wasn't accepted at the colleges I thought should have accepted me because I was a Division I–type football player. But then, I was accepted at Ivy U with an athletic scholarship, and I was really relieved. It didn't last long. Once they saw my transcript, they took it back. I spent my whole four years in high school thinking of myself as just an athlete—not as a student. Really, I know it sounds made up, but no one ever really told me that my grades would stop me from going to college." ☀

So now that you've heard all our admonitions, let's say your teen does have the talent and grades to get into a specialized program. Now what? You and your teen need to do your homework and ask pointed questions. David Mold of the Department of

Your teen is not "in" until you see the admission letter!

Theater at Marymount Manhattan College gives this advice: "Find the right program and institution to fit the student. Keep in mind different things are taught in different programs. There are a half dozen name-brand schools, and people think they have to get into them. They are good but not necessarily the right school for everybody. Also, don't just look at the program—look at the whole college. Many of these programs are in cities, and being in a city is not right for every student. Some students do better at a more traditional college experience in a college outside a city."

Let's also look at athletics. If your teen is not recruited, does this mean that there is nothing he or she or you can do? Of course not. First, make sure that he or she attends specialized summer programs. Some are even run by coaches from colleges your teen may consider. Your teen can also be very proactive and contact college coaches directly. It is best if your teen will make these calls or write these letters to show motivation and maturity. You can also retain a recruiting service. For a fee, these services will organize your teen's information and send the packet to numerous colleges. Jason's story demonstrates a proactive yet practical approach to the college search for a teen with a specialized interest or talent:

☀ A SWIMMER'S TALE

Since he was a child, Jason had a passion for swimming and dreamed of competing in a Division I school. His parents were always supportive (but not pushy!), and when Jason carried this passion into high school, his parents realized they needed to have a strategy to help their son realize his dream. His dad described their approach to us:

"We started out with a strategy of not applying to more than a reasonable number. In his junior year I went with him to places nearby, just to get a look at the campuses and think about what he'd like and get him to think about the whole thing early. Since he was learning to drive and anxious to get some practice in, we combined opportunities to practice driving with going to visit schools. We were lucky in that Jason was fairly decisive early on. He did not want an urban environment, size didn't matter, and he thought he wanted to go far away.

"Right from the start, we were realistic about fulfilling Jason's dream. We knew there wasn't much money in men's swimming.

Since only the best get a scholarship, we encouraged him to look at good academic universities. The rules didn't permit us to contact coaches too early. Instead, his mom spoke with parents of older kids on his swim team and asked other kids on the team how they made their decisions. She talked to more people than I did and went on the NCAA (National Collegiate Athletic Association) website. Jason also liked going on college websites to find swimmers' times. If everyone on a team was three or four seconds faster than him, he knew he didn't have a chance of getting on.

"While Jason was concerned only with whether he could get *on* the team, we knew that based on his personality, his college swim team would be his social life. We wanted him at a school where the kids on the team liked each other. We also knew that this would also hinge on the coach's philosophy. Some schools are like factories, and that wouldn't have been good for Jason. I was also concerned about the academics because that's why he was going to college. We had lots of 'discussions.' I'd say things like, 'You're not going to make a living at swimming' and 'No one is going to ask for your swim times at a job interview. A good academic college is more important.' We never argued but had a lot of discussions about what he wanted to get from college.

"I remember Jason getting letters from coaches, and he also wrote to some directly. He went on a few recruiting trips where he stayed with someone from the team and went to workouts. We told him that he could pick the college as long as they were affordable. He identified a few colleges, some Division I and some Division II, and sent off his applications. Some were quite expensive, and we hoped he would be offered a big enough academic scholarship to afford it. While he was academically strong, we knew he wasn't in the category of an elite swimmer and would not be offered a swimming scholarship, and we couldn't afford full private college fees." ✺

Jason's story is a great illustration of a smart *and* balanced approach to the college search for a teen with a special interest or talent. We've included Jason's coach contact letter in chapter 8. So don't forget Jason. The rest of his story, "A Swimmer's Tale," will continue in chapter 10.

What about the teen who has interests or abilities in the arts or athletics but does not want this to be the major focus of college like Jason did? There are plenty of liberal arts institutions with strong arts and athletics department. You need to explore what opportunities are available for your teen. There is no reason for a teen who loves to swim, sing, or act to attend a college where he or she will not be able to pursue these interests simply because he or she is not among the most talented.

Remember, a unique talent can be "the hook" for admission at a "reach school." Here's how one teen was able to use her talent to gain admission—and a generous scholarship—to the college of her dreams.

☼ MAYA'S STORY

Maya had attended a performing arts high school, specializing in voice and opera. When she compared herself to older, more talented classmates who were rejected by conservatories, she realized she didn't have a great shot at a conservatory. "There are just too many sopranos," she told us. Yet she loved singing and did not wish to give it up. During the fall of her senior year, her mother encouraged her to find colleges with good music departments where she could continue to sing and perform. Her mother realized that her talent could make her application stand out. With this goal in mind, her mom suggested she make a CD. Maya was energized and quickly found a studio and piano accompanist. Mom was there to pay the bill, and it wasn't cheap. But, as you'll see, it paid off.

Later that fall, Maya and her mom consulted with a private college adviser to draw up her college list. The CD certainly made her stand out; not many opera singers apply to liberal arts institutions. Subsequently, Maya was accepted by her number one choice and offered a large merit scholarship. Of course, the number one strategy mom employed was to plant the CD seed. Taping at the recording studio was exciting and rewarding, and Maya was thoroughly engaged. It actually turned out to be one of the highlights of the college admissions process. As an added bonus, Mom was able to make copies of Maya's CD to give to friends and family. ☼

The Determined Student

Some kids really do know where they want to go or have very strong preferences for what they want and don't want in a college. Tray and Janelle were just such teens, and while some of you are thinking, "That's great; I wish my teen had a clue," there are still things to be careful about, as their stories demonstrate. This how Tray's mom remembers the college race:

☀ A MOM'S TALE

"There were only three schools Tray wanted to go to, and he applied only to those three. Needless to say, his father and I were not happy. We thought it did not provide him with enough options. He wanted a big university in a midsize city that had Division I sports, a big stadium, *and* a communications program. He also did not want to be more than a five-hour drive from home! I tried to get him to add more schools to his list, but he insisted, 'This is what I want. I want to sit in a big stadium cheering with everyone.' This was his vision of college life, so what could we say? We let him apply where he wanted, held our breaths until April, and were unbelievably relieved when he got into his first choice. And you know what? It turned out to be the right choice for Tray." ☀

Janelle's college application experience did not have such a happy ending:

☀ JANELLE'S STORY

"I really thought I wanted to go to University X. That's all I ever considered, and now looking back, I don't know why. I applied there and nowhere else—even though my parents kept telling me it was a bad idea. When I was accepted, I was so happy, you just can't imagine. University X has a policy that you come and spend the night, and I did. Was I disappointed! I couldn't imagine myself spending four years there. I hated it. So I didn't go, but it was too late to apply anywhere else. I wound up at my local community college, and while I like it, I really wanted to go away." ☀

There are many determined students like Tray and Janelle. Sometimes their resolve can be a great thing. However, never lose sight of the fact that all teens have limited life experience. That is why it is important, if at all possible, to get your "determined" teen to add a few other schools to that college list—just in case things don't work out.

Financial Considerations

Wouldn't it be great if you didn't have to think about the cost of a college education? Most of us have to consider how we're going to swing paying for college. Fortunately, there are many options. There are public universities and community colleges where the costs are considerably less than at private institutions. But don't automatically discard the private option. Under the right conditions, substantial need-based aid is available to teens of modest and limited means. You can actually research which colleges have the most money to give.

Your teen may also possess qualities that can lead to scholarships, including those for athletics, music, artistic abilities, exceptionally high SATs and grades, and even demonstrated "leadership abilities." Keep in mind the odds of being offered a scholarship, especially merit aid, increase when your teen applies to a school for which his or her qualifications or College Board scores are higher than those of the typical applicant. Schools are always looking for such students to add to their incoming classes and are motivated to offer your teen aid in an attempt to "snag" him or her. As long as the college provides your teen the environment and programs he or she needs, why not consider one that will provide a good aid package?

A final thought about financial consideration: have an open talk with your teen about what your family can and cannot afford before he or she finalizes that list. It is important that both teens and parents go into this process with realistic expectations.

How Many Schools Make the Final Cut?

One of the most common questions we are asked is, "How many colleges should we tour?" and "How many colleges should he apply to?" In the past, teens typically applied to six colleges and probably toured fewer than ten. Today, some students seem to have adopted the "throw it all against the wall and something will stick" strategy and apply to up to twenty or more schools. This approach, as you might imagine, begins to border on the absurd. Please, don't go down the rabbit hole with Alice. Many high schools foreclose this option by limiting the number of schools a student can apply to. Other high schools will let your teen apply to as many colleges as he or she wants. As a rule, we suggest having a list of ten to fifteen to visit. Typically, this list gets pared down to approximately six schools that your teen will actually apply to. Keep in mind the "Rule of Six": your teen should apply to *at least* two "safeties," two "reaches," and two "just rights."

A friendly tip for Type A and worried parents: you are more likely to encourage (or approve of) your teen applying to an excessive number of colleges. Don't confuse quantity with quality. Don't actually decrease your teen's chances of acceptance. Too many applications will inevitably overwhelm your teen (in fact, all of you) and may result in poorly crafted applications. We hope this list of college characteristics has not overwhelmed you. With hundreds of colleges to consider, you can use these criteria to focus your search and have at least ten colleges to tour. So before you go any further in the process, complete the following questionnaire.

Needs Assessment Questionnaire

1. THE COLLEGE SETTING
   My teen wants:
   ☐ A four-year college
   ☐ A community college
   My teen prefers:
   ☐ Rural
   ☐ Suburban
   ☐ Urban
   My teen wants to be:
   ☐ Within driving distance of home
   ☐ Far from home
   ☐ Distance does not matter
   My teen wants:
   ☐ Small (less than 2,000)
   ☐ Midsized (2,000–5,000)
   ☐ Large university (over 5,000)
   My teen has important personal considerations and wants:
   ☐ A college with a particular religious affiliation
   ☐ A college welcoming of ethnic diversity
   ☐ A college welcoming of gay students

☐ A college with a particular political bent (liberal or conservative)

My teen wants or needs to attend a:
☐ Private college/university
☐ Public/state school/university

My teen needs financial aid
☐ Is a candidate for merit-based scholarships?
☐ Is a candidate for need-based scholarships?

My teen wants:
☐ A single-sex school
☐ A coed school

2. COLLEGE SERVICES AND FACILITIES

My teen has special interests:
☐ Outdoor recreation (e.g., skiing or rock climbing)
☐ Access to music, theater, museums
☐ Specialized internship work opportunities (e.g., journalism or science)

My teen plans to play a team sport:
☐ Varsity
☐ Club
☐ Extramural

My teen has a learning, emotional, or physical disability and needs:
☐ Accommodations
☐ Academic support
☐ Counseling

My teen has dorm requirements:
☐ Guaranteed dorm room throughout the college years
☐ Preferred dorm environment:
  ☐ Single sex
  ☐ Coed by floor
  ☐ Coed dorms with coed bathrooms
  ☐ Coed dorm with single-sex bathroom
  ☐ Substance-free dorms

3. COLLEGE EDUCATIONAL ENVIRONMENT

My teen prefers a certain learning environment:
☐ Prefers small classes
☐ Prefers larger classes
☐ Would be lost in a large university setting
☐ Values a close relationship with teachers

My teen has identified a field of study:
- ☐ Engineering
- ☐ Computers
- ☐ Preprofessional (e.g., medicine, nursing, or occupational or physical therapy
- ☐ Paraprofessional (e.g., paralegal or physical therapist)
- ☐ Business
- ☐ Performing arts (e.g., instrumental music, voice, theater, or dance)

My teen wants specialized opportunities:
- ☐ Study abroad
- ☐ Internships
- ☐ Research opportunities

Tip: Work with Your Teen to Expand or Contract the College List

Now that you have done your prerace training, you have an idea of what your teen needs and is looking for in a college. Finally, the time has arrived when you and your teen can begin the college search. If your teen is ready to work with you and you can start it together, great! If not, don't despair; you can start the research yourself. Parents and teens find different approaches helpful. Many like to use one of the well-known big guidebooks, such as the Princeton Review's *Best 357 Colleges* or the *Fiske Guide to Colleges*; others like the Internet, college fairs, or a combination of resources.

Do you need to hire a private college adviser? Few parents did this when we were applying to college, but now it has become more common, particularly among the affluent. Once, when sitting in on a parent discussion on choosing colleges, some of the parents—the more affluent ones—praised their private college advisers. Some paid thousands of dollars, while others had paid only a few hundred dollars for a few sessions. One parent, with a little twinkle in her eye, laughed as she praised the cost-effectiveness of what she called her "counselor-o-matic." She clarified that this was a free, advanced search engine accessed through the Princeton Review website. "All you have to do, "she explained, "is plug in details of the teen's stats (grade-point average, SAT/ACT scores), demographics, and what kind of college they want. Then out pops out a list of good matches, reaches, and safeties." The *U.S. News and World Report*'s website provides similar free services. All these are great resources, particularly if you or your teen enjoy computers. This is something you can try alone or together with your teen. Either way, we find that these websites can be very helpful because they alert you to colleges you may never have heard of or seriously considered— "undiscovered" gems.

You should also consider your teen's "nonnegotiables": the qualities that he or she, rightly or wrongly, insist rules a college out. Why waste both your time and his or hers touring a school that he or she won't even consider? One college student recalled, "There was this one school my parents insisted I visit. It was hours away. One of the state universities, I think, maybe University X. I didn't like it; it was a huge campus, and you'd need a car. I don't even drive. Everyone kinda pushed me to see it. People said you have to go and see it. It was annoying. While we packed to leave, I was saying, 'I'm not going there.' Even during the drive up, I was saying, 'Mom, I'm not going there!' It was a waste of a weekend. It took us like six hours to get there. I hated it!"

Forcing a teen to see a college he or she is dead set against rarely works. If you "take your shot," as the student's parents in the above story did and it doesn't turn the tide, just move on. Remember, it is natural for teens to latch on to a few things that they rate as "good" or "bad" about a school. It is so hard to convince them otherwise and is usually not worth the effort or conflict. Keep in mind that this is a time of high tension for everyone, and there's no need to add fuel to the fire. So if your teen, for a reason you find irrational or inexplicable, simply "hates" a certain school, it is usually best to let it go and move on to another college. Remember what we said at the beginning of the chapter: so many schools, so little time. If you have your heart set on a school that he or she "hates" (and can't let go of your dream), reread chapter 2.

What do you do if making the college list is too overwhelming or you find yourself arguing with your teen? Don't worry; there are still other strategies you can use. Many families do rely on outside guidance for creating the college list. While many teens complain about their high school counselors, others praise them highly. You certainly should encourage your teen to meet regularly with his or her counselor early in the junior year if possible. If you are invited to meet with them, make sure you don't miss it. Bring along your list of questions but be sensitive to their time constraints. Many are stretched thin with too many students to advise. We have frequently heard complaints about the overpushy parent demanding to meet with the school counselor during the freshman or sophomore year. For your teen, making a relationship with the college adviser can be priceless. The counselor is required to send a letter of recommendation to the colleges, and the more personal and positive the letter, the better. We are not suggesting to totally butter the counselor up, but having him or her in your teen's corner is a great help. Many have years of experience and can be as helpful as private college advisers. There are other people you can rope in to help. Older siblings, your teen's friends, aunts, and uncles—all can weigh in if your teen values their advice. Just remember, don't spring these "helpful" people on your teen unless you are confident they can be effective. Nothing will make a teen angrier than finding out that his or her parents are basically arranging a "college intervention."

The Homestretch

As we said earlier, almost all teens get into college somewhere, and most get into a college close to the top of their list. Now this is not to say that things never go wrong. There are the few students who do not get accepted by any of their top-choice colleges. Why does this happen? Usually when teens and their parents have unrealistic expectations and apply only to reach schools. That's why it is so important for parents to research and genuinely understand the importance of the college–teen fit. Don't fall into the trap of unrealistic expectations. If you do your homework and follow the "route" we have mapped out for you, chances are that both you and your teen will be pleased at the end of this race.

CHAPTER 7

Taking It on the Road

WHY BOTHER to make the college pilgrimage in a time of virtual reality? Can't you and your teen get everything you need off the Web, those slick CDs, or those materials the colleges send? The answer is an unequivocal "no. There simply is no substitute for seeing and actually experiencing a college campus firsthand. It's an indispensable step in the "is it a good match?" process and a great tool for whittling down that college list. Up to this point, all you and your teen have experienced is a virtual college—not the real deal.

So what to look for during the college visit? A good college fit is made up of some tangible and some intangible factors. The tangible ones are easy. Does the college provide a course of study that interests your teen? Is it the right size, price range, location, and so on? These are the type of features gleaned from written and Web-based materials. Yet equally important are the intangibles—that unique feel every college campus has that you can't quite put your finger on but can get only by experiencing it. This is what the campus visit gives you and, more important, your teen. It is all well and good to like a college on paper, but if you haven't seen it "in the flesh," you can't be sure the hype is true. Think of it the same way as booking a hotel online or from a brochure. The printed materials and descriptions look so beautiful, so perfect for that ideal vacation you've been dreaming about all year. You pack your bags, hop on the plane, and arrive at your destination with high expectations only to find that your picturesque hideaway is located next to a noisy freeway or the room smells of mold. You get the point: a picture may be worth a thousand words, but seeing is believing.

We're not going to pretend otherwise: campus visits are time consuming. These do require some organization and advanced planning. Let's discuss strategy. Logically, the first thing you need is a working college list created by using our tips from chapter 6. Remember that list should be not too long or too short. If it is too long, you and your teen will quickly feel overwhelmed, and if it is too short, you may not have enough options. We recommend considering approximately fifteen schools and certainly no more than twenty. We are not suggesting that you actually visit twenty colleges, although some families do. However, these tend to be those comprised of highly organized parents with very cooperative teens who started the college search during the freshman and sophomore years. In the real world, most don't have time to visit more than ten colleges, and some may be able to fit in only six. Even this number may sound overwhelming in an overscheduled life. How to do it? The answer is strategy. Our strategy is comprised of three parts: make the college list, know when to time the tour, and schedule the visit.

Make the College List

You can't visit colleges if you don't have a college list. So if you haven't done it and your teen is in his or her junior or senior year, turn back to chapter 6. Now that you have the list, the first thing is to look at it. Ask yourself how you and your teen feel about it. Do the selected schools appear to meet your family's *and* your teen's targeted goals for a college? If the answer is yes, then move forward with scheduling these college tours, but if you are not content with the list, don't hesitate to add or drop schools. The college list is not the Ten Commandments carved in stone. Always consider your college list as flexible. This will help you and your teen remain open to change and new opportunities and, as important, will keep all of you from falling into the "must" trap—"my teen *must* attend College X." So keep it flexible.

Timing Is Everything

Timing, as everyone likes to say, is everything. And it's true. If you are either too early or too late, you may not get the real experience, or you may be shut out of or foreclosed from an opportunity altogether. So the first consideration is when to visit. The answer: absolutely *not* during college breaks and absolutely *when* college is in full session. This answer may come as a surprise to some of you who have read other guidebooks that recommend summer vacation and breaks as ideal times to visit. If at all possible, avoid these times. Remember that the sine qua non of the college visit is the students. There is no way your teen can get the real feel of a college campus and a good sense of whether he or she would feel comfortable there if the student body is absent. So try to plan your tours while college is in session.

Schedule the Visit

We don't know any teens who plan and arrange the college visit by themselves. Most are perfectly happy letting their parents make the travel arrangements. The first thing to do is check out your teen's school and extracurricular schedule. It's extremely important to keep in mind that your teen must graduate high school before going on to college. And while the college admissions process may almost appear to be a full-time occupation, don't lose sight of that high school diploma. This means that if you have to cancel a tour because something crucial has come up, don't panic or become upset. Your teen does have multiple responsibilities—academic deadlines, high-stakes tests, and social events—and some of these things should come first. And you have a life too. As long as you don't leave the college tours for the last minute, everything can be scheduled in a relaxed manner.

A good rule of thumb to follow is to never schedule college visits on the day your teen has something he or she really wants (or has) to do. So do *not* tour during midterms or finals or when your teen has any other critical high school assignment or event. Nothing creates more stress and conflict than this. Moreover, this is usually the "kiss of death" for that school.

It is also important to let your teen have some control over the application process. A successful collaboration with your teen will strike a balance between "parent knows best" and "teen in the driver's seat." So make sure your teen feels part of the scheduling process, even if you are doing most of the legwork.

So when can you schedule those visits? Look for those days when your teen's high school is off but colleges are not. Don't start tearing your hair out over this suggestion—it is not as hard as you think. Surprisingly, most college calendars are distinct from high school calendars. For example, while most high schools give Columbus Day as a vacation day, most colleges do not. Most high schools key their spring break to Easter and in some parts of the country the Easter and Passover holidays, but many colleges do not. In addition, college schedules are not uniform throughout the country or even within a given region. This means that there are more available dates than you might think.

Begin by reviewing your teen's high school calendar and, as far as possible, exam and extracurricular schedules. Next, contact the colleges to find out about both the dates and the details for tours and open houses. Plan to make appointments for both a tour and the information session. Colleges attempt to make it as easy as possible for you and your teen to attend. Many hold these on weekends, making it much easier to accommodate the family schedule. Don't forget that colleges are also "shopping" for their next freshman class and want to have as large an applicant pool as possible. There are many opportunities to find the right time to visit.

Roadblock Alert: Don't Delay

It is important for everyone involved not to leave all the college tours for the last minute (i.e., the fall of the senior year). You and your teen will not benefit from whirlwind marathon tours. The only thing such marathons engender is a general sense of panic, leaving both you and your teen dazed and unable to recall one school from the other. You don't want your teen left asking, "Where was I on Tuesday? Which schools did we see on Wednesday? Where was that campus with the great student commons?" Sean, a high school senior, told us, "All the college tours turned into one big blur in my mind, with the same line used over and over again, 'We have over 100 clubs! And if you can't find a club you like, you can start your own!' That's all I remember about those visits."

As you can see from Sean's story, tours done in this fashion serve no purpose except to confuse and frustrate. Avoid this trap at all costs. Begin the touring process in the junior year or even at the end of the sophomore year and plan on no more than two tours a day. And when we say you can do up to two tours, we recommend this only if the two schools are in close proximity. Ideally, however, we believe that one per day is best.

Roadblock Alert: Season and Weather

Another small but sometimes critical factor to keep in mind is the season. It is better to tour a campus during the season in which it will show the best. If you are looking at a campus in California or in Florida, the season is almost irrelevant (do, however, avoid blazing heat or mudslides). However, if you are looking in a part of the country with seasonal variations, then try to schedule the campus visit when it can be seen at its best. In the Midwest, Northwest, and Northeast, this normally means you don't want to go in the dead of winter. Nothing will turn a teen off quicker than seeing a campus in upstate New York, for example, in February. Your teen is contemplating leaving the nest for the first time, and you don't want that first glimpse of his or her potential home away from home looking like a pile of slushy snow, barren trees, and gray skies.

This leads to that connected variable: the weather. If at all possible, do not tour in the rain. We do understand that this is easier said than done. However, with the ability to check weather forecasts up to ten days in advance, it is not impossible. Just as most campuses don't show well in the dead of winter, they don't show well in the rain. So if a torrential rainstorm is definitely in the forecast, reschedule the tour if possible. If not, don't panic. Just bring an umbrella.

Anatomy of a College Visit

It hasn't escaped our attention that we have thrown around a lot of different terms: "tour," "college visit," "information session," and so on. In the most general sense, the "college visit" is simply a physical visit to a college campus and may be comprised of some, all, or none of the above activities. It can consist of as little as getting out of the car and walking across the commons.

There is certainly a lot to consider in planning the college visit, particularly when you may be planning on going to see up to fifteen colleges. We think it might be helpful if you think of the college visit as a Little League baseball game made up of nine innings (occasionally with overtime). The first thing a manager has to consider is the season schedule and the logistics— when and how to arrive at the field on time (after all, you don't want to forfeit the game). Next, the manager has to make some crucial decisions about how to play the game itself, assign the players positions and batting order, and the like.

When it comes to the college visit, *you* are the manager, and its time to think logistics. So here's what you need to consider: what to bring, who should go on the tour, how to get to the campus in one piece, and what to do once you get there. Let's review each element that makes up the college visit.

First Mile: Packing for the Visit

It's important to know what to bring and what to wear. We suggest that you bring a large bag or book bag, a pad or small notebook, and, if your teen agrees, a camera (chances are it's part of your cell phone). It's a great idea to take pictures. You'll be surprised how quickly all the colleges begin to look alike, so make sure you get at least one picture with the college name displayed on a sign. The large bag or book bag is needed to store all the handouts and materials you and your teen will accumulate. It's incredibly uncomfortable to hold a growing pile of papers in your hand. In addition, bring something to write in—a notebook for information, any questions you want to ask (or wish you had asked), important names, and phone numbers.

Apparel is also important. Don't wear anything your teen finds embarrassing or calls attention to yourself. This means not trying to look as hip as your teen or dressing in a manner reminiscent of your own college days. Casual but comfortable should be your guide, and don't forget comfortable shoes.

Your teen's choice of attire should avoid the outlandish. In other words, your teen should not be the center of attention because of his or her clothes. On the other hand, try to be flexible and open minded; your teen needn't show up dressed too conservatively. Encourage him or her to avoid anything that is sexually explicit or overly bizarre.

Second Mile: The Entourage

Who should visit? Obviously, your teen should, but after that there are several options. Do you have to go? Not necessarily. Do both parents have to go? Not necessarily. Can your teen bring a friend? Possibly. Should siblings tag along? Maybe. You can see that there are options, even when it comes to who accompanies your teen on the tour. Let's discuss these.

Option #1: You Go with Your Teen

This is the most typical option and is the ideal one. You and/or your spouse accompany your teen on the tours. The advantage is that everyone sees the campus and gets a feel for it. You get to formulate and ask questions. You get to see your teen's reaction to the campus environment and not rely on a secondhand shrug of the shoulders when you inquire, "So, what did you think?"

In some families, both parents accompany the teen; in others, one parent is the designated tour taker; while in others, both parents take turns.

What should you do? It depends on your individual family, its needs, and your relationship to your teen. There is no right or wrong answer here. Any approach that gets your teen out the door will do.

Option #2: Bring the Siblings Along (or Not!)

Do you bring a sibling along? Again, that depends on circumstances: time, money, logistics, and the comfort level of the college-bound teen. Some teens welcome brothers and/or sisters tagging along; others do not. Some like the fact that the presence of others siblings will draw attention away from them, while others resent sharing the experience. Of course, if your teen does not mind the presence of a sibling and it's feasible to bring that child along, the advantage is that it initiates the younger child into the experience in a gentle, nonthreatening way. Again, whatever works for *your* family.

Option #3: Bring a Friend Along

Is it a good idea to bring along one of your teen's friends? That depends. It depends on whether they are interested in the same type of college, on whether they get along very well and don't get into arguments or tiffs, and on whether your teen is not overly influenced by the opinions of others—this friend in particular (unless the friend's influence is generally positive). If you do bring along a friend, we recommend that you discuss what seems obvious to us but not necessary to adolescents—that what is a good match for your teen may not be a good match for his or her friend.

There are also advantages to bringing along a friend. Sometimes this can be part of a tour-sharing arrangement. You take both teens to see Colleges A, B, and C, and the friend's parents take both teens to see Colleges X, Y, and Z. This option can be particularly helpful if you have time or money constraints or a teen who is reluctant to tour. Additionally, many teens tell us touring in tandem is simply more fun. It also gives them the security to go off and explore on their own:

☀ ANNA'S STORY

Anna, now a college sophomore, took a friend along. Despite being impressed that their student cum tour guide could talk while walking backward without tripping, he had no sense of humor and barely smiled. The tour, both girls quickly agreed, was a dud. When their group intersected with another tour group that seemed much more fun, they quickly abandoned their original group and joined the other. Anna's parents stayed with the boring group, and no one else seemed to notice that the girls had made an unauthorized switch. The second tour proved much better. Their secret escape turned into an enjoyable (and innocent) act of rebellion that everyone laughed about on the car ride home. Both girls left the visit with a much improved impression than if they had stayed with the original group or had gone alone. ☀

Option #4: The Group Tour

For parents who simply cannot swing accompanying their teens on college visits, there are other ways for teens to go. Many church groups, community organizations, and high schools offer group tours. The advantage is that your teen has fun going on campus visits with friends. The disadvantage can be that the schools chosen by the tour coordinator may not be on your teen's list. These tours tend to take on a whirlwind feel and are not the optimal way to visit. However, if this is the only option available, we urge you to take advantage of any touring opportunities available.

Option #5: A Combination of All the Above

You don't have to choose only one of these options. Options are just that: opportunities and possibilities.

Third Mile: Don't Get Lost

We can't tell you the number of arguments started because families get lost on the way to, are late for, or miss the tour. Remember, as you all head out, many teens are nervous—or already annoyed—at their parents. Tension can be high, especially for the first few tours. The threat of being late because you get lost on the way or are simply late leaving home only adds to that anxiety and can prevent your teen from giving the college a fair shake. Arriving late and trying to catch up with the tour will only embarrass most teens. Another tip: don't rely solely on MapQuest or similar map services; call the admissions office ahead of time to make sure the directions are accurate and give yourself plenty of time to get there on time. What do we mean by plenty? Half an hour to forty-five minutes, minimum. Mary's story illustrates how being late for a tour can wreck havoc on the whole experience:

✻ MARY'S STORY

Mary lamented that during the last half hour of the trip, her parents bickered incessantly as they meandered around the suburban streets looking for the college, each convinced it had been the other's job to get directions. Mary recalled how anxious she felt when they finally arrived at the college and their car screeched to a halt at the campus, late for the tour. Her mother, frantic by this point, hopped out of the car with Mary in tow, while her father went in search of a parking spot. Despite the stress, Mary breathed a sigh of relief as she spied a large group in the distance. She knew they were the tour group—a group that size certainly stands out. She hoped she could catch the group and slip in unnoticed. Those hopes were dashed when her mother called out loudly, "Go catch up to the front!" At that moment, she wished the ground would open up and swallow her. Needless to say, Mary did not get a good feel about the college; the high state of anxiety and frustration she and her parents felt by the time they arrived, combined with the embarrassment caused by her mom's unintentional faux pas, likely doomed Mary's chances of having a good campus visit. ✻

Fourth Mile: You're There—Now What?

Discuss the campus visit activities with your teen before you arrive. There are three basic activities you and your teen can attend: the college tour, an information session, and sitting in on a class. However, depending on your teen's individual interests, there are other opportunities your teen may want to take advantage of while on campus. Indeed, there are many options and combinations thereof, and it can all make the college visit a bit overwhelming. Now let's look over all the options you have once you've arrived (in one piece) at your destination.

The Campus Tour

Campus tours last about one hour and are typically run by a student. If you've ever watched any coming-of-age movies or a television show like *The OC*, you've seen this. In the "high school senior is getting ready to transition to college" episode, a group of anxious teens are doggedly following a student cum tour guide. His or her job is to dispense reams of information about the college: its history, the buildings, its physical plant, and student life.

The tour is his or her chance to see the college in the company of other perspective students and get the "lay of the land." Most colleges let teens and parents take the tour together, but some colleges offer parents and students separate tours. Colleges hope that without adults, kids will be more open and less inhibited, ask more questions, and more openly express their interests during the tour. Remember that some teens absolutely do not want their parents on the tour with them, and if this is the case, we feel you need to respect your teen's wishes and let him or her take the tour alone. Now is not the time to let your hurt or disappointed feelings show.

The Information Session

Information sessions are run by admissions staff and provide information about the admissions process, admissions requirements, college academic programs, and extracurricular activities. It is not at all unusual for the typical teen to want to skip the information session. When these sessions are merely a repetition of printed materials, both you and your teen will naturally be bored if you have already read through the materials. On the other hand, if there is a chance for questions and if one or both of you have not read the prepared materials carefully, this can be a good opportunity to obtain a lot of basic and more particularized information about the college. As a rule, we recommend that both of you attend, but if your teen just can't take anymore, remember you're the grown-up: stifle that yawn and attend. You might just be surprised at what you will learn.

During the college visit, it is not necessary for you and your teen to be joined at the hip. Many teens respond cheerfully to the suggestion that they can wander a bit—maybe go eat at the cafeteria while you sit through the information session. If your teen misses the information session, nothing is lost. Your teen won't be losing the chance to make that crucial connection, and you can get the information you need from other sources. In fact, the "real" campus is on the quad, in the campus common or cafeteria, and in the classrooms. A little free time for your teen to explore the campus may be just what is needed to really see if he or she can make (or not make) that crucial connection to the campus.

Sampling a Class

One issue that frequently comes up is whether to sit in on a class. Many teens have a strong interest in doing this, particularly when a college is near or at the top of their list. For these teens, we highly recommend that you call the admissions office ahead of time. First, ascertain if the college permits this (not all do). Second, arrange for your teen to sit in on a class that is of particular interest. If you can devote the time, it is even better if your teen can sit in on a few classes to get a better feel for the range and styles of classes and professors. Never force your teen to sit in on a class. It just isn't that important. This is one battle you simply don't need to fight. Sometimes you need to count your blessings that you at least got your teen to go on the tour. However, if your teen wants to and can sit in on a class, this questionnaire may prove useful:

Class Evaluation Questionnaire

1. How large was the class?
2. Was the class taught by a professor or a graduate student/adjunct instructor?
3. Was the professor excited, organized, thorough, and knowledgeable about the subject and a good instructor?
4. Did the professor know the students' names? How did he or she interact with the students?
5. Did the students remain engaged? Did they seem excited?
6. Were students able to express their opinions?
7. Were students able to ask questions, not concerned with looking bad?
8. Did you see any humor by either students or faculty?
9. Were you allowed to choose any class to sit in on, or was this a class chosen by the admissions staff?

Tailored Visits: Sports and the Arts

Some teens have highly specialized skills and talents that they want to pursue in college. For those students, the college visit should comprise all the activities and concerns we outline in this chapter along with some additional activities. As a general rule, there are four broad specialization categories: athletics, graphic and visual arts, drama, and music. We hope you have already made a college list that includes schools in sync with your teen's particular interests. Your college list should include schools that offer your teen the opportunity to pursue his or her dreams *and* where he or she has a good possibility being accepted and doing what he or she loves. After all, what's the point of attending a college where your teen has no chance to play his or her sport or be cast in the school play if that is his or her dream.

If your teen is a student-athlete, colleges are divided into three distinct divisions: Divisions I, II, and II. If your teen hopes to play on a division college team, you need to contact the team coach before arriving on campus. If you arrive on tour day and ask to meet with a coach, the odds are it's not happening (at least not that day). Not all students with athletic talent or interest aspire to or will be able to play on a college division team. A great alternative is playing on a college club or intramural team. If this alternative interests your teen, make sure you pick up information about these teams and the school policy for joining. Your teen may also enjoy seeing a game or practice.

If your teen is pursuing the arts (art, acting, singing, or playing a musical instrument), your college list should include conservatories or arts schools, along with universities that contain specialized "schools." During the college visit, make sure you check out the art studios, exhibition halls, theaters, concert facilities, recording facilities, and so on. If at all possible, let your teen sit in on a class or an activity in his or her field. Again, your teen's visit should include a look at what is available in these areas, and it may be advisable during the college visit to meet with a member of the drama department, see the art studio, or have an opportunity to talk with a member of a related club. Again, a timely placed call to the admissions office is advisable.

Interviews

We usually recommend that you schedule interviews on a separate day from the visit for two good reasons: 1) your teen doesn't need to waste the time and sheer emotional energy interviewing at a college he or she doesn't want to attend, and 2) the interview will go best if the teen has already seen the campus. Admissions officers are not impressed by a teen who knows nothing about the college or why he or she is applying.

That said, there are times when the two will simply have to be done on the same day. Perhaps the college is far from home or you're running out of time. Don't worry: you can do the tour and the interview the same day. However, if you find yourself in this situation, try to schedule the interview *after* the tour if at all possible. This way, your teen has the best chance of having something positive to say about the college during the interview. Again, don't try to do two college tours and interviews on the same day.

Strategies for interviews and auditions are included in chapter 8.

The Sleepover

This is another optional activity. It is usually done after an acceptance is received. Since sleepovers can be time consuming and stressful, the only reason to do this earlier (rather than later) is logistics or if your teen is considering early admissions. As with almost everything in life, there are pros and cons to include an overnight stay as part of the college visit. One serious problem with an overnight stay is that it can go badly not because the college is a bad fit but because your teen was assigned the host roommate from hell. When this happens, most teens permanently cross the college off their list even if it may be a good fit.

Special Accommodations

Most colleges welcome students with learning and physical disabilities and provide a host of accommodations and support. While some colleges have specific programs for these teens, others provide only the legally required services. If your teen has a learning disability or needs other accommodations, start your search by checking out college websites and the specialized guides that list the types of programs and accommodations that are available at numerous colleges and universities across the country. The next step, after drawing up the college list, is to arrange to meet with the director of these services before arriving on campus. By asking the right questions, you may either cross a college off your list or walk away with the feeling that the college may be the right fit for your teen.

We also urge you not to discuss or raise any disability issues during the tour or information session. In fact, the best way to guarantee your teen will never attend a college tour again (at least not with you) is to raise your hand between the science building and the college's newly minted athletics facility and start asking questions about accommodations for learning-disabled students. We provide a more in-depth discussion about college admission issues specific for teens with disabilities in chapter 9. But don't stop with the information we provide. Check out the many guides dedicated to this topic, such as Princeton Review's *The K & W Guide to Colleges for Students with Learning Disabilities or Attention Deficit Disorder* and Peterson's *Colleges for Students with Learning Disabilities or ADD.*

Fifth Mile: Rules of Conduct

We can't tell you how often we hear teens complain about their parents behaving badly during the college visit. If you have already started touring, you have probably either seen or heard tales of rude or controlling parents. These are parents who interrupt at inappropriate times, believe that the entire event was planned for the sole benefit of their teen, or are so domineering that it's clear the kid will never have the opportunity to ask a single question. So what is a safe approach? First, talk with your teen ahead of time. Of course, if you and your teen are taking separate tours or if your teen chooses not to attend the information session, you don't have much to worry about. Otherwise, if you feel you may want to ask a question, discuss this first with your teen. While many typical teens do not want you to ask anything, others want you to ask questions, but only those they have approved. They certainly want assurances that you won't divulge personal information or touch on any subjects he or she finds embarrassing. One student, John, told us he felt as if a spotlight had been aimed directly at him when his mother raised her hand during an information session and asked, "So, what is the suicide rate at your school?"

Remember, don't be surprised by anything your teen says or does during the visit. He or she is probably nervous and doesn't want to be noticed. Many don't even want to walk with you on the tour, wanting to appear as if they arrived on campus alone. If that's what they want, go with it. Let them have as much control over this part of the application process as possible. It's important not to take these perceived slights personally—it's all part of your teen preparing to emotionally (and physically) make that move out of the nest.

What about exchanging comments with your teen during the tour? Your teen's reaction will most likely hinge on the loudness of your voice. Teens hate to be embarrassed. One of our favorite examples of this type of off-putting parental behavior occurred when a young man we know whispered to his father during a tour, "Let's go, I hate this school." His father, visibly enraged, turned to his son, speaking loud enough for all to hear: "We've driven four hours to see this damn school, and you're going to finish the tour!" Another teen, Elena, an immigrant from Russia, recalled her desperate (but failed) attempts to control her family during a tour: "I repeatedly told them to lower their voices because not only were they getting two or three calls on their cell phones and both my mom and grandma were literally screaming into their cells in Russian, but I was totally embarrassed. No one else on the tour had family members speaking in another language, so I was already feeling different from the other kids, and this just called attention to that." The moral of the story: turn off your cell phone and never draw attention to yourself or your teen.

One last piece of advice on this subject: *never* attempt to push your teen to impress the admissions staff. Daisy, a seventeen-year-old high school junior's father, pestered her before a tour with instructions on how she should behave. Once on the tour, he loudly insisted that she take off her sunglasses so she could make "eye contact" with the student tour guide. Her father was so persistent that Daisy became exasperated. This precipitated a heated, audible argument. We don't believe that colleges make note of your or your teen's behavior during the tour, but we do suggest that you never cause a scene. If you must argue, save it for the car ride home.

> **Words to live by on the college tour: Discretion is the better part of valor.**

Searching for Gold: What to "Mine" during the College Visit

Now that you know where, how, and when to visit, you may be asking yourself, "What in the world am I looking for?" The college wants to give you certain information and leave you with a positive impression. They will provide lots of information pertaining to the quality of faculty and students and the wonderful programs and opportunities your teen will encounter. They will show you the fabulous new facilities and the venerable and historic old ones that are on campus. This is the official tour. You should also be on your own unofficial tour, looking for those nuggets of information to determine if this college is a good fit. So let's get out there and mine that campus for gold.

The Student Body

The composition of the student body is crucial to your teen's happiness and success. After all, your teen will be living, eating, sleeping, studying, and partying 24/7 with the other students on campus. This community will be (if all goes well) your teen's home away from home and, in many respects, will also be his or her *in loco familia* for the next four years.

The first "real" student you might meet is the tour guide. Ask yourself, "Is my tour guide the most accurate reflection of the student body?" These guides tend to be happy, satisfied students. They glow when discussing their college and, not surprisingly, are ardent advocates. After all, they weren't chosen randomly. Just bear in mind—and tell your teen if he or she doesn't already know—that the guides are not always objective. That means letting your eyes wander past what the tour guide shows you. Get a sense of the typical student. They will be, after all, everywhere you look. Look at how the students dress and their hairstyles, tattoos, and piercing. Listen for random pieces of conversation and ask yourself, "Will my teen fit in with these kids?"

The College Community

When picking a college, the quality of the community is a vital factor. For most students, this community will be the focal point of their lives over the next four years. Does it seem like a vibrant community? Look at bulletin boards outside the cafeterias, student centers, and dorms. Look at the type of events that are scheduled: are there outside speakers or concerts? If your teen truly wants a diverse college experience, look to see if the speakers represent a broad spectrum across the political landscape or if they fit into one narrow mold. Look at the college newspapers and even read the editorials. Notice if they are critical of the college in any way. While this may seem a bad sign, it could be an indication that the college fosters an atmosphere of freedom of speech and diversity of opinion.

What kind of regular campus activities are available? Look at notices about clubs. Find out the percentage of students who actually participate and whether faculty are also active participants. Are there multicultural or religious activities? If these are important to your teen, you need to review all the printed materials, and don't forget to talk with students and college staff.

The Classroom

What is the *real* class size? Don't be fooled by the guidebook statistics or announced "averages." Ask or see on their website if there are maximum and minimum size requirements for classes and, if so, what these are. On the tour, you can take note of the number of large lecture halls and auditoriums. As a rule, the largest classes will be in the introductory courses, but at some institutions, even some upper-level classes can have seventy-five students. You can ask if the large lecture type of classes are further broken up into smaller discussion groups. As a rule, a full-time faculty member will teach the lectures, while a graduate student often runs the discussion groups. This is the general rule, but many variations on this are possible, so ask.

These questions should also help you segue into another equally important classroom consideration: who is doing the teaching? Educators stress the importance of the relationship between student and faculty. This is a particularly important consideration in today's budget-conscious environment. If you thought part-time or contract employees were limited to corporate America, think again. Today, both large and small institutions rely on part-time or adjunct faculty who rarely maintain a permanent office or physical presence on campus and are less available to students for additional assistance or mentoring. Of course, there are exceptions. Still, it is important to know what kind of faculty teach the majority of courses: how many and which courses are taught by full-time faculty, and how many and which by adjuncts? You may also be interested in the credentials of full-time and adjunct faculty. Be a bit nosy. Check out a few department office doors and look at the posted advisement hours to get a sense of faculty availability. You will not be there in the fall, and it is often a sympathetic or involved faculty member who can mean the difference between success and failure for many teens.

Living Conditions

Living conditions, more commonly known as "dorm life," are an important part of the campus visit. Most tours include one of the best dorms, but what you really want to see are the dorms where the freshmen live. These frequently are the saddest dorms on campus. Seeing the freshman dorms is especially important for today's teens since on average they live in more individual space than previous generations. Many of today's teens have never had to share a television, a bedroom, or even a bathroom, and freshman living conditions can be quite a jolt.

It's important for you and your teen to have a realistic look at these because your teen may be disappointed if he or she envisioned some bright, cheery, roomy environment, only to end up in "the ghetto," as one freshman dorm is called at a well-respected private university. It is well known that physical environment can strongly influence a person's emotional state. If the housing conditions are dreary (at best) or downright overcrowded and substandard (at worst), your teen needs to know this in advance. Forewarned is, after all, forearmed. Below is a list of the basic questions you need to ask about freshman living conditions:

Dorm Evaluation Questionnaire

1. How many kids to a room or to a suite?
2. Are there any singles available, and, if so, how are these allocated?
3. Are nonsmoking rooms available?
4. Are there "study" or quiet dorms? Substance-free dorms?
5. What is the ratio of students to bathrooms? How are these cleaned, and how often? Are these single sex or coed?
6. How large are the dorm rooms, and what kind of desk and storage facilities are available?
7. Are there laundry facilities on-site, what are these like, and is there laundry service available?
8. Are dorms coed? If so, how are they arranged? By floor? Or on a room-to-room basis? Are single-sex dorms available?
9. Are there RAs (residential advisers) in the dorm? How many, and what is their role?
10. Are the dorms clean and well maintained?
11. How are roommates selected, and how easy is it to change roommates or dorms?
12. What do the common areas look like? Are they well maintained?

Don't be shy about asking and seeing. After all, your teen will likely have to live in a dorm at least a year, and you will pay a pretty penny for it.

Other Campus Facilities

Take a close look at whatever facilities your teen shows an interest in. This can include sports fields, fitness centers, science labs, performance art spaces, and so on. Are they well maintained and adequate for the purpose? Are they open to all students?

Safety on Campus

Safety comes first. When we send our teens off to college, we often believe we are sending them to a safe educational cocoon that is somehow sheltered from what has become an increasingly dangerous world. Yet even the highest ivy-covered wall cannot keep the real world out. As parents, we need to be aware of campus reality. It's important not to take safety for granted. Don't expect the college to highlight security problems. Ask, "How does the college handle safety issues?" "What is the on-campus crime rate?" "What is the nature of the crimes?"

Be sure to check out the security measures. For example, are there easily accessible and sufficient numbers of call boxes students can use if they need assistance? Is there a campus security force and what is their role? What is the relationship between campus security and the local police force? Does the campus have shuttle buses available or night escorts for students if requested? Is the campus well lit? Is there a lot of activity and foot traffic? We don't suggest that you grill the tour guide on these issues. Instead, these facts can be gathered discretely from the admissions office (most of it is published and can be sent you) or from the campus' department of public safety.

Don't forget fire safety. Not all buildings are up to code. One student, Morgan, fondly recalled how her father checked all the dorm buildings for sprinklers and fire alarms. For some reason, she found his comments sweet in that "Oh, Dad" kind of way—intrusive but cute. Perhaps he got away with it because he was circumspect in the manner of his inquiry and did it in a lighthearted, not anxiety-filled way.

The Cafeteria: Food and Social Atmosphere

The information you and your teen can gather by visiting and eating at the campus cafeteria is invaluable, often solidifying your teen's overall attitude toward a particular college—and with good reason. It is in this setting that you can check out the real range of the student population, observe student interaction, and even sample the "cuisine." Make sure to leave time to eat lunch or have a snack in the cafeteria. Take your time and look for the following:

1. Male-to-female ratio.
2. Who sits with whom? Do the students mix well, or do you see all the students of one ethnic or racial background or all the athletes sitting together?

3. How do the students dress? Similar to your teen or very different?
4. Do they appear to be having fun? Do you hear a lot of laughing? Do the students seem high energy or, worse, hung over?

The cafeteria is often the ideal place to encourage your teen to go off by him- or herself and talk with or, at minimum, see "real" students. If he or she has the opportunity to actually sit down and talk with students, that's better still. Here are some ideas about what your teen might like to ask a "real" student.

Questions for a Real Student

Social Life

1. How do you spend your free time? What extracurricular activities do you do?
2. What are the most fun or interesting activities you have done on campus?
3. What are the most fun or interesting activities you have done off campus? How hard was it to get there? Did the college provide any transportation?
4. Where are the really fun places to spend time?
5. How do most students get around? Do you need a car? What is parking like?
6. What is the alcohol/drug scene? If I don't want to use drugs or drink alcohol or only moderately, will I feel left out?

Campus Atmosphere

1. Are students free to express their opinions here, or is there a strong political or religious bent to the school?
2. Does the school have strong rules and regulations about students' behaviors? Are underage students fined or punished if they are found drinking? What about freedom of speech—are there speech codes?
3. What is the atmosphere really like? Are the students studying all the time?
4. If this is a single-sex school, do the students complain, or is there a real sense of closeness and camaraderie and solidarity?
5. Do the students feel safe on campus? Do you lock your dorm room?
6. How well do students from different social, economic, or ethnic backgrounds get along?

7. What is the atmosphere like for gay students?
8. What is the sorority/fraternity scene really like? If I wanted to, it is easy to be accepted? If I don't want to join, will I feel excluded?

Dorm Life

1. Is housing guaranteed for all four years?
2. Is there off-campus housing? What is the quality and the cost?
3. Is there a wide range of dorms—single sex, coed, substance free?
4. How is your roommate selected?
5. How many in one room? Are there many singles?
6. Do fraternities and sororities have their own dorms?

Academics

1. How tough are the classes? Is there some grade inflation?
2. How often do you see your adviser? Did you choose him or her, or were they assigned?
3. How easy is it to get to know your professors? Are they approachable?
4. Are the professors mostly interested in teaching undergraduates, or are their interests more in the graduate students or their own research?
5. Is it possible to work on a professor's research project?
6. How difficult is it to get into the classes you want or need for your major?
7. How much help do you get if you have a learning disability? Do the faculty seem put off by having to provide accommodations, or are they welcoming to students with learning disabilities?

The Fraternity/Sorority Scene

Some schools are Greek schools, some are not, and some are somewhere in between. Some teens are looking for this, while others wouldn't touch Greek life for a million dollars. All guidebooks list the percentage of students involved in the Greek life, but you can't get a sense of the importance of the fraternity/sorority scene unless you see for it yourself. Other important facts to inquire about are whether each organization has its own "house" and the nature of these associations. Greek organizations actually span a huge range, from those that are strictly social to others dedicated to community service or particular academic interests. And don't forget to investigate the process of pledging and hazing. Do the college and the fraternities/sororities set responsible limits? Are the rules enforced? What are the penalties for violations of these? This is important because over the past decade there have been numerous, well-publicized horror stories associated with out-of-control hazing practices. Some parents are very opposed to the idea of their college-bound teen joining the Greek life, as was the case with Alex, a commuter student on a campus where most students lived in the dorms:

✸ ALEX'S STORY

"I actually didn't know I was being rushed. The way my fraternity does it is they get to know people without telling you they are in a fraternity—I got to know them and I liked them. I was still commuting, and I wanted to have more ties to the school to have an excuse to come down to campus when I wasn't in class. They gave me a bid, and I decided I really wanted to join. The only thing was that my parents were not excited about it because they associated it with conservative kids, drinking, and kids just acting stupid. But I kind of liked the idea of joining. There are a lot of kinds of fraternities, and the one that gave me a bid does a lot of philanthropy. Also, we are rather diverse—not just white males—all kinds of guys. So when they asked me to join, I said, 'Sure.'

"There really wasn't any hazing. There's a big antihazing policy in my fraternity and in my chapter, and it's made clear it won't be tolerated. Well, when I told my parents, my mom was apathetic and said I should do what I wanted, but my dad was extremely unhappy. 'Why do you want to? What's the point? Do you know what they stand for?' He's basically an old hippie. I tried to explain that times have changed since the sixties and seventies, but he wasn't listening. He just kept repeating the same stuff and finally said he wouldn't pay for it, but of course he did. I joined, and now he's fine with it. Actually, I think he's kind of happy about it now because my parents moved and I'm living on campus. It's sure nice to have a group of people I can depend on now that I'm on my own; if I need something or someone, they can help me out.

"I think I just wanted to try something different. These guys are not my normal liberal group of friends—they give me a different perspective on things—a viewpoint I might not necessarily go and look for—but I think that's good." ☀

Certainly, Greek life is not for everyone. However, if your teen is interested in it and there are no safety objections, put your preconceptions (if you have these) aside. Let your teen get a different perspective and a range of experiences. After all, isn't this what college is all about?

Other Opportunities

If you are really ambitious or have free time while your teen is sitting in on a class, you can wander over to some of the other college offices to find information about internships, travel abroad, work-study, and other service opportunities. You can ask about whether students are able to help professors on research or work on independent projects. Some colleges, for example, have monies set aside to support student summer research programs.

After-the-Tour Tips

You'd be amazed at how quickly you will forget or confuse important details and information about a given campus. So here are two easy and great things you can do. First, as you are driving away, look at the surrounding area. We tell you to do this because odds are that you were lost, late, or distracted on the way to the tour and didn't get a real opportunity to look at the area. Is it a vibrant town? What is going on? Do you like the feel of the town? How close is the college to town? Can your teen walk, or is there public transportation? If the campus is located in a city, note the surrounding neighborhood. Is it residential or commercial? Is it affluent or run-down? What kind of stores, cafés, and so on exist? Will your teen feel (and be) safe? Second, as soon as you get home, file away any notes you and your teen made, along with pictures and tour materials you took or collected in your college file box or drawer.

Problems, Problems, Problems: My Teen Won't Visit

There will be a few of you reading this who, after considering all our suggestions, will put the book down, thinking, "Well this is all great advice, but my teen won't even agree to go see colleges! What should I do?" While this is not common, it does happen. There are teens who take this stance, and while it is a difficult problem to resolve, there are several strategies you can try.

First, try gentle persuasion. Go through all the reasons why it would be best for him or her to visit. If this doesn't work, bring in someone who has influence over your teen. Some teens subscribe to the "anyone-but-you" rule but will listen to a third party. Indeed, most teens have some other adult in their lives they are willing to listen to. Sometimes it is a grandparent, other relative, close family friend, or teacher. Whoever it is, enlist their help. If possible, ask that person to accompany you on the visit or even take your teen. After one good visit, your teen very well may cooperate.

If none of the above works, you need to dig a little further to find the roots of this problem. Ask yourself if your teen is feeling overwhelmed with homework, high-stakes tests, or extracurricular activities. If so, your teen many perceive the college visits as simply one more burden on top of a gigantic pile of obligations. If this is the case, you may need to scale back a bit on nonessentials. Perhaps you are insisting on starting the visits too early, say, in the freshman or sophomore year. Your teen may not be ready to start thinking about college. If this is your teen, back off and let it go for now. Bring up the issue later, before or during the junior year. In fact, many not-always focused (NAF) teens wait until the end of the junior year or beginning of the senior year before they are willing to undertake college visits.

Then there are the teens who avoid college visits simply because they are nervous about the prospect of leaving home or embarrassed to admit they still need parental support. This is what happened to Max. As his mother explained, he was a reluctant "tourist":

☀ A MOM'S TALE

"Max just didn't want to visit any colleges. He said he 'didn't need to.' Finally, I convinced him to tour a nearby college—under two hours away. I figured it was better not to keep him in the car too long. Well, he sulked all the way. When we got there, he wouldn't get out of the car! I begged and pleaded with him that we would miss the tour, but he said he didn't care. I was just about to give up when I said to him, 'Okay, we'll leave, but I just need to use the bathroom and get a cup of coffee. Just help me find the cafeteria because you know I always get lost.' He agreed,

and off we went. When we got to the cafeteria, I left him by himself, while I went off to use the bathroom and get coffee. When I
came back, he was actually talking to a student (a rather cute
girl). He told me his 'new friend' had offered to show him the
campus, so, if I didn't mind, he was going to take a short tour
with her, and off he went. When he came back two hours later, he
was very excited about the college and eager to apply. In fact, that
is where he wound up going. That experience taught me that a
little creativity can go a long way." ☀

Now is a good time to take a second look at the college list and make sure
there are a few schools relatively close to home (no more than a four-hour
drive). Another teen, Jillian, recalled, "My mom wanted me to go out of state,
and my dad wanted me to go to school in Canada because it was cheaper. I
wasn't even sure if I was ready to leave home. So, here I was, with my mom
putting lots of pressure on me to try living in a new place and my dad ready
to ship me out of the country! Finally, I talked to my mom about how I felt
and they stopped pressuring me and let me make my own decision."

If all else fails, see if you can interest your teen in a group tour, touring
with a friend, or even accompanying other friends without you. You can also
agree to simply make an "informal" visit to a college that does not involve
taking the tour, attending information sessions, and so on. Often seeing one
campus in this informal manner helps ease a teen into the whole process. If
you do this, pick a campus that is not too far from home (in this case, no
more than a two-hour drive), don't go on a rainy day, and by all means make
sure that your walk-through includes the cafeteria. You'd be surprised how
some of the most intransigent teens decide it's not such a bad idea to do the
more structured types of college visits after this.

If, after trying all this, your teen still refuses to visit, don't worry yet: he
or she will usually relent and visit after being accepted. If you have made a
realistic college list and completed the applications with care, a few colleges
should accept your teen. Of course, this means that you will be very busy in
April, after the acceptance letters are sent out. You have about one month
to decide which one to accept. Remember, your teen *will* go to college.

Because the success of touring often depends as much on how you and
your teen interact as on your teen's experience and impression of the college, it's time for a few tips directed to your particular parenting/personal
style:

Tips for the Type A Parent

1. Relax and keep perspective. Ignore well-meaning advice to hover excessively around the admissions office or pester admission officers.

2. Keep the number of colleges to tour to a reasonable number. You could drive everyone nuts by visiting over twenty colleges or insisting your teen sit in on a class at every college you visit. You could make this process into an utter misery. But don't. You want your teen to *enjoy* the visits and still have enough time to finish out high school on as strong a note possible.

Tip for the My-Dreams-Are-Your-Dreams Parent

Don't impose your impressions about the college on your teen. Wait to get feedback from him or her. He or she might sincerely like a school you consider a "safety." Don't denigrate enthusiastic reviews about a "safety" school. Don't forget that your teen may either want to or have to enroll there. Keep reminding yourself that you are looking for a good match for your teen, *not* for you or anyone else.

Tip for the Worried Parent

Would it help if we tell you not to worry? Probably not. More realistically, we urge you not to obsess. There are some things you can control and some you cannot. Take a deep breath—some of your worries may be realistic, but many are not. Don't let your worries leak out and ruin the visit for your teen. If you can't contain yourself, express your fears, worries, and hesitations with a trusted friend or spouse. In other words, talk about it with anyone but your teen.

Tips for the Procrastinating Parent

1. Don't create a trap for yourself and teen by delaying the tours. Procrastinating parents typically leave this task for the

last minute. While this is not the ideal approach to touring, neither is it a disaster in the making. Keep in mind that many NAF teens don't take a close look at colleges until they have been accepted.

2. Assign yourself a "nudger." In other words, find someone—a friend, relative, or spouse—who will either take over the scheduling of tours or function as a "nudge" that keeps you on track.

Tip for the Laid-Back Parent

Don't take the process for granted. Take a careful look at your teen, his or her needs, and the college list. Don't assume that your teen can or will succeed at just *any* college. Force yourself to pay close attention during the tours and information sessions. You may even need to do the extra homework of reading the course catalog and other written official and unofficial materials. Since you and the procrastinating parent actually have much in common, read the tips for the procrastinator.

Tip for the Ambivalent Parent

If you are an ambivalent parent, you need to watch your tendency to send mixed messages during this critical moment in your teen's life. Make a touring game plan and stick to it.

Jump over the Teen Challenges

The touring process also brings to the fore many teen specific challenges. Here are some easy-to-consult tips for jumping over these hurdles.

Tip for Teens with Communication Issues

Teens with communication challenges often behave unpredictably, particularly during college visits, because they are either unaware of or not open about their feelings. Some simply don't want to visit but can't bring themselves to express these sentiments. In turn, their ambivalence is expressed in inappropriate ways. Try to communicate honestly, but, if all else fails, keep your cool and your sense of humor.

Tip for Teens with Avoidance/Procrastination Issues

Try to figure out why they are avoiding or procrastinating. Many teens fall prey to the three big myths and feel overwhelmed and inadequate. These teens need reassurance that as long as they make a realistic college list and complete the necessary applications, they will be accepted at a number of colleges where they will succeed.

The Homestretch

We've given you a lot to think about, look for, and accomplish. The thought we want you to take away from this chapter is this: during the college visit, listen for and evaluate the messages sent by students, faculty, and administrators. Are they sending a consistent message about what the college is about—its strengths and weaknesses? Or are you getting mixed signals? Don't be swayed by one negative comment about a particular college. Remember, no college is beloved by every student. Finally, listen to your teen and to your instincts. As a parent, you have probably successfully relied on it over the years, so don't ignore it now.

CHAPTER 8

Packaging for Success
The College Application and the "Extras"

A HOT TOPIC among parents is whether the college admissions deck is stacked against even the most qualified always-focused (AF) teen. Recent books such as Daniel Golden's *The Price of Admission: How America's Ruling Class Buys Its Way into Elite Colleges—and Who Gets Left Outside the Gate* (2006) has reinforced these fears. With this in mind, it is not surprising that parents are asking, "What is the bottom line for admissions?," "Do admissions officers really 'see' my teen?," "Is there such a thing as a level playing field?," or "Does it all come down to slick application packaging and 'connections'?"

The bottom line: the playing field is not always level. We all realize that children of alums, as well as gifted athletes, are given special priority. These are factors beyond your control. School counselor Diane M. Ennis got it exactly right when she said, "The highly competitive schools are all unpredictable." Her colleague Clete Gualtieri added to this our favorite description of why or why not a particular applicant is accepted at an Ivy:

It is not just the Ivy Leagues but a collection of about 50 to 100 schools at the top that are unpredictable, and I like that word, unpredictable, and use that word a lot. Most schools have a set admissions criteria . . . they know what their students look like and look to accept the best students they can in that applicant pool, which changes from year to year. But at the crazy competitive schools it's not a stable thing. I like to think it's like making a stew. They only need so many carrots, potatoes, and so many pieces of celery. But you can only add so many pieces of carrots to your stew. If you want it to be good you have to add other ingredients—meat, stock, salt, pepper, etc. Without these things the stew will be bland. So they also need some athletes, and they also need some kid who plays the oboe, and they also need—and its huge right now—kids from a variety of socioeconomic backgrounds. All together, they hope that these ingredients will create the "perfect stew."

So, while the admissions process may be unpredictable, you can focus on what you can do to help your teen submit the best application possible. This chapter is designed to help you put together his or her college application packet, prepare him or her for the interview, and overcome some of the common application obstacles. Think of the application as a "snapshot." This chapter will help you with its composition and focus. You can ensure your teen will get a real hearing.

The Paper Trail: Putting Together the College Application Packet

Have you started the application process yet? Or are you still contemplating it? Whatever stage you are in, one of the biggest obstacles is getting started. Doing it all and getting it in on time can feel akin to scaling Mount Everest and returning to its base before the storm blows in. Don't get snowed in. There are many, many pieces of paper that must be filled out and sent to each college. Some are for you to mail personally, and some you arrange for others to send. If you are like so many overworked parents and overscheduled teens, just catching a glimpse of one application packet may be enough to make you feel queasy. Don't reach for the antacids yet! We have a simple step-by-step approach to both the paperwork and the packaging that will let you and your teen keep it all together and get it done right. So, before your eyes glaze over, before you drop the application in a remote corner of a desk or table, let's break the process down and make it easy to digest.

Here's what this portion of the chapter will do for you: 1) describe the specific items you need to include in the packet you send to the colleges, 2) describe the specific items that you have to arrange to be sent to the college, and 3) describe how best to complete the individual component parts of the packet.

Let's start by discussing the packet. This includes the application, a personal essay, recommendations, a résumé (optional), and a sample paper (optional). Sometimes you may also have to (or want to) include some extras, such as CDs, videos, and portfolios.

Component 1: The Application

The first thing to do is fill out what is commonly referred to as the "application." In this are the sections asking for basic information. The worst you can say about these sections is that they are tedious, particularly if your teen is applying to more than three colleges. Indeed, as you begin to peruse these, you will notice that the vast majority of college applications request the same basic information. "Why," you will ask yourself, "do I have to fill out the same basic form over and over and over?" The answer: in many cases, you don't! Many colleges and universities accept something called the "common application" (common app). Some even use it exclusively. Colleges that accept the common app can be found at https://app.commonapp.org.

The common app is an application form that you and your teen can fill out once and send to participating institutions. Two options for its use exist: fill it out online or use the paper version. When you complete the common app online, you can direct it to be sent to any college that accepts it. For those who are cyberspace adverse, you fill out the paper copy, photocopy it, and return it along with the **Common App website: https://app .commonapp.org** other college packet items by mail to the colleges you and your teen have selected. The common app asks for your teen's personal and high school information and includes a choice of five personal essay questions and one "topic of your choice." Note that some colleges that accept the common app still require your teen to answer one of their own specific essay questions.

Are there any disadvantages to using the common app? As a rule, no. We have never heard of anyone being rejected because they used the common app where the college has indicated it will be accepted. However, if you are a worrier or a Type A parent, your mind is already contemplating such things as "What will the admissions officer think about my teen if he didn't take the time to complete *their* college's application?" If using the common app will cause you to lose sleep and if you and your teen have the time, patience, and energy to fill out numerous application forms, by all means go for it; otherwise, use the common app whenever possible—your sanity will thank you for it.

Other twists on the application form are the myriad of state university systems. Each one of the fifty states has its own form and particular requirements, and, as a rule, you cannot use the common app for these. So, for example, if your teen is applying to one or more institutions that are part of the State University of New York (SUNY), you need to get the SUNY application form. The good thing is that you fill out one SUNY form for the colleges within the SUNY system. Don't relax yet. Some individual SUNY schools also require additional information. So, when applying to a state school, check (and double-check) their particular requirements.

We find that many teens are fairly flexible about who will complete the application form since it is a routine and fairly boring task. On the other hand, you may have a teen who insists on doing it all. Follow his or her lead. While it's true that there is little you can do to make your teen shine on this portion of the application, you can create a negative impression if it is filled with typos and spelling errors. So here are some tips for putting your teen's best foot forward on the application:

Tips for Completing the Application

1. *Read* the application directions. Common sense, right? Yes it is. However, countless parents and teens skip this step. Admissions officers can be put off by common mistakes such as putting down today's date where a birth date should go or forgetting to include or fully complete the supplemental essays. Be careful to check that you have answered each supplemental essay completely—some have subsections. Remember, each college application may have its own little "twist," so look over each one carefully, even where the common app is accepted.

2. *Don't* allow the application to go out with spelling errors and grammatical mistakes. *Don't* rely solely on spell check. *Check* and check it again yourself. Always proofread it, even if you or your teen are doing it online. Remember, once it's mailed or sent off into cyberspace, there is no way to recall it.

3. *Review* the completed application line by line to make sure all the required information has been supplied. It is tempting when you don't have the information at hand (such as a Social Security number or address) to say to yourself, "Oh, I'll come back to that later," and simply forget all about it.

Component 2: The Personal Essay

Are you ready for it? The personal essay. There has been a lot of discussion (and controversy) about the essay. How important is it really? What about input or editing by parents and teachers? Do teens and their parents routinely "cheat" by hiring a private college adviser to write it?

If there is one component of the college packet that is a flashpoint between parent and teen, this is it. This is the part that is "all teen" and often the hardest for teens to complete. Why? We believe that most people are under the illusion that there is such a thing as the "winning essay." Where do people get the impression that the personal essay is that important? Again, take a stroll down the college application aisle of your local bookstore and notice the numerous books dedicated to revealing the secret formula for writing that winning essay. Here's a good-natured question for all you worried or Type A parents: "How many of these books have you purchased or read already?"

Many educators point out that the anxiety surrounding the personal essay is misplaced. Like much else in the admissions process, the reasons why one teen is accepted and another seemingly equally talented teen is not depends on a host of variables, some tangible (SAT scores or high school grades) and some intangible. The personal essay falls into the latter category. No matter how well written or interesting you perceive your teen's essay is, its weight will depend on the given institution and, equally important, on how it strikes the reader (i.e., admissions officer or admissions committees). This points to a very real and sometimes forgotten element in the admissions process: the human factor. Ultimately, the decision to accept or reject an applicant rests with the very real people who sit on the admissions committee, and, as we all know by now, one size does not fit all. This means that an essay that genuinely resonates or touches one reader may not impress another. This is why, in the end, your teen should always strive to "be him- or herself" on the essay. Some admissions officers admit that while parents and teens place an inordinate emphasis on it, the essay rarely is *the* deciding factor to either admit or reject a qualified applicant. The majority of essays are simply not that amazing or powerful, nor are they expected to be—your teen, after all, has been on this earth only for about seventeen years. And, while it is probably true that small, liberal arts, and selective colleges might weigh the essay more than large, public institutions, in the end it is only *one* of a number of variables. A good general rule for the personal essay is to let your teen's "real voice" shine through. School counselor Laura Bond suggests that the essay is one way for many teens to demonstrate to a college that they are more than the sum of their hard stats (college boards, grade-point average, and so on). Colleges, she notes, "are looking for that total package . . . for a good human being that is going to be part of the campus community." With that said, here are some tips about essay writing.

Tip #1: *Discard* the notion of the winning essay

Many parents and teens believe that they must write a winning essay to guarantee admission. There simply is no such thing. Nor do admissions officers believe that in 500 words or less a teen can transmit the essence of his or her entire being. We can't repeat this enough: *there is no such thing as the winning essay.* The belief in this has caused countless problems and raised stress levels to no end. What must a teen who believes in this myth be thinking and feeling when he or she sits down to write—in 500 words mind you—a make-or-break essay? Now that's pressure.

Whenever there is pressure, look out for a roadblock. The "essay roadblock," as we like to call it, typically manifests itself in inordinate anxiety and procrastination, often resulting in teens developing writer's block or a rebellious refusal to even start the essay. Not surprisingly, the essay is often the last thing completed and the most rushed part of the application packet—just what you don't want.

We want to put this application task into perspective. There is no reason to feel such angst over the essay. Why? It is a huge waste of time and emotion. Here's what the essay *does not* have to do:

- Win a prize
- Be published
- Become a window into your teen's soul
- Be extraordinarily sophisticated

Here's what the essay *should* do:

- Capture your teen's "voice"
- Be relatively interesting and well written
- Offer a glimpse of something important about your teen

Tip #2: Admissions Officers Understand the Limits of the Essay

Admissions staff are flexible and have no preset rules about what is the best type of essay. They understand that there is no one winning essay format or style. Why? Because it is a highly subjective judgment, and what captures one reader's fancy or imagination may leave another cold. They know that the totality of who your teen is now and his or her potential for the future cannot possibly be captured in a 500-word essay. School counselor Clete Gualtieri said it best: "Most schools, especially the midrange types of school, aren't looking for that perfect person; they're looking for students who will succeed, and it's important for students to show evidence that they will succeed. That sometimes means writing their story about how they've overcome obstacles and how they persisted even when life or school were difficult." We think this is good advice. So relax and let your teen's voice shine through.

Tip #3: Encourage Your Teen's Voice to Shine Through

Much of the college packet is comprised of objective measures such as grades and standardized scores. The essay is your teen's opportunity to assert a bit more control over the process and place his or her own distinctive personal stamp onto the process. Emphasize to your teen that each one of us has our own unique personal history and that this is a relatively easy way in which he or she can make him- or herself come alive to the admissions staff. Much of the paperwork consists of listing accomplishments and filling in boxes. The essay is the one application task that is original, free from much of the outside structure and direction that defines the rest of the application. It should be a reflection of something that can impart a real sense of who your teen is and his or her future promise. Parents often make the mistake of stifling their teen's voice because they don't think it sounds sufficiently "refined" or "complicated." One mother we know credited her son Dan's SAT tutor with getting him to really write something that expressed who he was:

☀ A MOM'S TALE

"I think the SAT tutor motivated Dan to do it. He prodded Dan to find something that he really felt strongly about and put it on paper. Dan actually wrote twelve pages. The hard thing was condensing it. He wrote about how he was on his high school basketball team and got kicked off at the end of his freshman year for basically not being tall enough. While it's true, Dan is small, he really is a terrific player, and even other parents told the coach he was wrong, but the guy wouldn't budge. The way this coach acted, you'd think he was coaching in the NBA and they were in the finals every week. The whole thing just devastated Dan. To Dan's credit, he told us, 'I'm gonna make him change his mind.' And I was surprised, but he practiced ball every single day during the summer and throughout the year. And you know, the coach put him back on the team.

"Dan's essay was about this experience. He wrote about this and how he focused and practiced and forced the coach to put him back on the team. It was a really great essay, and it was easy for him to write because it was right from his heart." ☀

Not only was it, as this mother said, "right from his heart," but it also showed admissions that he had the desire and will to succeed, even when faced with a challenge or an obstacle. Many students and parents make the mistake and think that a student has to have suffered a major "trauma" to express this. Not true. Admissions staff know that most kids (thankfully) have not experienced earth-shattering events, and what Dan showed was staying power and a will to succeed.

The essay, unlike the SAT or ACT, is a task that asks them to reflect and present their authentic "voice." Viewed in this way, the essay should be the most enjoyable part of the application.

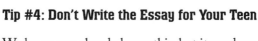

Tip #4: Don't Write the Essay for Your Teen

We know you already know this, but it needs repetition. Many parents, in their anxiety and impatience, succumb to the temptation to write the essay for their teen or, even worse, hire someone to do it. Do not give in to this temptation. When tutors or overly intrusive parents write or heavily edit the essay, it loses the teen's voice. It doesn't sound like the applicant and often doesn't even read like a real teenager. Many college admissions counselors have a "nose" for the parent- or tutor-written essay.

We know that some of you will consider hiring a tutor to "help" your child with their essay. This option is especially tempting for a Type A parent with a procrastinating teen. We believe that it sends the wrong message to your teen—that he or she either can't do it or that his or her work will not be good enough. Worse, it encourages your teen to disregard the value of honesty and integrity in life. Think: do you really want to send this message?

We know from experience that there are some teens so paralyzed by the process that they simply can't get started. As the application deadline looms, your teen may require a bit of active intervention to get it done. Here are some tips to make sure the ultimate product is genuinely your teen's and not yours or that of a tutor.

Tip #5: Appropriate and Effective Assistance

Here are four concrete steps you can take to assist your teen to get the essay done well and in a timely fashion:

1. Choose a topic
2. Have your teen write a draft
3. Give feedback
4. Edit

Step 1: Choose a Topic

Choosing the essay topic can be the most difficult part for many teens. While some teens have too many ideas, others simply draw a blank. Too many teens falsely believe that they need to draw on an extraordinary experience or have endured a terrible trauma. "How," one teen we know lamented, "will anything I write make an impression? Nothing has ever happened to me. I was never shot, no one close to me ever died, and I was never abused. What will the college think of me?" What indeed! Most teens have never experienced extreme events. In reality, most of us have little to offer to one of the numerous bare-it-alls on national TV talk shows. Even though teens are famous for complaining and appearing terribly discontent, most actually like their parents. Yet thousands of happy, well-adjusted, trauma-free teens still write great personal essays.

We all know that choosing the essay topic is hard. It's particularly difficult when sitting alone in a room drumming fingers on a table, staring into space. This is the perfect recipe for writer's block. Resist the temptation to choose the essay topic for your teen. On the other hand, you can help by becoming familiar with common essay topics, including achievements/scholarship, goals for the future, personal growth experiences (e.g., trips abroad, work, a high school class, athletics, or artistic/performing activities), important personal influences (e.g., mother or teacher), important experiences (e.g., deaths, illnesses, religious experiences, or applying to college), social events or interests, family issues, thoughts on political/international events or interests, and what we call the "offbeat" topics, including cartoons/drawings.

One of the best techniques for coming up with ideas is *brainstorming*. Encourage your teen to talk about any exciting or meaningful experiences, their talents, and interests. Include strengths, weaknesses, and unique characteristics. Encourage them to be creative and don't narrow their focus. Many teens draw a blank not because they don't have great ideas but because of all the anxiety attached to this process. If they can't list anything, tell them to take a deep breath, relax, and just "tell me a story." This helps everyone become more creative because, truly, we all have great stories to tell.

Another jumping-off point can be to begin with something he wrote in the past (now aren't you glad you saved your teen's old essays?). Other sources for (essay) topics are journals or diaries or even a blog contribution. Once your teen has come up with a number of ideas, it's time to settle on a topic. The success of the essay does not really hinge on the topic itself but rather on how well the writer paints a picture of who he or she is—personality, talents, spirit, and manner of thinking. The admissions staff wants the "who, what, when, where, and why" of your teen. A common trap is to write too much about the experience or event and leave out its connection to or impact on the writer. So, after your teen chooses a topic, your follow-up question is, "What do you want this topic to convey about you?"

Another common teen pitfall is exaggerating an experience or accomplishment or just outright bragging. Many teens feel they have to go this route to impress the reader, so you need to remind him or her that the admissions staff does not expect him or her to have won the Nobel Prize or cured cancer. Nor do they expect your teen to be Mother Theresa. If your teen is a typical teen, a not-always-focused (NAF) teen, don't hesitate to reflect this in the essay. Demonstrating the ability to see oneself clearly is a strength, not a weakness. Don't forget what school counselor Clete Gualtieri says about this (it bears repeating): "admissions staff are not looking for that perfect person. They're looking for a student that will succeed" and has shown "evidence that they can succeed." So while your teen certainly shouldn't spill his or her guts or confess to something off-putting, demonstrating self-awareness can be a plus.

The tone of an essay can be serious or even humorous. Sometimes teens and parents think that humor in the college essay is out of place. Not so. Humor, joyfulness, and lightheartedness can make for a wonderful essay. On the other hand, as we have said, let your teen's voice shine through. So don't pressure your teen to write in a style that is not naturally his or her own. Some essay subjects are indeed sad or serious, and the essay can and should reflect that.

One teen we know, Meghan, told us about how her father's constant interference almost dissuaded her from writing the essay she wanted:

☀ MEGHAN'S STORY

Meghan's dad was a Type A parent. He hovered. He questioned. He fretted. He outright nagged. Did he have good reason for this? "Well," Meghan conceded, "It was getting close to the deadline, and I have always been a bit of a procrastinator, but honestly he was making me crazier." As the deadline loomed, her dad couldn't contain himself any longer. He was fed up with the advice to "let her do it by herself" and began throwing out topics. He favored her writing about some of her unique performing experiences. "Tell them about how you toured in China with your chorus!" he urged. Finally, even Meghan realized, it was "do or die," and she shut herself up in her room to face her computer alone, determined to write the "damn" essay. Two hours later, she emerged, somewhat uneasy, to show what she had written. It was not the topic her father suggested. She explained to him that she just couldn't write that type of essay. "It feels like bragging; I tried and didn't like it," she said. Instead, she produced this essay, which would fit in the category of "offbeat topics." ☀

Meghan's Essay

"I boarded the C train at the Jay Street station at 6:30 AM on Wednesday, October 8th. I like the early morning commute because, unlike the bustling sardine-can-squeeze later in rush hour, subway cars are half-full at that hour. I had my usual luck in finding a cozy window seat where I burrowed comfortably alongside a pudgy old man and began reading my novel.

I felt very isolated and alone on the subway that day. All the other passengers seemed distant and preoccupied. My old friend on the right was fast asleep; my neighbor to the front was rocking his head to the headphone's blaring pulse. The Brooks Brothers clad broker meticulously examined yesterday's stock charts in the *Wall Street Journal.* The bible lady held onto the chrome pole and read her pocket edition.

I felt like a confused outsider. I wished we were pulling together toward a shared goal, but there was no denying we were a bunch of disconnected strangers. My fellow travelers pretended, in that New York sort of way, that they were alone. Isn't that bizarre? I wondered how we would communicate if we shared a common problem, like a delay or something worse. The unsettling and prevailing attitude in New York sometimes seems to be, "Every man for himself. I'll call you if I need you for something."

Just then, the roaring A train overtook and passed us on the express track. I felt a sudden and undeniable urge to champion the steady, reliable C train and her passengers. Sure, the station-skipping A train indulges the neuroses of those who "must" arrive a few minutes before everyone else, but what do they do with those minutes anyway?

My cool analysis of the situation notwithstanding, I desperately wanted our C train to beat that imperious A train to 59th Street. We were a long shot when we arrived simultaneously at the 14th Street station because two additional local stops awaited us at 23rd and 50th streets. I was disheartened when a couple of my C train comrades scurried across the platform to board the gleaming A train, but I refused to bail. Our supremely confident competitor granted us a head start out of the station.

We were neck and neck all the way to 42nd Street. The atmosphere on the C train was tense. I leaned forward and concentrated on the immense darkness that lay beyond my window. I imagined we were all concentrating, even if I was the only one who showed it. I was sure that all of us had been stepped on by the A train at least once in our lifetimes. C train passengers, on the whole, harbor a great deal of resentment toward the voweled crusader that thunders alongside our peaceful track.

The steadfastness of the C train drive that day was inspiring. Never before had a New York City train forged ahead with such single-minded purpose. I was proud to be a member of the team. I think we all were. But the A train pulled out of 42nd Street first and sped past us at 50th Street. As we left the station, I sadly concluded that the A train was already hurtling toward 125th Street.

Something strange caught my eye on our approach to 59th Street: the A train stopped dead in its tracks between stations. The D train, compatriot of the C and archrival of the A, had blocked this A train's entry into the station. As we triumphantly breezed into the station, I hoped my teammates appreciated the magnitude of our mass transit achievement. I wondered if the knowing glances we exchanged communicated their understanding. And even though we were instructed by our conductor to "Step lively," the gait of my pudgy friend seemed especially spry."

We are not including this as an example of a stellar or winning essay. Instead, it is one of our favorites because it is unique, playful, and clearly written by an adolescent.

Step 2: The Draft

Most essays have a predictable format, with an introduction, a body, and a conclusion. Unless your teen is a particularly creative writer, he or she should probably stick to this accepted format. For the first draft, encourage your teen to write it out fairly quickly, without extensive editing. The most important thing is that your teen have a working draft. Editing comes after the initial thoughts are down on paper. It is also a good idea to encourage your teen to put the draft aside for a few days. Giving it a rest lets your teen go back to it with a fresh perspective or, as we like to call it, with "new eyes."

Step 3: Feedback

Once the initial draft is done, it is time for feedback—provided that your teen is willing. Again, this is not your opportunity to insert yourself into the substance of the essay. Your job is to assist your teen shape the essay into a final product that will effectively reflect *your* teen. Ask yourself, "Is the essay effective in getting across the ideas my teen has in mind?" If not, talk with your teen about these ideas, encouraging him or her to flesh them out. Talking through ideas is one of the most effective ways of developing and expanding ideas. Even after the draft is complete, it is important that your teen read his or her essay again. Many benefit from reading it aloud. Encourage him or her to ask, "What does this essay say about me? Does this essay make my point?"

If your teen is resistant or defensive about doing this with you, encourage him or her to show the draft to a friend, a family member, or a trusted teacher. Don't be defensive or make him or her feel guilty about "excluding" you from the process. Remember, feedback can come from many sources—it doesn't have to come from you.

It is also important to encourage your teen to see writing the essay as a process. While most teens will allow others to take a look after they have written a first draft, many want to write a few drafts before they are ready to have it read by others. Be patient. More drafts are better than no drafts.

One last pointer: the recommended word count is 500. Encourage your teen to stay within or very close to this limit.

Step 4: Edit

The editing process consists of making sure that your teen's essay is as well written and is a genuine reflection of your teen. So here are the basics to look for in a well-written essay. First, look for an evocative opening sentence that both lets the reader want to continue reading and gives the reader an indication where the essay is going. Since it's a short piece, the essay has to grab the reader immediately out of the gate. Second, the best writing is "active" (using active verbs) with relatively short sentences. Third, check to see if the body of the essay stays on point. It should also reflect something important about your teen's personality, character, or point of view. Finally, the conclusion can be brief and sum up the main point. Don't worry if your teen chooses a creative ending that leaves the reader with unanswered questions. This could actually turn into a fruitful source of conversation during the personal interview.

Don't rely on spell check

Once the draft is finalized, it must be *proofread*. This is extremely important. Nothing screams out at the admissions officer "I don't care!" more than sloppy work. Admissions staff can be turned off by spelling and grammatical errors, even if the content of the essay is interesting. So here is where you can be very helpful and more assertive. Even the most resistant-to-input teen will generally give you the opportunity to check his or her spelling, punctuation, and grammar. In fact, we recommend that before the essay is submitted it be given to a few people to read over one last time. It is easy to miss errors when you and your teen have been reading the same essay over and over.

Tips You Can Share with Your Teen

Do:

1. Make it personal—about something important to you—but not too personal; it's not psychotherapy
2. Sound honest and genuine
3. Be positive—even if you are describing a flaw, put a good spin on it
4. Make it exciting
5. Take some risk
6. Keep it focused
7. Use humor—if that comes naturally to you
8. Include examples to illustrate your main point
9. Show, don't tell—use examples that show who you are
10. Proofread for spelling and grammar errors
11. Let others proofread

Don't:

1. Brag—don't work to sell yourself; writing about an endearing flaw can make a great topic
2. Retell what is already in your application packet
3. Rush
4. Try to include too much—like everything you've done or accomplished
5. Write about something you don't feel passionate about
6. Use clichés or be predictable—"I want to help people" or "How bad I felt when I lost the game"
7. Drop names or include your parent's accomplishments—it's totally tacky
8. Don't overreach or try to write about a topic with an authority not reflected in your experience or knowledge is not effective

Component 3: Supplemental Essays

Many colleges, even those who accept the common app, ask for a supplemental essay. These typically ask, "Why do you want to attend our college?" We find that by the time teens get to these supplemental essays, they have often run out of steam and rush through them. You need to do your best to help them slow down so that they can put some effort into their writing.

Encourage your teen not to rush these supplemental essays, particularly when writing for their number one choice. The essay should not be a boilerplate—one essay with just the name of the college changed. Some teens, like Tony, hit a roadblock on the supplemental essay:

✻ A MOM'S STORY

Tony, a NAF teen, didn't want to do the supplemental essay topic, "Describe a typical meal you shared with people you considered to be your family," because, he thought, the topic was ridiculous. He angrily asked, "What do they mean '*considered*' my family? I have a family!" He absolutely refused to write one more supplemental essay. "I don't care," he told his mom, "I'm not answering any more of these stupid questions." At this point, his mother, Elizabeth, realized her son had hit a brick wall and simply could do no more. Indeed, Elizabeth completely sympathized with him. The only reason she wanted him to complete this particular application was because the school counselor had warned her that Tony had applied only to "reach schools." He needed, she realized, a safety school, and this was it. The day before the application deadline, the college admissions officer called, asking, "Where is the other essay we need? The deadline is tomorrow." Elizabeth honestly told the admissions officer that Tony was simply too "burnt out" by the process to write another essay. Instead, she proposed that she e-mail the admissions officer an article he had written for his school newspaper. The college officer grudgingly agreed to take this. While the officer wasn't thrilled with Elizabeth's solution, her strategy must have worked since Tony was accepted at the college. ✻

Component 4: The College Résumé

Your anxiety may be peaking as you question, "What has my teen done that could possibly fill up an entire résumé?" Don't worry; just a bit of creativity is required. The operational word, keep in mind, is "creative," not "fictional." Almost all teens have strengths, abilities, and experiences that can help you put together an adequate if not excellent résumé. Not all colleges or universities require a résumé, but chances are that at least one school will, so plan on doing this. You can even include it in the packets that don't require one. It can't hurt, but don't think that it substitutes for filling out the sections on the college application asking for the same information. It does not.

You have probably noticed that we are talking in terms of *you* creating the résumé and not your teen. With good reason, most teens need significant help organizing or completing the résumé—they just don't have any experience making one. The teen college applicant is, after all, on average, only seventeen years old.

So what makes for a good résumé? First, it needs to be reader friendly. It allows the admissions officer to scan it quickly and identify those experiences that make your teen stand out. The résumé should begin with a heading that includes name, address, telephone number, name and address of high school, and e-mail address. We strongly advise you to influence your teen's choice of e-mail user name. Encourage him or her to get a new account, one with a reasonable name, not "Fluffy 102" or others we won't mention. If they agree, it's best to have one that you can have access to. Colleges often respond by e-mail, and you don't want to be out of the loop.

The résumé should include these sections: Education/Academics, Experience (Paid and Volunteer), and Awards/Honors. Under Education/Academics, you can include special programs (e.g., the International Baccalaureate program). It also includes membership in school clubs, student government, as well as academic honors. It can include school activities that make them stand out or shine. In the Experience section, you can include community service, paid employment, sports, music and theatrical experiences, as well as hobbies. In the Awards/Honors section, put in any recognized athletic, artistic, or writing achievements.

Don't list a section heading without anything under it. For example, many wonderful teens don't have any awards or honors. So just leave this section out.

What can you do if your NAF teen doesn't have a slew of accomplishments? Of course, you can beef it up with special or unique projects they completed in school, but use your common sense. Resist panicking and buffing up the résumé with unimportant fluff or fictional activities. Remember, the admissions staff often looks at the résumé to find topics for the teen interview. Packaging is about presenting your teen in the best light; it's not to deceive, especially since this sends your teen the message that he or she isn't good enough and that is clearly not the message you want to send. Here is a résumé format you might find helpful.

RÉSUMÉ

Jane Doe   Anywhere High School
100 Apple Lane
Anywhere, NY 11111   Year of Graduation: 2007
(212) 111-1111
JaneDoe100@aol.com

SCHOOL ACTIVITIES
"Anywhere News" School Newspaper
    Co-Chief Editor/Writer   2005–2007
    Writer   2003–2005
Honor Society
    Member   2005–2007
    Secretary   2006–2007
Chinese Club
    Member   2004–2007
Anywhere Theater Company
    "You Can't Take It With You"   2004–2005
    Part—Grandfather

ACADEMIC PROGRAMS/COURSES
Anywhere College
    Summer Institute   Summers, 2003–2004

WORK EXPERIENCE
Anywhere Summer Camp
    Counselor with children ages 7–12   Summers, 2005

VOLUNTEER EXPERIENCE
Anywhere Hospital—Pediatric Unit
    Assisting treatment staff with children ages 4–12   Summer, 2006
Anywhere Medical Center—Child Learning Center
    Assisting physical, speech/occupational therapists
    treating children with developmental disorders   Summer, 2005
Anywhere School
    Kindergarten and first-grade classroom volunteer   2003–2004

HONORS/AWARDS
Scholastic Art and Writing Award—
    Honorable Mention Recipient—   2006
    "The Anywhere Article"
Principal's Honor Roll   2004, 2005, and 2006

INTERNATIONAL TRAVEL
Costa Rica
Language immersion program—lived with a   Summer, 2006
    Costa Rican family

Component 5: The Sample Paper

Many colleges request a graded paper from an English or social science class. Make sure that you submit their best effort. It should be a paper with teacher comments on it and should be, though it's not always mandatory, a paper from their junior or senior year.

Don't count on your teen saving graded papers. Teens frequently "misplace" things and may have assumed it sufficient to save a copy on the computer. It's not. It must be a photocopy that the teacher actually wrote comments on and graded. With this in mind, we urge you to collect and file these away in your college drawer or file box, starting in the fall of the junior year.

RÉSUMÉ RULES

No lying, exaggerating, or padding with unessential activities. Emphasize the one or two main activities or abilities that define your teen.

Component 6: Recommendations

Tips

1. Don't send more recommendation letters than the college requests. Admissions officers are swamped with paperwork, and when you send more than requested, the officer may choose not to read all of them and miss the best one. This is a case when more can actually be less.

2. Read the recommendation instructions carefully. Colleges typically want at least one recommendation to be from a high school teacher. Your teen must ask their teachers for these. Many teens, particularly those who aren't outgoing or confident, may find this difficult. Here's how to constructively help your teen.

First, suggest that your teen identify two or three teachers to approach. Ideally, one should be an English or a writing teacher since colleges are usually interested in how well your teen writes. Teens may fall into the trap of choosing the most popular teachers. Often, the most popular teachers are so swamped with requests that they can't spend sufficient time on each one.

Another option is to pick a class in which your teen struggled at the beginning but showed marked improvement by the end. This can be a good choice but must be approached carefully. Some teachers genuinely appreciate an improved student as much as (and sometimes more than) the "perfect" student. If your teen has had this experience, he or she needs to approach that teacher and get a sense of whether he or she will write a genuinely good recommendation. The best strategy then is to encourage your teen to discuss his or her thoughts with you about a few teachers before settling on two.

Next comes the task of asking for the recommendation. Many teens aren't experienced in observing subtle reactions and messages. You may need to explain to your teen how to identify whether the teacher truly wants to write this letter and whether he or she will write a strong letter of recommendation. Certainly, your teen should back away if the teacher says, "I think another teacher knows you better" or "I think another teacher would write you a better recommendation."

Trickier still is how to rule out someone likely to write a lukewarm letter. Don't pick a teacher who doesn't have much of a relationship with your teen. Don't be swayed by someone's reputation or your belief that they have clout. Remember that the person writing this letter is acting as your teen's "advocate" and must be willing to write about your teen with conviction.

You certainly can include recommendation letters from nonschool individuals. The Type A parent may have already collected recommendations from coaches, ministers, community directors, theater or choral directors, and so on. Again, don't send too many. A few great ones are better than many lukewarm ones.

Perhaps you have not even thought of recommendation letters before the spring of the junior year. Sometimes teens are encouraged to start positioning themselves early for recommendations. The advice is to identify teachers they like, take many courses with that teacher, and "stand out." We can't help but cringe when we read this kind of Machiavellian advice. We believe that pushing a teen to think of high school and the teacher–student relationship in this manner is unhealthy both immediately and in the long run. Relationships can't be forced; rather, they grow spontaneously. Rely on your common sense and let your teen develop relationships with his or her teachers in an ordinary and honest way. Most teens will do this naturally, especially if they participate in high school activities.

What if your teen hasn't formed a close relationship with a teacher? This is a common and normal situation for teens, especially those attending large high schools. They will still be able to find teachers who will write recommendation letters for them. If this sounds like your teen, your school counselor can help identify at least one teacher who will get the job done. You certainly should consider getting a recommendation letter from someone outside the high school who knows your teen well. Perhaps ask his or her boss or coworker at a part-time job, a minister, or a respected adult who has known the teen for a long time. Don't panic; think creatively.

☀ ARIELLA'S STORY

Ariella, a high school junior, volunteered in a court psychiatric clinic. It turned out she was the only high school student; all the other volunteers were in college. While Ariella's overall experience was wonderful, she hadn't formed a close relationship with the supervising psychologist and was concerned that he would not write her more than a perfunctory recommendation letter. Her mother suggested that she ask the supervising college student. This turned out to be a great *and* a creative solution. Not only was the request not a burden, but the college student was quite flattered. The end result was a unique and glowing recommendation letter from an unusual source. ☀

Your teen's school counselor will also prepare a letter to send to the colleges. Many teens don't enjoy meeting with their school counselor or find that they don't receive the time they need. Sean, an average student in a prestigious private high school, expressed a great deal of resentment toward his counselor. He told us this story of a painful conversation he had with that counselor: "He said he didn't have any contacts with the schools I had a chance at getting into, that he only had some pull at the top-tier schools, but since my grades were so low, I couldn't apply to any of them. He made a point of telling me that he couldn't help me at all. Like I wasn't worth helping because I wasn't applying to one of the elite schools. He made me feel like crap."

Even if your teen doesn't love his or her counselor, you can help him or her work effectively with one. Give your teen a packet for the school counselor including all the addressed and stamped envelopes for each college, a copy of the résumé, and maybe a brief letter saying thank you for their work and including a short written statement about your teen. Don't be surprised if a counselor lifts part of your letter to include in a recommendation. Remember, counselors have to write a letter for every senior and can do with some creative borrowing themselves. Why not lend a hand?

Recommendation letters are sent out in different ways. Many high schools and teachers have their own policy. Some high schools collect the teacher recommendations and send them out directly to each college. Some teachers ask you to give them an addressed and stamped envelope so they can mail the letters themselves. A teacher may hand your teen his or her recommendation, and it is up to you to copy and send it out. However the recommendations are handled, it is important to make it as easy for the writer as possible. *Do* enclose an addressed and stamped envelope. *Do* give the writer your teen's résumé. *Do* write down for the teacher the class your teen was in, the time frame, and the grade received. *Do* write down the recommendation letter's due date. *Do* ask the writer if any additional information is required to help him or her write a strong letter for your teen. And last but not least, *do* have your teen either verbally or in a written note thank the writer. These letters take time, and most people who agree to do this for your teen, particularly teachers, have numerous requests to fill.

Component 7: Standardized Test Scores

It is up to you to arrange for these test scores to be sent to the college; the high school will not. It also costs some money—though SAT fee-waiver cards through the College Board are available to high school juniors or seniors who cannot afford to pay the fees. If you believe your teen can qualify for a fee-waiver card, speak to your teen's school counselor about how to obtain one. You can also contact the test company either by phone or via the Internet to arrange for this. For SATs and SAT IIs and advanced placement (AP) tests, contact the College Board at www.collegeboard.org.

Component 8: High School Transcript

While some smaller public and private schools take on this task, it is usually up to you to make sure that your teen's transcript is sent to each college. You or your teen need to get the high school transcript request form, fill it out, and return it to the appropriate office in a timely manner. Don't forget to ask if the high school has its own cutoff date for such requests or how long its takes them to send transcripts from the date of request. While your teen's transcript is what it is, we recommend you review it before it is sent out. Better to correct a mistake before it goes out than to try to do this later.

Component 9: The Extras

Many teens have musical, theatrical, artistic, or athletic abilities that colleges value. Including extras—CDs, videotapes, portfolios, and so on—can make the difference between acceptance and rejection. Any teen can highlight such abilities—even those teens not applying for a conservatory, theater program, or sports team.

Remember the swimmer Jason from chapter 5? Here's the letter he sent out to the college swim coaches of all the schools he applied to:

John Smith
Head Swimming Coach
Anywhere University

11/20/04

Dear Coach Smith,
I am currently a senior at Anywhere High School in Someplace, Delaware. I swim for the Aquatic Club at X University and have been swimming competitively for 11 years. Swimming has always provided me with an opportunity to challenge myself physically and mentally while teaching me to manage my time. I enjoy taking part in every aspect of the sport from the training to the competition and am very interested in becoming part of your swimming team.

When I was 14, I qualified for Sectionals in the 100- and 200-yard butterfly. Since then I have swum in 5 sectional meets, the most recent one being at

Z University. There I placed 49th out of 104 in the 200-meter butterfly and 84th out of 170 in the 100-meter butterfly. In 2003, I made the All-American Scholastic team due to both my high GPA and placing in the 2003 short-course sectional meet. In 2001, I competed in the World Maccabiah Games in Israel as a member on Team USA in the junior category. There I was a finalist in the 100-meter butterfly, and our 400-meter medley relay took the silver medal. Overall, I would consider my career in swimming to be very successful up to this point, and I look forward to seeing what I can accomplish in the seasons to come.

As my senior year has progressed, I have undertaken many more responsibilities in addition to swimming. During my junior year, I founded a rock-climbing club at my high school and hold the position of president. This is a big responsibility, as the club has approximately 40 members. I am also a member of our school's chapter of the National Honor Society (NHS) and help the 2005 Class Council with fund-raising activities. I feel that this provides me with the leadership skills necessary to be a part of an outstanding college swimming and diving squad.

My cumulative GPA stands at a 3.84. I scored a 1,360 on the SAT and 31 on the ACT. In the current academic year, I am taking three AP courses (Calculus, Physics, Biology) and doing an independent research in organic chemistry under the guidance of my AP Chemistry teacher from last year. Your university is a prestigious academic institution, and I am currently awaiting the admissions office decision.

As an individual, I make sure to put forth all my effort into everything that I do both academically and physically. As a member of a team, I give everything that I have to help lead the team and make us better as a whole. Just as I know that I can rely on others for support and motivation at points, I know that others can rely on me. If accepted onto your team, I will give my all in order to make myself better for the betterment of the team.

Sincerely,

Jason Jones
Anywhere, Delaware 00000

Pulling It All Together

You thought maybe it was time to rest, but don't rest yet. After you have mailed the packet and arranged for the high school transcript, recommendations, and test scores to be sent, wait a few weeks. Then call the colleges and make sure everything arrived. Often colleges will notify you if something is missing, but there is no reason you can't politely check. Just resist the urge to be a pest.

Up Close and Personal: The Interview

While only a minority of colleges insist on interviews, many, particularly small liberal arts colleges, recommend them. Large public institutions and some Ivies don't interview at all. While some colleges do not place great weight on these interviews, common wisdom has it that it can't hurt, and we concur. The interview can be an opportunity for the admissions staff to really get to know your teen, to get beyond the paperwork, grades, and test scores and see the real person. Furthermore, it also provides another window into the school through which your teen can decide if the college is right for him or her. Interviews are a two-way street. So, when possible, opt for the interview. Here's how Jeffrey's father remembered his son's interview:

✺ A DAD'S TALE

"Jeffrey had an interview scheduled with an alum at the school's alumni club. His (private) college adviser and I told him, 'Whatever you do don't talk about fantasy sports.' He was really into the fantasy football and basketball teams that are on the Internet. Sometimes I thought it was his whole life. He was actually the 'commissioner' of his league, and he just knew everything about it. I also thought it was an unimpressive topic to discuss at an interview. So what does Jeffrey go in and talk about? Fantasy sports. But it turned out okay because he really connected with this guy, and they spent the whole interview discussing fantasy sports." ✺

We don't know if it was the interview that clinched it for him, but Jeffrey was admitted to this school and accepted the offer.

Let's review all the steps that go into preparing for and doing the interview.

When to Interview

You can begin the interviews late in the junior year. As we mentioned in chapter 7, we don't recommend that you schedule the college tour and interview on the same day. However, sometimes it can't be avoided, especially with a procrastinating parent or teen who started the college search in the senior year.

Arrange for the Interview

The first task is to arrange for interviews. This is one of the easiest tasks to do. Simply call the college admissions office. Often the hardest thing about scheduling the interview is to make sure it does not conflict with any important academic obligation or event. If your teen will make the calls, even better; it gives the impression that he or she is mature and capable.

Tip #1: Prepare for the Interview

Many guidebooks and websites emphasize the importance of preparing for the interview by extensively researching the school and conducting mock interviews. We don't know what planet they are living on, but in our experience most teens resist that type of preparation. Type A parents run the risk of overpreparing, causing their teens to look like they are on script during the interview. Just like in *Goldilocks and the Three Bears*, the preparation needs to be "just right."

Your teen should do a bit of homework for the interview. At a minimum, your teen needs to read up on the school—the college brochure is usually sufficient. Admissions officers are not impressed by a teen who knows absolutely nothing about the college or why he or she is applying. Often the NAF teen will refuse to do this prep work. If this happens with your teen, don't worry. Simply bring it with you on your way to the interview. The vast majority of teens will look at it in the car or on the train—or you can *discuss* it with him.

If a common roadblock occurs and your teen absolutely refuses to read anything about the college, you can find out what the college provides that is relevant and point it out to your teen. You can mention things about the college that excites him or her—making him or her, it is hoped, more enthusiastic about the college during the interview.

Tip #2: Ask a Question

Most of the guidebooks specializing on college interview techniques advise teens to ask questions and try to make the interview into a conversation. We agree. It really is a good idea for your teen to ask questions. This sounds simple enough, right? Well, not always. Many teens are reticent when it comes to asking questions of adults. If you don't believe us, pop into a high school English or history class sometime. You'll observe that teacher-initiated questions are often met with stony silence and darting eyes. The vast majority of students ask no questions at all. Yes, there are those few students who eagerly raise their hands, eager to participate. These AF teens, not surprisingly, will probably be the same college applicants who read all the college brochures, are eager to write the essay, and have numerous questions on the tip of their tongues for the interviewer. But, as you now know, most teens, the NAF teens, are simply shy or not that engaged.

So you may be thinking, "I'll simply give my kid a couple of questions she can ask during the interview, right?" It depends. We don't believe that the interviewers want students to prepare and ask questions just to impress them, and believe us, they know a "canned" question when they hear one. So don't encourage them to ask questions that anyone who read the brochure would know, such as "Do you have a core curriculum?" Instead, try to "tease" questions out of your teen by discussing the college materials with him or her. Take a page from Jeffrey's dad's tale earlier in this chapter. Jeffrey instinctively understood that the best interview is heartfelt, not dry as dust because it is forced and artificial. Of course, many NAF teens are extremely nervous during the interview, and this leads us to the next tip for interviewing: practice interview questions.

Tip #3: Practice Interview Questions

While it is impossible to know what questions your teen will be asked, there are several topics typically covered in the interview, and most NAF and even AF teens benefit from talking about these or even (only if willing) doing mock interviews. A boilerplate interview session asks about their high school academic and extracurricular activities, their goals for the future, their interests in outside political or social issues, and their reasons for choosing that college. Here is a list of common questions:

Practice Interview Questions

High School Experience

1. If I visited your school, what might I observe about the students, the teachers, and the community?
2. What was your favorite subject in high school?
3. What might your teachers say about your academic strengths and weaknesses?
4. Tell me about your favorite teacher.
5. Tell me about a great experience or achievement in high school.
6. If you had the power to change something about your high school, what would it be?

Personal/Intellectual Life

1. What do you do for fun? What are your hobbies?
2. Tell me about an extracurricular activity you found meaningful or important.
3. Have you done any volunteer work? Tell me about it.
4. What are your personal strengths and weaknesses?
5. Tell me about a book, article, or movie you enjoyed or found meaningful and why.
6. What newspapers or magazines do you read?
7. How would your friends describe you?
8. How would your teachers describe you?
9. What did you do last summer?

Your Future Goals

1. Why do you want to attend this college?
2. What do you think you could contribute to this college?
3. What are you planning to study or major in and why?
4. Where do you see yourself in five years? Ten?

Catchall

1. Is there anything about you not evident from your application that you want me to know?
2. Tell me about someone you admire and why.
3. Tell me about an experience you found disappointing or difficult, how you handled it, or what you learned from it.
4. Tell me about an experience you found meaningful or important.
5. If you could change one thing about yourself, what would it be?
6. If you did not go to college next year, what might you want to do instead?

The Dear God Help Me, What Do I Say Questions

1. What other colleges are you considering attending?
2. Our college receives many more applications from students than we can accept. Tell me why we should accept you.
3. Does your transcript reflect your abilities and potential? If not, please explain.
4. Have there been situations that have interfered with your ability to perform up to your potential in high school? If yes, please explain.

One last interviewing tip: **Never let on that it is your "safety" school.**

Special Issues That Can Arise during the Interview

Many NAF teens do not have stellar transcripts or résumés. Many have uneven grades and experienced some bumps along the way. Sometimes a teen's grades have suffered or plummeted when facing medical or emotional problems, deaths, or crises in the family or when transferring high schools. Interviewers often ask about a teen's academic record during the interview, and it's best to prepare your teen for this type of question. The worst thing that can happen during an interview is for a teen to be blindsided by a questions such as "I see you had to repeat freshman English. Do you want to tell me what was going on?" If this sounds like something that could happen to your teen during the interview, it is very important you discuss these types of questions or issues ahead of time.

Clothing and Appearance

This is one of the most common areas of conflict between parents and teens. If your teen is particularly wedded to her style of dress and it is not too outlandish, focus instead on neatness and cleanliness and limiting jewelry, perfume, and makeup. If possible, encourage your teen to avoid torn jeans and overly casual clothing. And don't forget that combing hair is a plus.

When should you take a stand? Only if your teen's appearance is truly bizarre or he or she chooses sexually explicit clothing. When should you back off? More often than you might think. Even if your friends offer advice such as "the interview is not a time for outlandish fashion," remember it is your job to get your teen out the door without a huge argument. If your teen has purple hair or a pierced eyebrow, what can you do? Maintain your composure. The good news is that college admissions staff know that most teens don't wear suits or skirts with saddle shoes. Trust us, they've seen it all.

That said, there are some things that are not acceptable, and if your teen is too extreme, it could prejudice his or her chances of being accepted. First, try to reason with him or her. Explain that you don't want him or her judged by her clothing. That it is a distraction. For a particularly recalcitrant teen, this probably won't do the trick. Another tactic is to suggest a compromise. Propose an outfit that can incorporate your teen's style but that stays within more traditional boundaries. And, if that fails, ask him or her to show the outfit to friends or an adult whom he or she respects, and keep your fingers crossed. Hopefully, that person will have a positive influence.

☀ A MOM'S TALE

One parent, Jane, related how she and her daughter Laura had shopped specially for the interview outfit—a tailored skirt and button-down blouse—yet the morning they were to leave, her daughter came downstairs in a totally different, very casual outfit. The only reminder of their shopping trip was the shoes—which, in her opinion, were now too fancy for the outfit. As Jane became increasingly tense and angry, her daughter explained that she had changed her mind, that the outfit they bought seemed too fancy and was really not her style. Luckily Jane was able to collect herself and kept her eye on the ball—the only real goal was to get her daughter into the car and to avoid an argument. She realized that Laura was already nervous about the interview and that, if they argued, her anxiety would escalate and could lead to a disastrous interview. Jane was smart and let the clothing issue go in pursuit of helping her daughter perform at her best. ✺

Tip #4: Get to the Interview on Time

The same rules that apply to the college visit apply to the interview: get good directions and arrive early. We recommend at least half an hour early. This gives you time to get lost and gives your teen a chance to go to the bathroom, get something to eat or drink, and generally just settle down.

This is also the time for you to take a back seat. Step back and let your teen approach the admissions desk to let them know he or she is there. This gives the impression that your teen is mature and not too dependent on his or her parents. It also helps build confidence before the interview. Now it is not necessary for you to hide or pretend you aren't there, but it is best to take a seat in the waiting room where you can chat with the other nervous parents.

Whatever happens—and things do happen—don't make a scene in the admissions office. It will serve no positive purpose and can only make a bad situation worse. Here's what our friend Kate remembered about one of their many campus visits:

✺ A MOM'S TALE

Lisa was on her tenth tour and sixth interview and was emotionally exhausted—just plain sick of it all! When mother and daughter arrived at the college's admissions office, they were told Lisa was scheduled for an 11:00 A.M. tour and a noon interview. She immediately became disgruntled and told her mother (in no uncertain terms) that she did not want to go on the tour and that she wanted to be interviewed earlier so she could get home to finish an important school project.

Mom's anxiety was at its zenith, and to make matters even worse, she noticed that the other parents in the waiting room were listening; some had that "I've been there" look on their faces. Luckily, since this was Lisa's sixth and not first interview, Mom had sufficient experience and perspective not to argue with Lisa right then and there in the admissions office. Instead, she agreed to ask the secretary if it was possible to set up an earlier appointment. When the admissions staff could not change the time and the 11:00 A.M. tour was about to get underway, Lisa, ready to explode, told her mom, "I need to go outside and cool down!" With warmth and humor, her mom gently responded, "Do you think you'll be coming back?" Lisa laughed, regained her composure, and agreed to join the tour. ☀

Tips You Can Give Your Teen for the Interview

- Relax, relax, relax.
- It's only a conversation. It should be enjoyable.
- Shake hands hello and introduce yourself.
- Don't chew gum.
- Think before you speak.
- Don't just answer yes or no. Expand on your answer but know when to stop.
- Be yourself; don't lie or exaggerate. Never brag. Remember, if the interviewer gets to know you, he or she will like you.
- If it feels right, explain problems in your transcript.
- Don't memorize any answers.
- Don't curse.
- Make eye contact, yet don't stare into their eyes.
- Smile! It's also okay to laugh at the interviewer's jokes.
- Try not to fidget, bite nails, or tap on the chair.
- Breathe—slowly.
- At the end, shake hands good-bye, say thank you, and ask for the interviewer's card.
- Relax, relax, relax.

Extras

Now we've come to the "extras." What are these? These are your teen's particular attributes (beyond those measurable stats) that might bring him or her to an admissions officer's attention as a "sought-after student." We've mentioned a few of these already, such as a particular talent or ability (e.g., a quarterback for the football team or a violinist for the orchestra). Thankfully, these are not the only attributes that might make your teen particularly attractive to a school. Schools are always looking to construct a living and learning environment that is reflective of the mosaic that is America. And this, in fact, is good news for most of you. Colleges strive to create a student body drawn from a range of geographic areas as well as from diverse socioeconomic, ethnic, religious, political, and racial backgrounds. And, as previously mentioned, they also look to achieve this through the inclusion of students with varied life experiences, talents, interests, and special skills. In other words, what schools are really looking for is a diverse campus that will more closely mirror American society. To that end, they recruit from a wide range of groups underrepresented at *their* institution. The implication of this? Your teen may be a sought-after applicant at one college but not at another. This means, for instance, that for a college located in New York City, a teen from a rural area or from America's heartland may be given some advantage in admissions.

But don't worry if your teen doesn't want to wander too far from the nest. For some schools, near is also dear. Numerous schools eagerly recruit and give "extra points" for being "local." Tufts, Harvard, Duke University, and Williams College all seek to place local kids on their campuses. Why? Community relations play a big role in this. Don't forget that those ivy-covered walls are only so tall and that the surrounding community is a "selling" factor for many colleges. Therefore, most schools strive to maintain a "good neighbor" policy.

In other instances, an applicant's gender might make him or her a sought-after student. This is the case, for example, when a young woman applies to an engineering or computer technology program or a young man applies to a once traditional women's college where female students still predominate. We refer to this as "gender diversity." "Extracurricular diversity" can also give a boost to student athletes, musicians, and artists or any student with unusual or atypical extracurricular activities. Remember the teen who studied opera? Extracurricular *and* geographic factors aided her quest for admissions to a liberal arts college that was outside her geographic area.

Colleges also consider socioeconomic background when choosing their freshman class. This "socioeconomic diversity" can include first-generation college students as well as those from lower-income families—regardless of race or ethnicity. Amherst, for example, tries to bring more socioeconomic diversity to its student body both by reducing the need for loans by these students and by offering what it refers to as "opportunity weekends." The college pays for up to 200 students of limited economics to visit the campus.

Tip #5: Don't Be Immediately Discouraged by Hefty Tuition Fees

Many colleges will offer very generous financial aid packages in order to recruit underrepresented students, or students of interest. It seems as if so many factors have to be looked at to make this determination. It isn't always as obvious as you might think. How else can you know if your teen qualifies? Again, while as a general rule admissions officers view African American, American Indian, and Hispanic applicants as students of interest, there are instances where this rule does not hold. Never assume. Not all institutions consider ethnic background during the admissions process. The University of California system, for example, does not take race or ethnicity into account when choosing its incoming class. At historically black universities such as Howard, it would be a non–African American applicant who would be viewed by the admissions officer as a student of interest. Non–African American enrollment at these institutions has been, in fact, steadily increasing. The bottom line: keep an open mind. There are countless "hidden" opportunities for your teen.

The Homestretch

If you take nothing else away from this chapter, we hope you keep in mind three important lessons. First, you now *genuinely* believe that "packaging for success" is most effective when the college list fits your teen and his or her needs, not the other way around. Second, you can be very *creative* during the packaging leg of the college marathon and don't need to spend a fortune on a private college counselor to accomplish this. Finally, there are *countless* opportunities out there for your teen, and with a little initiative and creativity, you can discover these.

CHAPTER 9

Personal Considerations
Issues We All Think about but Don't Discuss

ONCE YOU START running the college admissions marathon, a host of factors come into play, such as family composition, race, ethnicity, sexual orientation, socioeconomic circumstances, religious and political beliefs, learning, emotional and physical disabilities, and finances. These individual concerns and issues, while extremely varied, are rarely discussed in college guides and can be extra challenges during the application race. It's time to forge ahead and discuss some of these "delicate" issues.

Divorced and Separated Families

We live in a society where a large number of teens grow up in divorced or separated families. Many teens are raised by divorced or separated parents. More and more, this has resulted in "blended" family. While most of these families work well together, many struggle with unresolved family problems. Below we will discuss some of the most common challenges that pop up during the application process.

Financial Task Challenges

Financing a four-year college education can be daunting, particularly if your teen plans to attend a private college or university. Divorced and separated parents frequently face challenges in terms of who pays, how much, and who will take charge of the college application tasks. One private college admission counselor described her experience with divorced couples this way:

☀ A COUNSELOR'S TALE

"Divorced parents often send conflicting messages. One calls saying 'A,' the other calls saying 'B' (mostly about who's going to pay the bill). In fact, anything to do with finances seems open to dispute, everything from who's going to pay my bill to who will write the check for the application fees. These divorced parents even disagree about whether finances are an issue. One says, 'Yes,' the other says, 'No.' And you can't imagine what goes on when the issue of tuition is raised! It can be truly unbelievable. Of course, it is the kid who is stuck in the middle, and all this wrangling makes my job even harder since it often takes months to negotiate between the exes just what range of schools their teen can even consider." ☀

Certainly, there are many divorced parents that have no difficulty coming to an equitable arrangement. Yet even among the most amicable of exes, misunderstandings frequently arise. Moreover, it is not uncommon for unresolved divorce issues to come to a head during the child's college search, with the unintended effect of heaping added stress onto the teen during the nerve-wracking process of college applications.

Here are some tips to prevent roadblocks. Together (and by that we mean you *and* your ex) must decide realistically what you can or cannot afford and who is responsible for which college-related expenses. We suggest drawing up an itemized, estimated bill, including tuition, books, supplies, room and board, travel, and spending money. Unless there is some genuine objection, write it down. You don't want—and trust us it happens—any memory lapses later. It's a nightmare when one parent claims, "I never agreed to pay for that!"

Who needs to be included in these frank financial discussions? We recommend including *all* the financially responsible adults (and remember in some families this can include stepparents, grandparents, and others). It is best to work out the financial issues early in the process, even before making the college list and definitely before an offer is accepted. After the family has come to some decision about the financial constraints, if any, let the teen know. There simply are no easy solutions for family conflict over money, nor does one solution fit all families. However, the one rule that does hold true for all families is the need for a frank discussion about what is always a touchy issue.

Sometimes, those involved in the financing just can't or won't work together during the application process. If you face such a roadblock, don't panic; all the application tasks will get done, even if the process is more complicated and you have to run an extra lap. Sometimes, it means accepting that your ex won't pay his or her fair share. Sometimes, it means ruling out private colleges. Here is how Adam and his mom faced the challenge of the "recalcitrant" parent:

※ ONE FAMILY'S STORY

Adam's parents were divorced, and his father simply refused to complete the necessary financial documents the college required. This impasse spilled over into a whole host of unresolved issues between Adam's parents, and, not surprisingly, they barely spoke to each other. Needless to say, compromise seemed out of the question, and for a while it seemed as if Adam would not be able to qualify for any financial aid. The solution: Adam's mother put her embarrassment aside, contacted the colleges, and explained the family situation to the admissions office. She provided the necessary documentation, and Adam was accepted at one of his top choices *and* received the financial aid package he needed. ※

Application Challenges

Roadblocks occur when application tasks aren't getting done. Parents in conflict frequently disagree about numerous application tasks, including the following: Where should the teen apply? Who will help the teen make out the college list? Who is going to keep track of the application tasks, such as filling out the college application and scheduling the tours? Who will accompany the teen on the college visit? Who will oversee signing the teen up for standardized tests and prep classes? Who will be the point person to talk with high school and college personnel when necessary?

If this sounds like your family, we recommend that you take your cue from your teen. Most teens have already "assigned" each parent a specific role. You have probably noticed there are things your teen talks to you about and things your teen prefers to discuss with the other parent. Your daughter may turn to you with their personal problems but to your ex to assist with hands-on tasks. If your teen expresses such preferences, don't resist it or be offended. It will make the whole process much easier if you accept this "natural" division of labor. At all costs, avoid making your teen feel as if he or she is choosing sides or picking the favorite parent.

There is a tendency for both parents to come together for the college visit. This can be great, unless there is a high level of tension in your relationship. Discuss this ahead of time. If there is a good chance that you and your ex will be arguing in the car on the way to the college tour or interview, don't go together. You can always divide up the college visits. But if you can do it amicably, then go for it. Your teen will thank you for it (if not now, then at some point in the future).

Disagreements while drawing up the college list are common. Certainly, all parents, married or not, can have divergent dreams for their teen. However, for many divorced couples, there is an extra layer of tension that comes from strong residual feelings about the divorce. This can spill over into the college search process and become a new battleground in which the only casualty will be the teen.

❉ ANDREA'S STORY

Andrea's parents divorced when she was in elementary school, and while they had agreed to joint custody, her parents' postmarriage relationship was not without its problems. Despite this, both were actively involved in her upbringing, and, not surprisingly, when it came time for Andrea to apply to college, both parents had a lot to say about it. Andrea had played competitive tennis since she was young, and her dad wanted her to consider only colleges with excellent tennis programs. He had been the parent who had attended all her matches, so it was not surprising that he would focus on that particular ability. On the other hand, Andrea had a learning disability, and her mother was the parent primarily involved in her academics. Her mom focused on colleges with strong programs for the learning disabled. Both parents dug in their heels and refused to discuss drawing up the best college list with institutions that could fulfill both criteria: academic support and sports. Of course, what Andrea truly wanted seemed to be missing in this tug-of-war equation. In the end, Andrea felt so torn between her parents that she decided to stay home and attend her local community college until she could figure out what she wanted. ☀

A strategy that might have been effective for this family was to use a mediator to broker a compromise. Such a strategy would have saved Andrea from being placed in this untenable position. This family might have also benefited from the services of a private college consultant who made sure that Andrea's wishes were heard.

We hope that this discussion has helped you to see that teens from divorced and separated families do not have to experience more stress and roadblocks during this time. In fact, the two main stressor issues—financial and division-of-labor challenges—are factors for most families.

First-Generation College Students

If you did not attend college directly out of high school, you are probably much less familiar with the application process. "A lot of a student's confidence entering this process depends on the family," commented school counselor Denise Becher. "Kids of parents who have never gone to college and don't know the educational process are probably going to need a little extra support." Here are some comments our college students made about being a first-generation college student:

- "Neither of my parents went to college, so they were very proud and excited that I was going to college. They tried to be as helpful and supportive as possible throughout the entire process, but I remember feeling almost as if they were useless because they could not provide answers to the many questions I had."
- "Both of my parents are foreign and never attended college. They were generally absent from the entire process."
- "My parents never went to college. My father didn't care about it too much, but for my mother it was very important that I go. She was the one who was usually helping me. In the end, I did not go far from home. We really couldn't get everything together—there was so much paperwork, and I needed money. We just didn't know where to start or

where I should apply. In the end, I went to my local community college, but I would have liked to go away."

We find that children of parents who did not experience the "straight from high school to college" route often feel a bit "out to sea" and need a little more handholding and overall direction to navigate the system. With this in mind, it is particularly important for you to find other parents who have successfully completed the college admissions process and spend extra time reviewing the college guides and materials. You and your teen should also make the time to meet *regularly* with the school counselor. For your family, it's particularly important to start early in the high school years. Your school counselor can help your teen register for the right high school classes, the SATs, and SAT IIs and keep you on track with the deadlines. *Don't* miss the college fairs and open houses. These are great opportunities for you to get not only an idea about the range of colleges but also a chance to connect with other parents who are excellent sources of information and support.

Race, Ethnicity, Sexual Orientation, Religion, and Politics

Many parents and students have particular concerns about the college fit because of their teen's race, ethnicity, sexual orientation, and religious or political beliefs.

African American Teens

The first point during the application process when the issue of race can arise is when drawing up the college list. While African Americans represent approximately 12 percent of the general population, they make up a much smaller percentage of the student body on many college and university campuses. A full 24 percent of all African American college students attend a historically black college or university (HBCU). Unless your teen attends an HBCU, he or she may likely be one of the few students of color, particularly at a small liberal arts college.

Finding the right fit college can be a complex process for any teen, and for a teen of color there are additional issues—something rarely discussed in most guidebooks. If your teen, for instance, is attending a high school where the predominant student body is comprised of racial or ethnic minorities, ask yourself, "How has that experience been so far?" Don't assume that he or she is unhappy and ready for a change. For many teens of color, particularly those of modest means, the thought of attending a small liberal arts college comprised mainly of white middle-class and upper-middle-class kids makes them uncomfortable. Others, on the other hand, are okay with this. As with any teen, it is crucial that you openly discuss this issue with your teen and explore whether he or she is ready and eager for this change. As with any teen, some are ready for a change, and some are less willing or ready to step outside their "comfort zone." Remember, there is no right or wrong in this, only what is best for *your* teen.

On the other hand, your teen may be attending a high school in which he or she is already one of the few minorities. Again, ask yourself and your teen what kind of environment he or she is looking for in a college. For some teens, race is not a predominant consideration in drawing up the college list, while other teens of color may express a clear preference and wish to attend one of the historically black colleges, such as Spelman or More-house. These schools can be especially appealing in providing a secure base and positive role models. Every teen needs something different and has his or her own vision of the "ideal" college environment. It is your job to help him or her find that best fit. Our friend Elaine explains why her family picked a historically black college for their daughter Brittany:

☀ A MOM'S TALE

"I was raised in Alabama and attended a historically black junior college. It was a great experience for me, and I felt strongly that Brittany would also thrive at a historically black college. We raised Brittany in New York City, and she attended a competitive public high school in which she had been one of the few African American students. It was a good experience, but, at this point, I wanted her in a setting with her own peers, students with positive attitudes about African Americans. Most of the people I knew growing up went to historically black colleges, and, from what I saw, they were more successful than those who didn't attend these types of schools. The other thing that is important for us is that we know that a historically black college will provide the social network and camaraderie she needs to succeed.

"While I don't say this is the right choice for everyone, I thought it was for Brittany. I encouraged her to apply to Spelman—it was a dream of mine—and I told her that her chances for success, for going to medical school, were better at that type of school. I told her that there would be people there to advise her. I wanted her to understand that this type of support would be better at a historically black college. Now, she is doing research on ovarian cancer at Morehouse Medical School with her biology professor who is also an obstetrician. She is getting the type of support we had hoped for, so I think we made the right choice." ❈

Brittany's mom may be correct in identifying this route as bolstering her daughter's chances for success. You may be interested in knowing that in 2004, the American Medical Association cited one single HBCU, Xavier University of Louisiana, as sending more African Americans on to medical school who succeed in passing the medical board exams than any other institution of higher learning in the nation. However, no matter whether you are considering a historically black college or not, don't neglect the campus visits; HBCU or not, every college has its own atmosphere and social culture. Look at the cafeteria. Are the students self-segregated, or do you see students of different ethnic backgrounds hanging out together? Check out the clubs and other extracurricular activities. Does it appear to be a diverse campus—not just in terms of black and white, but are there many types of students present? What is your teen's reaction to what he or she sees? Do you think your teen will feel comfortable? Remember too that race is just one factor for your teen to consider. Like any other applicant, he or she is looking for that good fit that will meet his or her academic, social, and aspirational needs. The racial composition of the student body is one factor, but may or may not be his or her primary concern.

It is also helpful to consult specialized books and resources, including *Black Excel: The College Help Network* (www.blackexcel.org), *The 100 Best Colleges for African-American Students* by Erlene B. Wilson, *African American Student's College Guide: Your One-Stop Resource for Choosing the Right College, Getting in, and Paying the Bill* by Isaac Black, *A Black Student's Guide to Scholarships* (5th ed.) by Barry Beckham, and *Eight Steps to Help Black Families Pay for College* by Thomas LaVeist.

One last piece of advice: as with any teen, what is right for one African American teen may not be right for another. Don't feel pressured into following what others are doing. Your teen is a unique individual, and, as we keep saying, "one size does not fit all."

Multiracial Teens

The United States has undergone a major shift over the past forty years, becoming much more racially and ethnically diverse. Many young people today reject the traditional black–white dichotomy of the past and insist on acknowledging and celebrating everything they are. Perhaps the best-known multiracial figure in today's society is Tiger Woods, who, at the beginning of his career, took a lot of heat for insisting that the press acknowledge his Thai along with his African American heritage. This trend toward acknowledging mixed heritage has become so common that the U.S. Census Bureau added it as a category on the 2000 census. That census found that more than 7 million people have a parent of more than one race, while more than 2 million others identified themselves as being of mixed racial heritage. With this in mind, it is not surprising that there are growing numbers of entering college freshmen of a mixed racial heritage. These teens too have some special concerns. Some teens with this background may feel more comfortable or identify principally with one or another aspect of their heritage. Others may identify with both, refusing to "choose a side." In either case, you and your teen also need to speak frankly about this and make sure you identify schools where your teen can feel comfortable. As with all other teens, the recommendation remains the same: visit, visit, and visit some more.

Ethnic, Religious, and Political Views

Jewish, Muslim, Asian, and Native American teens may also have concerns about finding the right college fit, as does any teen with strong religious sentiments or political views. Many want to be surrounded primarily by similar peers, while others want more diversity. Again, there is no *single formula* for all teens.

Many religious teens choose to attend a religiously affiliated college. Other teens are interested in attending a nonaffiliated college with a diverse student body. Religious and conservative teens often have concerns about attending liberal arts colleges that have been described as bastions of the Left and nonreligious. These teen applicants are understandably concerned about whether their beliefs will be viewed with tolerance or whether they will be ridiculed, stigmatized, or in some manner penalized for their opinions and religious or political beliefs.

As always, we strongly recommend a campus visit, talking with students, and meeting with the college chaplain. In the case of a teen with a strong political conviction, you can also look closely at the publications of faculty members or discuss your concerns with admissions counselors or even with a dean of students. You may also find these books helpful: *Choose a Christian College: A Guide to Academically Challenging Colleges Committed to a Christ-Centered Campus Life* by Christian College Coalition Staff or *College Bound: What Christian Parents Need to Know about Helping Their Kids Choose a College* by Thomas A. Shaw.

Teens who are members of ethnic and/or religious minorities face similar challenges. With a few exceptions, these teens do not have the option of attending a college where they will be the "majority." However, there are certain campuses where they will make up a larger proportion of the campus body than on others. Again, it is important for your teen to visit the campus and get its feel. Ask yourself, "Will my teen feel comfortable?" "Is this a welcoming environment for my teen?" "Are there support systems in place where he can find his comfort zone?" Since each teen is a unique individual, what might suit one teen might not suit a similarly situated teen. So, as always, focus on what is best for *your* teen, not anyone else's.

Home-Schooled Teens

Another underrepresented group not usually discussed in the college guides are home-schooled teens. These teens come from diverse backgrounds, and some of their application tasks are different from teens from traditional high school settings. Make sure you familiarize yourself with how each college your teen applies to handles home-schooled teens' application requirements. On the whole, however, the main application tasks are the same—drawing up the college list, touring, interviewing, and packaging for success. Helpful resources include *Home Schooling High School: Planning Ahead for College Admissions* by Jeanne Gowen Dennis and Michael Farris and *Homeschooler's College Admissions Handbook: Preparing 12- to 18-Year-Olds for Success in the College of Their Choice* by Cafi Cohen.

Sexual Orientation

Up to 50 percent of gay, bisexual, or transgendered teens "come out of the closet" during high school. Others are still grappling with issues relating to sexual orientation during the college application process. Some are unclear about their sexual orientation; others are clear but worried or inhibited about discussing it honestly with their parents. As if applying to college weren't stressful enough, add this to the mix. Of course, it would be easy for us to encourage you to have that open and direct talk with the teen, but we know it isn't that easy. We do know that parents need to first honestly face how they feel about their teen's sexual orientation. If they are more accepting or at least try to be, it can be easier for them to discuss how this issue impacts drawing up their college list.

When drawing up the college list, it is important to take your cues from your teen. Gay or bisexual teens are usually aware that some colleges are more welcoming than others. You can read the college literature and website for information on organizations for gay, bisexual, and transgendered students.

Many teens with sexual orientation issues have strong ideas about the types of schools they are and are not willing to consider. Your daughter, for example, may want to consider only women's colleges, or your son may refuse to consider colleges with strong Greek scenes. Don't try to push colleges that might be patently unwelcoming. A helpful resource is *Gay, Lesbian and Bisexual Student's Guide to Colleges, Universities and Graduate Schools* by Jan-Mitchell Sherrill and Craig Hardesty.

Disabilities

If you have a teen with a learning or physical disability or an emotional problem, you need to investigate how much support each college provides. While the Disabilities Rights law requires that each college provide accommodations, the extent and quality differ greatly in degree. Let's discuss learning disabilities first. Almost all provide basic accommodations, including extended time for completing tests. Many colleges are welcoming of students with learning disabilities and eagerly provide a host of accommodations and support, learning specialists, counseling on studying skills, and the most up-to-date computer software. Landmark College in Vermont, for example, is a two-year college that specializes in educating students with learning disabilities.

Jackie Bonamo, ED, assistant director of the Program for Academic Access at Marymount Manhattan College, gives this advice to parents of teens with learning disabilities: "Parents must educate themselves about all the things needed—the documentation guidelines. They need to make sure they get the best psycho-education evaluation. So often the quality, completeness, and accuracy of an evaluation by public schools are extremely variable. It's best to have a clinic or private practitioner do a full evaluation. You can find one through the Orton Dyslexia Society or any local organization that deals with learning disabilities. You need to make sure the evaluation is typed and legible and includes a diagnosis and the learning disability's impact on learning and recommendations for accommodations and learning. Not just a list of scores. And make sure the report includes an indication of an attention problem. The evaluator must at least screen for attention-deficit disorder since at least 50 percent of learning-disabled students have attention issues. Parents also need to understand that there is a range in academic challenge in colleges with learning-disabled programs. Also, some colleges will not give a language or math waiver, even if the teen has documented learning disability in that area. Don't assume any one college will give a waiver. Read about the program. Arrange for a visit to talk to people in the program and visit while the school is in session." In terms of confidentiality, Dr. Bonamo believes that learning disabilities need to be openly discussed with college staff. She stated, "In terms of the interview, once you have declared a learning disability, no secrets are involved."

In terms of physical disabilities, again, most colleges *advertise* that they are accessible, but if your teen uses a wheelchair or other assistive devices, you already know that seeing is believing. You need to carefully tour prospective colleges, noting the availability of ramps, elevators, and accessible bathrooms. Note how hilly the campus is as well as weather considerations. You may want to cross off your list any college where heavy snowfall is common.

Teens have other medical and psychological issues that factor into the college fit. A pediatric gastrointestinal doctor recounted numerous stories of the calls she has made and letters she has written to document her patients' medical needs to secure private dorm rooms and bathrooms.

If your teen is struggling with eating disorders, anxiety, or depression, you need to investigate what psychological and nutritional services are provided at each college. Jenna, an eighteen-year-old freshman, was struggling with an eating disorder and anxiety throughout her senior year of high school. After graduation, her mother became apprehensive as the time for her daughter to leave to college approached. She followed our advice and had already arranged for Jenna to be seen regularly by a counselor and nutritionist at the college. She also had already found a psychologist walking distance from the college for her daughter to meet with weekly. She was able to send Jenna off, knowing that supports were already in place.

Tips for Teens with Disabilities

If your teen has emotional problems or other disabilities, have the needed support services in place before he or she arrives at college.

If your teen has a disability or needs services or other accommodations, you need to do extra homework and arrange to meet with the director of these services before arriving on campus. By asking the right questions, you may either cross a college off your list or walk away with the feeling that the college may be the right fit for your teen.

We also urge you *not* to discuss or raise these issues during the tour or information session. In fact, the best way to guarantee that your teen will never attend a college tour again (at least not with you) is to raise your hand between the science building and the college's newly minted athletics facility and start asking questions about accommodations for learning-disabled students. But don't stop with the information we provide. Check out the many guides dedicated to this topic, such as Princeton Review's *The K & W Guide to Colleges for Students with Learning Disabilities or Attention Deficit Disorders*; Peterson's *Colleges for Students with Learning Disabilities or ADD*; *ADD and the College Student: A Guide for High School and College Students with ADD*, edited by Patricia O. Quinn; and *Learning How to Learn: A Guide for Getting into College with a Learning Disability, Staying in and Staying Sane* by Joyanne Cobb. Specialty guides for other disabilities include *Realizing the College Dream with Autism or Asperger Syndrome: A Parent's Guide to Student Success* by Ann Palmer and *College Bound: A Guide for Students with Visual Impairments* by Ellen Trief and Raquel Feeny. Also check out the U.S. Department of Justice, Civil Rights Division, Disability Rights Section's website, *A Guide to Disability Rights Laws*, at www.usdoj.gov/crt/ada/cguide.htm.

Financial Considerations

Teens from economically disadvantaged environments (these are found in rural, urban, and even suburban areas) face an additional challenge: over-crowded and underresourced schools that complicate the already complicated application process. However, with a bit of creativity and organization, it is certainly possible to find a good-fit college for your teen. If your family faces this challenge, let's look at some tips you can use to overcome these hurdles.

Tip #1: Provide Your Teen with a "Blueprint"

Diedre Simon, a local instructional superintendent for the Paterson, New Jersey, School District (serving a mainly urban, low-income population), says that the biggest hurdle low-income teens face is the lack of what she calls a "blueprint." These teens are less likely to grow up with the idea that a college education is in their future. Don't feel intimidated by this extra hurdle. You can—and must—supply that vision for your teen, even if the school and peer environment does not. Create that blueprint by doing the following:

- Discussing college regularly with your teen.
- Visiting college campuses early and often. You don't need to travel far— your local community college is fine. The idea is to instill the expectation that your teen *will* be going to college.
- Look for community and church groups that take teens on group tours and sign up your teen.
- Send away for college view books (they're free) to familiarize you and your teen with the options.
- Go to your local public library. Almost all public libraries (rural and urban) keep reams of college guidebooks as well as provide free access to the Internet.
- Review your teen's class schedule and make sure he or she is taking a college-bound curriculum.

Tip #2: Build Up Your Confidence

Many parents with financial constraints did not attend college, and some may not have finished high school. *Don't* let this deter you. All this means is that you may not start the application process with as much information or self-confidence as other parents, but it doesn't mean you want less for your teen. All parents want the best for their kids. So kick your confidence factor into gear by becoming as familiar as you can with the process. Read this book, ask questions of school counselors, attend college fairs, visit local colleges, and seek out any public or private organizations that can guide you. And *always* ask questions.

Tip #3: Find and Use Resources

You need and can find the resources to jump-start your teen's application process. You've probably noticed we are continually directing parents to make use of school counselors, tutors, and prep courses. We understand that in many underresourced schools this is easier said than done. The school counselor in your child's school may be overworked or put in the untenable position of acting more like a disciplinarian than a college adviser. If this describes your school and if despite your best efforts the school is less than helpful than you need, it is crucial to seek out like-minded parents. This will allow you to pool knowledge and resources and provide you and your teen with a built-in peer support system. Here are some specific suggestions:

- Search out community or religious organizations that sponsor free or reasonably priced tutors, college tours, test prep programs, and similar services.
- Make sure you sign up your teen for the PSAT/PLAN and later the SAT/ACT tests. Call the College Board and ask about fee waivers.
- Put together a group of like-minded parents and their kids and pool your resources, organizing group visits and having "application parties" where you can all sit and review college view books and fill out the applications.

Our final piece of advice: *believe in your ability* to guide your teen into a good-fit college. Convey that confidence to your teen, and you and your teen *will* cross the finish line.

Paying for College

Finances are a challenge for most families. A 2006 study issued by the National Center for Public Policy and Higher Education found that for many teens and their families, a college education is becoming out of reach because of rising costs. The study noted that while in the 1990s federal Pell grants covered 70 percent of the tuition costs at a public four-year college, today those grants cover less than half. This means that the average family must spend 31 percent of its income to cover the costs of a public college. With this in mind, it's important that you and your teen have realistic expectations. Your teen needs to be aware if he or she needs scholarships and/or loans before drawing up the college list. We have heard too many stories of teens who applied to private colleges believing that they could attend as long as they got in, only to be told that the money was not available. It is much better—and healthier—for all concerned to be up front about the realities from the beginning. Some helpful resources include *Paying for College without Going Broke* (2007) by Kalman A. Chany and Geoff Martz and *The FastWeb College Gold: The Step-by-Step Guide to Paying for College* (2006) by Mark Kantrowitz and Doug Hardy.

The Homestretch

Some of these personal issues are difficult for many of us to grapple with or discuss openly. These considerations cover a myriad of issues, and some of you may not confront any of these, while others may be affected by several. The most important thing to take away from this chapter is that misunderstandings can seriously complicate crossing the college admissions finish line. This means that, as sensitive as some of these topics might seem, we believe it can never hurt to try to talk about them openly with your spouse, partner, and teen. Consequently, if any of these concerns touch your teen and your family, we hope we've convinced you to get the conversation started.

CHAPTER 10

Crossing the Finish Line
Making the Decision

T LAST! The applications are finally submitted, and you're ready to take a breather. You need some well-earned rest and downtime. We encourage you and your teen to put all the application materials away for a while. It's time to forget about SAT scores, essays, interviews, and touring—all those stressful college tasks that have bombarded you all over the past months. Time to get back to your real lives. Rest up because you still have decisions and some new tasks ahead, depending on whether your teen applied early decision, early action, or regular action (admission). Let's review how the next lap of the race is run.

Early Decision Letters

If your teen applied early decision (ED), you probably submitted the application in December and heard from the college fairly quickly. The ED reply takes one of three forms: 1) admitted, 2) denied, or 3) deferred.

Admitted! If your teen receives the prayed for fat envelope, congratulations; put away this chapter and go out and celebrate with him or her. Finish line crossed, race over!

Denied! If your teen receives the dreaded thin envelope, don't panic. While the race is not over, all this means is that you are going to have to complete the applications to the remaining colleges on his or her college list. Clearly, being denied admission is going to be a disappointment for both of you. For many parents and teens, it can be emotionally wrenching. After all, your teen applied to that college because it was his or her "dream" school. This denial need not be a devastating trauma. You need to offer a good deal of support while encouraging your teen to put it behind him or her. It is extremely important that you not act as if you are horribly disappointed. You can sympathize with your teen while letting him or her know that it isn't the end of the world. Encourage your teen to move forward.

Different parent types react differently to a denial letter, so here are some tips.

Tip #1: Keep Perspective

Most parents feel let down. If you are a Type A parent, we know you may feel devastated. His or her dream school may have also been your dream school, and you need to wrestle with all your feelings. Just make sure not to convey your feelings, either verbally or nonverbally. And, above all, no tears. Instead, remind yourself that your teen depends on you for perspective—to put this rejection in the best light and bear in mind what you learned about Myth #1, "Only an Ivy will do." There are so many other great fit colleges to choose from. An early admissions rejection means nothing more than a bit of extra work. And you, Type A parent (or any type of parent), are more than up to the challenge.

Tip #2: Don't Dawdle

If you are a procrastinating or an ambivalent parent, you need to avoid the tendency to dawdle. Don't give in to that urge. Now is the time to get into action. Unless you have the other applications completed and ready to go (we doubt it, though, unless you've changed your style), you have only a month to submit the applications to the other schools on the college list. Similarly, if you are a laid-back parent, you will have the same inclination but not because you are a procrastinator but because of your innate belief that it will all work itself out on its own. Well, it won't. You too need to get yourself in gear to help your teen finish the race. You definitely should use the common application.

Deferred! What should you do if your teen is deferred? Just like the teen who received the rejection letter, you need to get busy and submit applications to the other colleges on that college list you put together earlier. How you and your teen react to this news is entirely another issue. Of course, you and your teen also need to cope with feelings of disappointment, and you need to help him or her put it all in perspective. However, since the deferred letter is not an out-and-out rejection, it also brings with it the hope of an acceptance letter further down the road. But be prepared. This hope also brings with it the possibility of a second disappointment. Unlike the regular rejection letter, the deferred letter leaves both of you in a kind of emotional "no-man's land." You have another lap to go before you can rest. Forge ahead and submit all the other applications.

Tip: Coping with Deferment

If, after all of this, your teen still ranks the early admit school as his or her first choice, you should encourage your teen to demonstrate continued interest in the college. He or she can write them a letter making his or her case. Go with that old adage of "nothing ventured, nothing gained." On the flip side of the emotional coin, many deferred teens react to the deferred letter by getting angry and changing their opinion of the college. Some teens begin to devalue that school and declare that they no longer wish to attend. This is normal. Don't try to dissuade or argue about it. Just listen and stay neutral. In April, if your teen is finally accepted, his or her old positive feelings will probably reemerge, and if your teen is rejected, he or she will be more prepared for the disappointment, perhaps convinced "I didn't want them anyway." Always be on your guard against Myth #1, "Only an Ivy will do." Remind your teen that he or she can be perfectly happy at another school. This is the beauty of discarding Myth #1— you know there is more than one good fit out there.

Early Action

Early action (EA) is relatively easy to handle since it simply means that the college will let your teen know "early" whether he or she has been accepted. No binding agreement comes with this. If accepted EA, he or she does not have to commit to going there. In other words, your teen gets to keep his her options open. If, come April, your teen gets other offers from other colleges he or she prefers, he or she can reject the EA acceptance and go with the college that now tops his or her list. On the other hand, if his or her EA school rejects him or her, you will all go through the "mourning process" early and, hopefully, by the time April comes and the other acceptance letters roll in, he she will have settled on another choice. In reality, EA comes with few downsides.

Regular Action Letters

Regular action is applying to college according to the traditional time line: most applications in sometime between the New Year until February 15 with a decision coming sometime between early and mid-April. Teens applying regular action typically include a good number and range of schools. Of course, we hope you followed the "Rule of Six." Sometimes, even with a regular action application, your teen may receive what is referred to as a "likely letter" sometime in January or February. The school is letting him or her know that he or she has more likely than not been accepted before the uniform April notification day. Why would a college do this? To entice the teen to seriously consider their school. Teens are always flattered when they receive the "likely letter." Just remember that it is not a lock, and you need to make sure your teen understands this too.

Okay, it's April. For the majority of teens who applied regular admission, those long-awaited envelopes begin to appear in your mailbox. Your teen will receive one of three types of letters: 1) admit, 2) denied, or 3) wait-listed.

Admitted! If your teen receives the fat envelope from his or her number one choice, it is time to relax and celebrate. Your teen crossed the finish line; the race is over. All you need to do is send in the initial deposit and enjoy the rest of the spring and summer. If other colleges accepted your teen, let them know of your decision so that they can offer the slot to another applicant. Needless to say, your teen should be in great shape to go to school tomorrow and face all his or her friends, teachers, and other family members, who will be sure to ask, "So, where are you going?"

Your teen is admitted and it's all over, right? Not so fast. Most teens are actually accepted by more than one college and are faced with a choice. Choices, as we said before, are usually a good thing, but they do come with responsibility. Choices require mental and emotional work. If your teen is accepted by a number of colleges, none of which is the clear favorite, it means that both of you will be running another lap. Here's a tip on how to approach the choice dilemma:

Tip: Choosing between Schools

Clear, if at all possible, both of your schedules during April. Rank order the list of accepted colleges and schedule return visits to the colleges at the top of the list. Many teens are unable to decide between their top choices. Instead, they have a "contenders" list and need to take one final look before settling on the *one*. Many colleges hold "accepted students weekends" to help teens make this hard decision. Certainly, take advantage of these events while keeping in mind that the colleges are selling themselves. Make sure your teen understands that the events he or she attends during that weekend don't reflect a typical weekend. Encourage him or her to look past the program and seek out other views of the campus. Some teens actually prefer to schedule their return visits during a regular week and many request an overnight visit. The only problem with the overnight visit, as we mentioned in chapter 7, is that your teen can clash with the roommate.

☀ A MOM'S TALE

Claire had been accepted at three of her top choices, and one offered a very generous merit scholarship. Her mother, Jan, was excited and had difficulty not showing her preference for this college. Jan encouraged her to schedule the overnight visit and happily dropped her off. Poor Jan. The next morning at 7:00, the phone rang. It was Claire, crying. "Can I please come home now? I don't want to stay for the rest of the day. I hate this place." Jan swallowed her feelings and said the right thing: "I'll be right there to pick you up." On picking up the tearful Claire, Jan learned that her one and only night on campus had been spent with the proverbial "roommate from hell." Jan, of course, understood that this experience had totally skewed her view of the college. But no matter how much Jan tried to explain that this was only one student and not representative of the whole student body, her daughter remained unconvinced. That college was definitely off her list. It was now up to Jan to deal with her own feelings of frustration and disappointment and move on. ☀

Other factors may weigh in on making that final decision. Paramount for many parents and their teens is money. There is just no easy way to say it. Finances are often the number one factor when choosing a school. A teen can be accepted but without the needed financial aid package. In some instances, a teen has to face the reality that without that package, the college is out of their reach. This result can sometimes be as disappointing as an out-and-out rejection. Remember our swimmer, Jason? When April came, he was faced with a difficult decision. He was accepted at three colleges, one of which was a private university and too expensive for his family. Here's how they handled the choices (and family constraints) they faced.

☀ A SWIMMER'S TALE CONTINUES

Jason's mother told us she "felt awful" about not letting Jason accept the private school. As she explained, "I had friends tell me, 'How do you put a price tag on education?' I said it was pretty easy. Not going back in debt! We'd been in debt before. I wanted my kid to graduate without that burden. But I did feel bad because I knew that private school was a good fit."

Jason's parents wanted him to accept the brand-name, prestigious state university that was known for their excellent academics. As his father remembered, "I encouraged him to seriously consider it; it was affordable. I thought it had a lot more to offer; it was a bigger school, more prestigious. I was ignored. I did a bit of nudging, but Jason was consistent and firm. He knew other kids on that team who 'hated the coach.' In the end, Jason chose the smaller, less prestigious state university and excelled—academically, athletically, and socially." Most importantly, despite some initial misgivings over his choice of schools, his college years could not have been better. Even better, Jason and his family emerged debt free at the end of his four years, and he is looking forward to entering graduate school. ☀

So, as you can see, while choices are good, these also come with their own (potential) set of complications and considerations.

Denied! While most teens are accepted by one of their top choice, not every teen will be accepted by their number one choice. There is also the complex situation where a teen is accepted into the college itself but not into the desired program. Every teen reacts differently, often depending on their preparation. Were you successful in your prerace preparation? Were you able to dispel Myth #1? Did your teen fully understand the family's financial constraints?

Most teens will struggle with a mix of feelings. However, we have found that the majority, as long as they are accepted by their second or third choice, will shed some tears but quickly see the benefits of the school where they are accepted and move on.

Eventually, most will find so much to like about that college that it morphs into their number one choice. Psychologists refer to this process as "cognitive restructuring." This is a fancy term for turning a disappointment into a positive. Teens may say to themselves, "I actually like the school that accepted me better."

Wait-Listed! Now let's discuss how to deal with the most anxiety-filled letter—the one telling your teen he or she has been wait-listed. The reactions and feelings this letter engenders are akin to the "deferred" letter we discussed earlier. The wait-list letter is difficult to cope with. Your teen won't necessarily know how long the wait list is or where he or she is rank ordered on the list. The upshot is that neither you nor your teen will really know what being placed on the wait list means. Many educators question the practice of long wait lists since it prolongs the uncertainty and anxiety when the chance of a real acceptance offer is probably quite low. To put a good spin on it, at least it shows your teen that he or she had the qualifications for acceptance but there just weren't enough spaces to offer him or her a place. Sounds good, and certainly, as the parent, this is just the twist you should put on it. But will it make your teen feel better? Probably not.

Does being placed on a wait list really mean that your teen has a good chance of being accepted, or does it mean the opposite—literally no chance? It depends on how long the wait list is and how many spots typically open up. Each college differs and rarely includes this information along with the wait-list letter. It is relatively easy to find if your teen has the gumption to pick up the phone and ask the admissions officer, "How large is your wait list?" Some colleges rank order the wait list, so your teen can ask about this too. For the phone-shy teen, he or she can find some of this information at www.usnews.com.

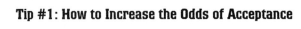

Tip #1: How to Increase the Odds of Acceptance

If there is a long wait list, does this mean that your teen doesn't stand a chance? Not necessarily, though, like winning the lottery, odds are against it, but someone does win. The winners in the wait-list lap of this race are those who show a demonstrated interest. So if your teen still has his or her heart set on this college, then by all means return the card indicating that he or she wants to remain on the wait list. Encourage your teen to write a letter explaining why he or she still ranks that college number one. That letter can also convey how much he or she loved the school and will definitely enroll if offered a spot. It can't hurt, and your teen has nothing to lose.

Some teens have the opposite reaction to the wait-list letter. Some feel disgusted or angry and want to send back the "are you still interested in us" card, checking off the "no thanks" box. The name of the game here is, as always, that it's your teen's feelings that count, not yours. Consider what is best for your teen. If there is literally no chance of receiving an acceptance, then why push him or her to continue pursuing it? Encourage your teen to pursue the college only if he or she can take a laid-back approach, a "what the heck, I have nothing to lose" attitude. If your teen can do this, then help him or her craft a convincing letter of demonstrated interest, and then both of you have to wait to hear.

Tip #2: Don't Sit Out the Wait-List Leg of the Race

While waiting for the answer from the number one college, your teen needs to accept his or her number two choice *and* send in the deposit. This ensures that he or she has an excellent, good-match college to attend in the fall and will be able to relax a bit. If offered a place off the wait list, you will then lose your deposit, typically a few hundred dollars. Luckily, your teen will probably be notified if he or she has been offered a slot by the end of June.

A New Twist

Some colleges have begun a new twist on the traditional spring admissions policy. They send an acceptance offer but with the caveat that the teen can't start that fall but must wait to begin the following spring. Colleges make these offers because they predict openings in the spring due to dropouts and openings in the dorms. Other institutions have begun to offer acceptances predicated on a summer start date—yes, the summer, right after they graduate. Some teens are so excited to be accepted by their number one choice that they find these unusual start dates acceptable; others do not. If your teen is set on attending this college and can live with the restrictions, why not accept? There is nothing to lose. If the start date is the spring, he or she can always take courses during the fall at another institution, work to earn some money, or even travel.

Never Left the Gate

And what about the not-always-focused (NAF) teen who never got it together to start or complete the application race or who was rejected by *all* his or her choices? What about the teen who wasn't accepted at any college he or she wanted and refuse to go elsewhere? Again, the race isn't over. Many teens need some time to mature or even enroll in a gap-year program. The gap year is a period between graduating high school and matriculating in college during which the student typically travels, completes specialized language or academic programs, or volunteers or participates in various experiential opportunities. Many of these programs are geared toward students who need some assistance—either emotionally or academically. Most teens benefit from these specialized programs. They enroll and complete courses, typically earning better grades than they did in high school. Frequently, they complete volunteer projects or work in settings that will make them more desirable applicants for the following year. In addition, don't forget that most community colleges have an open enrollment policy. So, if your teen wants to keep his or her foot in the college door, this can be the perfect solution for him or her. We hope you see that there are multiple options and solutions. The fact of the matter is that if your teen really wants to attend college, he or she will.

One last bit of advice on this subject comes from Marymount Manhattan College Dean Grecco, who has more than twenty years of experience working in colleges and counseling students who struggle to succeed. She has this advice for parents of college-bound teens:

> The smartest thing for a parent to do is to honestly assess their teen's readiness to take on this endeavor. I see a fair number of high school seniors apply to college just because it's the next step. Some graduating seniors are not ready for college. Some are not emotionally ready to be on their own or able to manage their lives without adult supervision. They're not ready to make decisions. I see lots who are pursuing their parents' dream. To be successful in college, they have to figure out what they enjoy and not go into engineering because their father wants engineering. It isn't always bad for them to be away from school for a year, get a job, volunteer, to get direction. So, before making up the

college list, be realistic about whether your child is ready for college. You can make this decision by looking at your child's academic success in high school, how they interact with friends, how they handle drinking, and how they behave in school. Ask yourselves, Do they have a sense of responsibility, can they say no to influence—are they strong enough to resist peer pressure?

Creative Alternatives

Life is nothing if not unpredictable. Remember the old Chinese curse: "May you live in interesting times." We have just outlined for you the myriad of ways applicants can reach that college admissions finish line. Sometimes, however, things go wrong, and a more creative approach must be considered. So, while we can't predict every permutation, here is a bit of a heads-up of what could be lurking around the corner.

Deferred Admission (or "My Child Refuses to Go")

Many teens complete the whole race, receive an admit letter (sometimes in multiples), make the tough choice between offers, and then, just when it's time to send off the deposit and celebrate the victory, they balk. You can hear it in their voice: "I'm so tired, I can't even think about going to college next fall." Or a flat out "I just don't want to go!" What's a parent to do? They think creatively. Many colleges are open to an accepted student's request to defer admission for a semester or a year. This means that your teen has his or her acceptance guaranteed but can put off starting. Most teens use this time to work or travel and, in the process, mature and gain direction in their lives. When they start college a semester or a year later, they are better prepared to buckle down and work. While many parents panic, thinking the teen will never go to college, we find that this rarely happens. Often a year of working minimum-wage jobs motivates a teen to enroll in a cushy college environment.

Transferring

As we said in chapter 1, choosing a college is *not* the same as getting married. In fact, a high percentage of students transfer. If your teen is not accepted at any of his or her top choices, he or she can attend his or her second or third choice, give it a chance, and, if still unsatisfied, apply to transfer. Remember, you are the consumer, and there is no shame in changing schools. The truth is that no one really cares where you started. In the end, it's more important where you finish and *how* you finish. A useful resource is Freedman's *How to Transfer to the College of Your Choice*.

One thing to consider when drawing up the new college list is how many credits will transfer. Each college has a different policy. As a rule, most credits will transfer. Most schools will not transfer a course where the student received less than a C. It is important to find out this information ahead of time and make the transfer decision with this in mind. After all, college is expensive enough, and neither you nor your teen want to lose substantial sums of money or time.

A successful transfer hinges on a few things. First, you, the parent, need to stay the course; the race has now become more like the steeplechase. You need to show support and enthusiasm for another round of applications. Fake it! Gird your loins! Summon up the energy!

Tips for Creative Solutions to Transferring Colleges

- If your teen starts at a safety school, encourage him or her to give it a fair try. You'd be surprised at how often a teen ends up loving and graduating successfully from his or her safety school.
- Encourage your teen to work hard and get good grades during the freshman year. This is what the colleges to which he or she hopes to transfer will look at in considering whether to offer him or her admission.
- Encourage your teen to enroll in courses whose credits will be easier to transfer. These tend to be introductory or required courses, such as General Psychology or Biology 101.
- When making up the new college list, make sure to include colleges that actually accept a good number of transfer students. This information, while not easily found, can be ferreted out in college guidebooks and computer websites.

Handling Disappointment

We hope you will not need this section. However, we also know that life, from time to time, throws all of us a curve ball. In this case, it could be simply the dashed expectation of your teen getting into his or her number one choice or even your teen not getting in anywhere. Whatever the origins of your disappointment, you need to keep perspective. To help you do this, we have three final tips for you:

- If the news is less than great, control or hide your disappointment or anger. It won't help and can discourage your teen from expressing his or her feelings.
- Remember, college sweeps week is very hard on teens, both those who get in to their number one and those who don't. Facing peers, teachers, and other family members can be tough.
- Prepare your teen for intrusive comments or "condolences." Keep perspective—it's not a death in the family.

Postrace Report

Most of us—teens and parents alike—begin this race with a lot of preconceived expectations and understanding of what constitutes "winning" the college race. We hope that by now you agree with us that what really constitutes success is your teen's acceptance at a college that will put his or her feet on the path to real future success. As the acceptance letters start rolling in and your teen has made a decision to go to College A and not College B, both of you will see that acceptance is not really the finish line. In fact, it is just the beginning of your teen's first, sometimes tentative steps into adulthood. Once your teen arrives on campus, he or she will discover, in quick succession, that he or she is faced with a host of decisions and new challenges, such as "Should I go to class today or sleep in?" and "Should I party all night or study for that big test?"

In the end, your teen's ability to choose wisely pushes him or her through the teen threshold and into adulthood. This is, after all, what the teen years are all about—preparing for that next phase in life. While this book has helped you complete the college admissions race, the *real* race continues. The next lap is helping your AF or NAF teen become a self-sufficient and happy human being.

CHAPTER 11

Looking Back, Looking Forward

NOW THAT YOU and your teen have finished the college application process, we hope that he or she has received the fat envelope from the college that will provide the best fit. More than that, we hope that both of you have enjoyed or at least benefited from running this race.

While you catch your breath and feel relieved that the race is over, you probably realize that you've learned not only a lot about colleges but, more important, also a tremendous amount about yourself and your teen. Hopefully, through all this work and stress, your relationship with your teen has grown and matured. He or she is ready to step into the college years.

Now is the time to tell your teen how proud you are of his or her hard work in high school and on those high-stakes tests. It is a time to celebrate how your teen made his or her first huge adult decisions—where to apply and go to college. Now is also the time to pat yourself on the back. You've worked hard too, not just with the college tasks but also with putting aside your dreams and fears and placing your teen first. This is why and how you've both won the race.

We'd like to leave you with some thoughts from our students. You'll notice that, while the "T" word is not used, "Thanks" to their moms and dads is implied in every one of their comments. We are confident that at the end of this arduous race, your teen will also be thanking you for all your care, concern, and love, even if the "T" word never passes his or her lips.

☀ SOME COLLEGE STUDENTS' MESSAGES

"My mom was very supportive of me going to any college of my choice. She would always tell me that 'as long as you are happy, we're happy.' That support gave me the courage and strength to come to a school so far away."

"The bottom line is that my mother never put any doubts in my mind—she always said I could achieve my dreams."

"My dad was especially helpful when I went to visit schools I had applied to. Since I am an extremely bad decision maker, he was able to guide me with my decision. He was very helpful throughout the process."

"I could not have made it through this transition without the love and support of my parents. This college experience has brought my family closer."

"I am in college because of my mother. Not only did she keep meticulous notes of everything college related, I applied to nine colleges and she took me to visit all of them. We drove to Boston and Maine and even flew to Seattle. She said that if I got into the school of my choice, I could go. No exceptions. I am very grateful for her pushing me, and I'd be lost without her organization and motivation."

"Touring the school with my mom was the best. My mom and I are very close, and I was happy to have her share the experience with me."

"Once when I was in an interview, I had forgotten to bring a high school transcript to show the interviewer, and my mother luckily kept one in her bag. She really saved me!"

"I have a learning disability, and I was scared no one would want me. But my parents were really supportive and helped find a school for me with a strong support system, and now I'm doing better now than I ever did in high school."

"My parents reassured me that I should do what felt right and that they would always be there for me and that nothing was permanent. This calmed me down and comforted me. They constantly reminded me to only look at today and not worry about tomorrow." ☼

Acknowledgments

THE AUTHORS wish to thank our husbands and children and all the high school parents and teens who shared with us their application experiences during their college admission journeys. Equally important is the debt of gratitude we owe our students for teaching us that there are many paths to success in college and in life.

References

Americans with Disabilities Act of 1990. United States Public Law 101-133, 104. Stat. 327.

Berry, Lemuel, Jr. 1995. *Minority Financial Aid Directory*. Dubuque, IA: Kendall/ Hunt Publishers.

Chany, Kalman A., and Geoff Martz. 2007. *Paying for College without Going Broke*. New York: Random House.

Christian College Coalition Staff. 1994. *Choose a Christian College: A Guide to Academically Challenging Colleges Committed to a Christ-Centered Life*. Lawrenceville, NJ: Peterson's.

Cobb, Joyanne. 2003. *Learning How to Learn: A Guide for Getting into College with a Learning Disability, Staying in, and Staying Sane*. Washington, DC: Child and Family Press.

Cohen, Cafi. 2000. *Homeschooler's College Admissions Handbook: Preparing 12- to 18-Year-Olds for Success in the College of Their Choice*. Roseville, CA: Prima.

College Board. 2007. *Guide to Getting Financial Aid*. New York: College Board.

Dale, Stacy Berg, and Alan B. Krueger. 2002. "Estimating the Payoff of Attending a More Selective College: An Application of Selection on Observables and Unobservables." *Quarterly Journal of Economics*, 107 (4): 1491–1527.

Dennis, Jeanne Gowen, and Michael Farris. 2004. *Homeschooling High School: Planning Ahead for College Admissions*. Lynwood, WA: Emerald Books.

Easterbrook, Gregg. 2004. "Who Needs Harvard?" *Atlantic Monthly*, October.

Golden, Daniel. 2006. *The Price of Admission: How America's Ruling Class Buys Its Way into Elite Colleges—and Who Gets Left Outside the Gate*. New York: Crown.

Kantrowitz, Mark, and Doug Hardy. 2006. *The FastWeb College Gold: The Step-by-Step Guide to Paying for College*. New York: Collins.

Fiske, Edward B. 2007. *Fiske Guide to Colleges*. Naperville, IL: Sourcebooks.

Freedman, Eric. 2002. *How to Transfer to the College of Your Choice*. Berkeley, CA: Ten Speed Press.

Mathews, Jay. 2003. *Harvard Schmarvard: Getting beyond the Ivy League to the College That Is Best for You.* New York: Three Rivers Press.

Palmer, Ann. 2006. *Realizing the College Dream with Autism or Asperger Syndrome: A Parent's Guide to Student Success.* Philadelphia, PA: Jessica Kingsley Publishers.

Peterson's. 2006. *Colleges for Students with Learning Disabilities or ADD.* Lawrenceville, NJ: Peterson's.

Pope, Loren. 2006. *Forty Schools That Make a Difference.* New York: Penguin Books.

———. 2007. *Looking beyond the Ivy League: Finding the College That's Right for You.* New York: Penguin Books.

Princeton Review. 2004. *Best 357 Colleges.* New York: Princeton Review.

———. 2007. *The K & W Guide to Colleges for Students with Learning Disabilities or Attention Deficit Disorders.* 9th ed. New York: Princeton Review.

Quinn, Patricia O., ed. 2001. *ADD and the College Student: A Guide for High School and College Students with ADD.* Washington, D.C.: Magination Press.

Samuelson, Robert J. 1999. "The Worthless Ivy League?" *Newsweek,* November 1.

Shaw, Thomas. 2005. *College Bound: What Christian Parents Need to Know about Helping Their Kids Choose a College.* Chicago: Moody Publishers.

Sherrill, Jan-Mitchell, and Craig Hardesty. 1994. *Gay, Lesbian and Bisexual Student's Guide to Colleges, Universities and Graduate Schools.* New York: New York University Press.

Siminoff, Faren R. 2004. *Crossing the Sound: The Rise of Atlantic American Communities in the Seventeenth Century.* New York: New York University Press.

Trief, Ellen, and Raquel Feeny. 2005. *College Bound: A Guide for Students with Visual Impairments.* New York: AFB Press.

U.S. Bureau of Labor Statistics. 2005. "College Enrollment and Work Activity of 2005 High School Graduates." www.bls.gov/news.release/hsgec.nr0.htm.

U.S. Department of Justice. 2005. *A Guide to Disability Rights Laws.* www.usdoj.gov/crt/ada/cguide.htm.

Waldman, Adelle. 2004. "A Prestigious Alma Mater Is Overrated on the Job." *College Journal from the Wall Street Journal.* www.collegejournal.com/successwork/onjob/20041116-waldman.html.

Wilson, R. Reid. 1996. *Don't Panic: Taking Control of Anxiety Attacks.* Rev. ed. New York: Collins.

Windmeyer, Shane L. 2006. *The Advocate Guide for LGBT Students.* Los Angeles, CA: Alyson Publications.

Index

About the Authors

CHERYL PARADIS, Psy.D., holds her doctorate in clinical psychology and has more than twenty years of experience as a clinical psychologist working with a variety of populations, including teens and their families. She has extensive experience administering psychodiagnostic tests to children and adolescents with problems such as learning disabilities and a need for test accommodations. She has counseled teens and their parents for psychological and academic problems and family and school issues. Dr. Paradis also specializes in treating anxiety disorders and spent fifteen years on staff at the State University of New York Health Science Center at Brooklyn's Anxiety Disorder Clinic. Her extensive research and clinical work has also included African American and Caribbean American populations. Dr. Paradis is currently an associate professor of psychology at Marymount Manhattan College and teaches courses in child development and abnormal psychology. She recently completed a successful college application process with her second child.

FAREN R. SIMINOFF is an attorney and historian. She holds a J.D. from Syracuse University College of Law and a Ph.D. in American history from New York University. Dr. Siminoff is the author of *Crossing the Sound: The Rise of Atlantic American Communities in the Seventeenth Century* (2004). She is currently an associate professor at Nassau Community College and teaches American history, including courses in culture and society and race and ethnicity in America. Her legal practice has included contract and employment law, including interpreting the Americans with Disabilities Act of 1990. As a professor at a community college, Dr. Siminoff regularly counsels and assists students with college transfer options and the college admissions process. In addition, many of her students are first-generation college students, children of immigrants, as well as students with learning disabilities. She routinely advises parents and their teens on the college admissions process.